SICKNESS IN SMALL SCALE SECTOR
Causes and Cures

About the Author

Dr. Satish B. Mathur, Ph. D. (Business Management), C.A.I.I.B., is currently a Professor of Finance at the Indian Institute of Management, Lucknow. Earlier, he had been with the State Bank of India (SBI) for over 27 years (1961-1988) where he had held several senior executive positions, in the areas of policy and planning, training and administration, such as Senior Member of Faculty at the Bank's apex College at Hyderabad, Asstt. General Manager, Chief Manager of Intensive Industrial Finance branches, etc. Later he switched over to the Administrative Staff College of India (ASCI), Hyderabad, as a Senior Member of Faculty in the Finance Area. During his about eight years tenure at ASCI (1988-95), Dr. Mathur had conducted a large number of programmes in the Finance Area, for senior and top level executives in the public and private sectors, as also for senior I.A.S. and I.P.S. officers.

By virtue of his vast and varied experience as a Senior Bank Executive with SBI, Dr. Mathur has developed credible specialisation and expertise in the areas of Industrial Finance, Prevention of Industrial Sickness and Corporate Turnaround Strategies, with deep insight, futuristic vision and pragmatic approach to the related problems.

He has published around fifty papers in Indian and International Journals of repute, as also in the leading financial papers some of which have been used by UNICEF in their international training programmes. His book entitled *The A to Z of Managerial Excellence* (Global Business Press, 1995, Delhi-110095) has been very well received in the market, so much so that it has undergone three reprints within a short span of around three years.

SICKNESS IN SMALL SCALE SECTOR
Causes and Cures
(With Special Reference to the Role of Commercial Banks)

By

Dr. SATISH B. MATHUR
Ph.D., C.A.I.I.B.
Professor of Finance,
Indian Institute of Management, Lucknow (India)

CONCEPT PUBLISHING COMPANY, NEW DELHI-110059

ISBN 81-7022-744-5

First Published 1999

Published and Printed by
Ashok Kumar Mittal
Concept Publishing Company
A/15-16, Commercial Block, Mohan Garden
NEW DELHI-110059
Phones : 5648039, 5649024
Fax : 091-11-5648053

Dedicated
to
The Loving Memory
of
My Revered Parents
Late Shrimati Heera Devi Mathur
and
Late Shri Bhagwati Lal Mathur

PREFACE

The growing incidence of industrial sickness has, of late, been a cause for grave concern for the policy-makers and the academicians, for the Central and the State Governments and the Reserve Bank of India, for the commercial banks and the other financial institutions, for the entrepreneurs – both present and prospective – and, in a way, for all the right thinking persons.

The rising trend in the industrial sickness, particularly in the small scale sector, has assumed serious proportions during the last decade, both in terms of the number of sick units and the bank credits outstanding against such accounts. This unhealthy trend has further ramifications, like aggravation of the present unemployment problem, loss of production, blockage of funds in non-performing assets, loss of human resources and entrepreneurial talents, etc. Concerted efforts are, therefore, required to be made by all concerned to prevent the industrial sickness.

The researchers and practitioners alike are almost unanimously of the view that most of the units fall sick largely due to management failure. Further, some external factors like shortage of raw materials, power cuts, marketing problems, unduly delayed payment of bills by the government departments and large scale industries, frequent changes in the government policies, etc., also cause sickness in the small scale industrial (SSI) units.

An attempt has, therefore, been made in the present book to identify the various causes of sickness, both internal and external, based on the study of the selected live cases of the sick SSI units. Some live cases of healthy units have also been studied to identify the facilitating and hindering factors responsible for the success or failure of the units.

Most of the researchers, and even some of the bankers, are of the view that the commercial banks, by virtue of their day-to-day contacts with the borrowers, through the conduct of their bank accounts, can play a vital role in arresting the incidence of sickness by taking right remedial measures in right time, in close coordination with the entrepreneurs as also the other financial institutions. However, not much research seems to have been undertaken with a view to suggesting the specific measures that the commercial banks may take to discharge the onerous function of preventing the industrial sickness.

An attempt has, therefore, been made in the present study to examine the bank's systems and procedures of sanction, disbursement and control of advances, to analyse the reasons for the gaps, if any, between the laid down systems and procedures, and the prevailing practices at the branches and the controlling offices, and to make suggestions for bridging the gaps, wherever necessary. Further, the roles of the other financial institutions, the government and the large scale industries, in the prevention of the sickness in the small scale sector, have also been examined in the study.

I am extremely grateful to Dr. Laxmi Narain, UGC Emeritus Fellow, Department of Business Management, Osmania University, Hyderabad for his inspiring guidance and constructive criticism. I lack words to express my hearty gratitude to Meera, my wife, for her valuable suggestions, and perennial support and encouragement for completing the work early. My sincere thanks are due to Archana and Kartika, my daughters, for their untiring help in proofreading the computer print-outs as also for suggesting some significant modifications in the pattern of presentations, for making the book more reader-friendly.

SATISH B. MATHUR

CONTENTS

CHAPTER FOUR

Appendices

LIST OF TABLES

Unitwise Break-up of the Causes of Sickness found in the 22 Cases of Sick SSI Units

LIST OF FIGURE

1

INTRODUCTION

IMPORTANCE OF SMALL SCALE INDUSTRIES IN THE DEVELOPMENT OF OUR NATIONAL ECONOMY

Small Scale Sector : The Engine of Balanced and Decentralised Development

Small Scale Industries (SSI) play a vital role in the development of our national economy. We are facing the problems of unemployment and paucity of capital resources. "The built in characteristics of small scale industries (SSI) sector, such as relatively small size of initial capital requirement, entrepreneurship and employ-ment generation potential, etc., render them as the engine of balanced and decentralised development".[1] "Employment generated in small scale factory units is nine times that of large establishments for an investment of Rs.1 lakh in fixed assets".[2] Further, the number of job seekers on live registers employment exchanges has increased from 197.53 lakh as on 31st December 1982 to 327.76 lakh as on 31st December 1989.[3] Under the circumstances, the small scale industries assume great importance in mitigating the problem of unemployment, in facilitating the growth of our industrial sector and in ensuring an all-round development of our economy. Jawaharlal Nehru has put it well:

"Cottage and small scale industries are of vary special importance in India. If we lack capital, we do not lack manpower. We must use this manpower both to add to the wealth of the country and to reduce unemployment".[4]

Further, as most of the villagers remain under-employed, specially when the agricultural operations are not on, they may set up some village, cottage and small scale industries, gain fuller employment in their own villages and come above the poverty line. To quote Mahatma Gandhi, ". . . the poor of the world cannot be helped by mass production, only by production by masses".[5] This may also arrest the exodus to the already over-crowded urban and metropolitan areas and mitigate the related socio-economic problems and their multifaceted ramifications. Even women may work in such small/tiny units in their free time and increase their household income. This way they would be able to improve upon their present standard of living as also their economic independence and their status in the society.

Besides, small scale industries avoid regional imbalances and facilitate decentralised development in various parts of the country, including the remote areas, by effectively utilising the locally available raw materials and other resources, including the manpower.

Role of Small Scale Industries as Contained in the Various Industrial Policy Resolutions and Statements

The Industrial Policy Resolution of April 1948 rightly found the small scale industries as being "particularly suited for the better utilisation of local resources and for the achievement of local self-sufficiency in respect of certain types of essential consumer goods like food, cloth and agricultural implements".[6]

Stressing the role of small scale industries in the development of our national economy, the 1956 Industrial Policy Resolution stated as under:

> "In relation to some of the problems that need urgent solutions, they offer some distinct advantages. They

provide immediate large scale employment. They offer a method of ensuring a more equitable distribution of national income and they facilitate an effective mobilisation of resources of capital and skills which might otherwise remain unutilised. Some of the problems that unplanned urbanisation tends to create will be avoided by the establishment of small centres of industrial production all over the country."

The 1980 Industrial Policy Statement enunciated the concept of economic federalism in which there would be close organic linkages between the large and the small sectors and which would generate a large number of ancillary and small scale units. Under the new Industrial Policy, announced on May 31, 1990, the investment ceiling in plant and machinery has been enhanced from Rs. 35 lakh to Rs. 60 lakh for small industries and from Rs. 45 lakh to Rs. 75 lakh for ancillary units, with a view to facilitating the growth and modernisation of the small scale sector. For tiny units within the small scale sector, the investment ceiling has been raised from Rs. 2 lakh to Rs. 5 lakh.[7]

As would be observed from the foregoing Industrial Policy Resolutions and Statements, a significant role has been envisaged for small scale industries in the development of our national economy. The objectives of the role may be summarised as under:

(i) Creation of large scale employment opportunities, both for self-employment and wage employment.
(ii) Decentralisation of industrial development.
(iii) Full exploitation of local resources.
(iv) Effective utilisation of human skills and craftsmanship.
(v) Development of rural growth centres and reduction of regional imbalances through dispersal of industries.
(vi) Prevention of disorganised urbanisation.

(vii) Diffusion and de-concentration of economic power within the community.

Performance of the Small Scale Sector

The performance of the small scale sector, on various parameters, viz., number of units, value of production and exports, and number of persons employed, in the recent years, has been impressive.

Number of Units

In 1960, there were only 30,000 SSI units registered with the various State Directors of Industries throughout the country.[8] The number of SSI units has since steadily increased over the years. The trend of the increase from 1984-85 (April-March) to 1989-90 may be seen from Table 1.1. During 1989-90 (April-March) the number of small scale units increased by 6.7 per cent to 18.27 lakh from 17.12 lakh in 1988-89.

Value of Production

The estimated value of production of goods and services in the small scale sector at Rs. 1,18,210 crore in 1989-90 (at 1988-89 prices) was higher by 11.1 per cent than that of Rs. 1,06,400 crore in the previous year.

The year-wise break up of value of production in the sector from 1984-85 to 1989-90 has been given in Table 1.1. Further, village and small scale industries taken together account for about 49 per cent of total industrial production, and the contribution of industries falling under the purview of Small Industries Development Organisation (SIDO) is about 35 per cent.[9]

Value of Exports

Exports of the small scale sector have continued to be on the rise. During 1988-89, the exports were higher by 25.3 per cent at Rs. 5,681.15 crore (estimated) than those of Rs. 4,535 crore in 1987-88. The trend of the increase in the value of exports in the sector may be assessed from Table 1.1. The share of the small scale sector in the total exports, however, marginally declined to 28 per cent in 1988-89 from 28.8 per cent in 1987-88.[10]

TABLE 1.1: Achievements of the Small Scale Sector

Year Apr.-Mar.	No.of Units Lakh Nos.	Production Rs. crore at current prices	Exports Rs. in crore	Employment Lakh Persons
1984-85	12.42	50,520	2553	90
1985-86	13.56	61,228	2769	96
1986-87	14.64	72,250	3631	101.4
1987-88	15.86	87,300	4535	107
1988-89	17.12	1,06,400	5681.15 (E)	113 (P)
1989-90	18.27	1,18,210 *	NA	119.6 (E)

* = At 1988-89 prices
E = Estimated
P - Provisional
NA. = Not Available

Source : Reserve Bank of India, Bomaby, Report on Currency and Finance, Vol. I: *Economic Review*, 1987-88, p. 67 and 1989-90, p. 70.

Main Source: Office of the Development Commissioner, SSI, Ministry of Industry.

Number of Persons Employed

As may be seen from Table 1.1, the level of employment in the small scale sector increased by 32.9 per cent from 90 lakh persons in 1984-85 to 119.6 lakh persons (estimated) in 1989-90.

Outlays in the Five Year Plans on SSI (Including Industrial Estates)

Development of small scale industries has been given high priority in successive Five Year Plans in view of their advantages in terms of low investment and high potential for employment generation, particularly in the rural and semi-urban areas. This is evident from the fact that the plan outlays for the small scale industries and the Industrial Estates have increased from Rs. 5.20 crore (excluding Industrial Estates) in the First Five Year Plan to Rs. 113.06 crore (including Industrial Estates) in the Third Plan and Rs. 1120.51 crore (including Industrial Estates) in the Seventh Plan. The outlays for the Central and State Plans on small scale industries in the Five Year Plans and Annual Plans have been presented in Table 1.2.

DEFINITION OF SMALL SCALE INDUSTRIES

Gradual Widening of the Scope of SSI: A Historical Perspective

Since the beginning of the Small Industries Development Programme (1954), there has been changes in the definition of a small scale industrial unit/undertaking. In the year 1955, a small scale industrial unit was defined as the one :

(a) having an investment of capital nature (i.e., in land and building, plant and machinery, furniture and fixtures, etc) not exceeding Rs. 5 lakh; and
(b) employing less than 50 persons, if using power, and less than 100 persons, if not using power.

In 1957 the aforesaid ceiling on the number of employees was liberalised and made applicable on per shift basis.

In 1960, however, the ceiling on the number of employees was finally lifted. This was a step in the right

TABLE 1.2: Outlays for the Central and State Plans on Small Scale Industries (Including Industrial Estates in Five Year Plans

Plan	Period	Outlays *(Rs. in crore)*
First Plan	(1951-56)	5.20*
Second Plan	(1956-61)	56.00*
Third Plan	(1961-66)	113.06
Annual Plan	(1966-69)	53.48
Fourth Plan	(1969-74)	96.19
Fifth Plan	(1974-79)	221.74
Annual Plan	(1979-80)	104.81
Sixth Plan	(1980-85)	616.10
Seventh Plan	(1985-90)	1120.51

* Excluding Industrial Estates

Source: Hand Book of Statistics, 1989, Small Scale Industries in India, Development Commissioner (SSI), New Delhi, p. 8.

Main Sources: (i) 6th Plan Documents, Table 12.3.
(ii) 7th Plan Documents, Table 4.3, p. 104.

direction with a view to encouraging the establishment of labour – intensive units and thereby mitigating the problem of unemployment by providing more employment opportunities with proportionately lesser investment of capital, in comparison to large scale industries.

Definition of SSI in Some Other Countries

According to Khan,[11] some foreign countries like China, Denmark, Egypt, Germany, Israel, Indonesia, Iran, Italy, Japan, Norway, Philippines, Sweden, Taiwan, Turkey, United Kingdom and United States of America, have stipulated different ceilings on the number of employees as one of the criteria for identifying a small scale industry. In some neighbouring countries like Pakistan and Sri Lanka, however, no upper limit for employees has been fixed for small scale industries. The difinitions of small scale industries prevalent in these countries, as compiled by Khan, are presented in Table 1.3.

Further Expansion of the Scope of SSI in India

It was realised that stipulating a ceiling on investment in fixed assets, including cost of land, may not be realistic and uniform, inasmuch as the cost of land substantially varied in rural, semi-urban, urban and metropolitan areas. The cost of plant and machinery may, however, be uniform all over the country except for a marginal variation comprising the transportation cost.

Therefore, in 1966, the ceiling was fixed in regard to investment in plant and machinery only (excluding land and building, furnitures and fixtures, etc), and it was also raised from Rs. 5 lakh to Rs. 7.5 lakh (Rs. 10 lakh for ancillary units).

The investment ceiling in plans and machinery was further raised from Rs. 7.5 lakh to Rs. 10 lakh (Rs. 15 lakh in case of ancillary units) in 1975, to Rs. 20 lakh (Rs. 25 lakh in case of ancillary units) in 1980, and to Rs. 35 lakh (Rs. 45 lakh in case of ancillary units) in 1985.[12]

Current Definition of SSI

Under the Industrial Policy, announced on May 31, 1990, the investment ceiling in plant and machinery has been enhanced from Rs. 35 lakh to Rs. 60 lakh for small industries, from Rs. 45 lakh to Rs. 75 lakh for ancillary units, and from Rs. 2 lakh to Rs. 5 lakh for tiny units.[13]

The progressive rise in the ceiling of investment in plant and machinery has been attributed to the steady rise in the cost of plant and machinery and the felt need for modernisation and use of the recent technology in small scale sector.

"A special relaxation has been made in this sector to stimulate export growth".[14] Thus, "small scale units which undertake to export at least 30 per cent of annual production by the third year will be permitted to step up their investment in plant and machinery to Rs. 75 lakh",[15] (in place of Rs. 60 lakh in normal cases).

Operative Definition of SSI

As we have undertaken the study of SSI units which were in existence prior to the announcement of the Industrial Policy on May 31, 1990, we have adopted the definition of SSI units which was applicable during the material period, i.e., investment in plant and machinery upto Rs. 35 lakh (Rs. 45 lakh in case of ancillary units).

TABLE 1.3: Definition of Small Scale Industries in Some Other Countries

Country	Definition	Remarks
China	Units employing less than 30 workers with power of less than 5 H.P. and fixed capital upto 5 million.	–
Egypt, Israel & Turkey	Units employing less than 10 persons and using less than 10 H.P. of Electricity.	–
ESCAP countries	Units employing less than 20 persons using power or 50 persons when not using power.	–
Germany, Sweden, Norway & Denmark	–	There is no official definion. Generally units employing 300 workers are considered as small units.

(Contd.)

TABLE 1.3 *(Contd.)*

Country	Definition	Remarks
Indonesia	Manufacturing units employing less than 10 full time workers and not using mechanically driven tools and machinery.	This classification covers home and cottage industries too.
Iran	Ceiling of 50 lakh rials in fixed assets at the time of occupancy of factory and total employee less than 50 workers per shift	This must be wholly under Iranian ownership and the product should not be of artistic nature.
Italy	Units having less than 1,500 million liore capital investment and employing less than 500 persons.	–
Japan	Manufacturing units employing less than 300 persons or having capital investment of less than 10 million yen	Concept of small industries varies from 30 employees or less in wholesale trade to 300 persons or less in manufacturing units.
Pakistan	Units having Rs. 7.5 lakh in fixed assets.	This ceiling is relaxed to Pak Rs. 12 to 13 lakh for capital intensive industries.
Philippines	Units employing less than 100 workers	–
Sri Lanka	Using power and having capital investment in land, building and machinery, not exceeding Rs. 5 lakh.	Manufacturing units are divided into (i) Cottage (ii) handicrafts and (iii) Small scale industries.
Sweden	Units employing less than 50 workers.	There is no official definition.

(Contd.)

TABLE 1.3 *(Contd.)*

Country	Definition	Remarks
Taiwan	Units employing less than 20 workers with power or less than 40 workers without power.	There is no official definition.
U.K.	Units employing less than 500 workers.	–
U.S.A.	Units having less than 500 employees otherwise certified as small by the Small Business Administration.	Concept changes and stands at 250 employees if any assistance or facility is sought.

Source: R.R. Khan, Management of Small Scale Industries, S. Chand and Company, New Delhi, 1979, pp. 2-3.

ROLE OF COMMERCIAL BANKS IN ASSISTING SMALL SCALE INDUSTRIES

The commercial banks assist the small scale units in many ways. They organise Entrepreneurship Development Programmes to train the prospective entrepreneurs in the various functional areas of management and counsel them to select and launch only viable projects. They are expected to thoroughly examine the technical feasibility and economic viability of the projects and properly assess and meet the genuine credit requirements of the units. Through effective supervision and follow-up of the advances and periodical performance monitoring of the units, the commercial banks may detect the early symptoms of sickness and arrest the sickness at the incipient stage itself by taking right remedial measures in right time. If, however, some units finally fall sick, they are expected to undertake in-depth viability studies of such units, and formulate and implement comprehensive rehabilitation programmes with a view to reviving the viable sick units through a regular and rigorous performance monitoring system.

Advances to Small Scale Industries by Banks

The amount of outstandings in the advances to small scale industries by all scheduled commercial banks increased from Rs. 3,953.09 crore in 9.61 lakh accounts as on the last Friday of December 1981 to Rs. 9,127.25 crore in 18.63 lakh accounts as on the last Friday of December of 1986.

The outstanding advances of public sector banks to the small scale industries as on the last Friday of December 1989, further increased to Rs. 14,281 crore in 28.06 lakh accounts (provisional) from Rs. 12,309 crore in 25.98 lakh accounts as at the end of December 1988 and Rs. 10,798 crore in 23.15 lakh accounts as at the end of June 1988.[16]

The year-wise break up of the number of accounts and the amount oustanding in these accounts from 1981 to 1986 for all scheduled commercial banks, and from 1987 to 1989 for public sector banks only, has been presented in Table 1.4.

Incidentally, the amount of financial assistance sanctioned by State Financial Corporations to small scale industries was Rs. 892 crore and the amount disbursed Rs. 689 crore during 1987-88.[17]

Quality Aspects of Bank Loans to SSI

The quantum of loans sanctioned and disbursed by the commercial banks and the State Financial Corporations are indeed impressive. However, the steadily growing incidence of sickness, particulary in the small scale sector, go to suggest that there is something lacking in the quality of management of the advances pertaining to prompt and

TABLE 1.4: Advances to Total SSI Sector by All Scheduled Commercial Banks

As on the last Friday of December	No. of Accounts (No. in lakh)	Amount outstanding (Rs. in crore)
1981	9.61	3,953.09
1982	10.50	4,464.32
1983	12.44	5,389.37
1984	14.55	6,537.18
1985	16.42	7,829.31
1986	18.63	9,127.25
1987*	21.71	10,166.32
1988*	25.98	12,308.67
1989*	28.06 (Provisional)	14,281.00 (Provisional)

* Data relate to Public Sector Banks only.

Sources: (i) Hand Book of Statistics, 1989, Small Scale Industries in India, Development Commissioner (SSI), New Delhi, p. 94.

(ii) *Reserve Bank of India Bulletin,* March 1991, (Supplement) p. 80.

realistic project appraisal, assessment and disbursement of loans, effective supervision and follow-up of advances and performance monitoring of the units, detection of early symptoms of sickness and initiation of right remedial measures in right time, and the rehabilitation of viable sick units.

Most of the Indian researchers and writers are of the view that the major cause of industrial sickness is lack of managerial skills on the part of the entrepreneurs, particularly in the small scale sector. They have, *inter alia,* suggested that the entrepreneurs would do well to ensure that only viable projects are selected and properly implemented by them (entrepreneurs). Further, during the post-implementation stage, they (entrepreneurs) should remain alert throughout to pick up the early signals of sickness with a view to taking timely corrective steps to arrest the sickness at the incipient stage itself.

Several Indian researchers and writers maintain that next to the entrepreneurs, the bankers, by virtue of their day-to-day transactions with the borrowers, are the first among the outsiders to come to know of the early symptoms of sickness in an industrial unit through the conduct of the bank accounts, and effective supervision and follow-up of the advances. They, therefore, hold the view that the banks can play a significant role in arresting the growing incidence of sickness in the small scale sector, by streamlining their systems right from the project appraisal stage to the periodical performance monitoring of the units, and by taking appropriate remedial measures in right time at the early stage of sickness, in close coordination with the entrepreneurs and other financial institutions. However, much research does not seem to have been done covering the various aspects of such role of the banks in particular.

We, therefore, propose to study some cases of sick SSI units, financed by a commercial banks, with a view to identifying the various causes of sickness and examining the roles of the entrepreneurs and the banks in particular, and those of the other financial institutions, the government and the large scale industries in general, in arresting the incidence of sickness in the small scale industries.

Objectives of the Study

The general objectives of the study are:

(i) to identify the major causes of sickness in the small scale industries (SSI);

(ii) to examine the contributory factors on the part of the

entrepreneurs and the commercial banks in the growing incidence of sickness in the small scale sector;

(iii) to analyse the effectiveness of the existing systems and procedures of the commercial banks in regard to project appraisal, assessment and disbursement of working capital advances, post-sanction supervision and follow-up of the advances, and rehabilitation of sick SSI units; and

(iv) to make suggestions, based on the empirical study,

(a) to the commercial banks, regarding adequate financing of only viable projects, timely dectection of symptoms of incipient sickness through effective supervision and follow-up, and initiation of right remedial measures in right time for arresting the sickness at the early stage, and for rehabilitation of the units, if they finally fall sick ; and

(b) to the small entrepreneurs, the financial institutions, the governments,and the large scale industries, to play their respective roles positively for arresting the growing incidence of sickness in the small scale sector.

Scope of the Study

We have confined our study particulary to the role and responsibility of commercial banks, in arresting the incidence of sickness in the small sector, for the following main reasons:

(i) Commercial banks play a vital role in meeting the financial requirements of the small scale industries as a major portion of the finance to the sector comes from them.

(ii) Commercial banks mainly meet the working capital requirements of the units, management whereof has greater flexibility, as compared to term loans.

(iii) Bankers, by virtue of providing working capital finance to the units, come in direct contact with the entrepreneurs on a regular basis through the day-to-day transactions in the bank accounts.

(iv) Bankers are, therefore, in a better position, as compared to the officers of other financial institutions, to detect early symptoms of sickness and to initiate suitable remedial measures in right time to arrest the sickness at the incipient stage itself; and

(v) Lastly, the commercial banks have a crucial role to play in the rehabilitation of sick SSI units, in close coordination with the other financial institutions and the entrepreneurs.

Further, due to the constraints of time and resources, and with a view to eliminating the variable of differences in the systems and procedures of different banks, we have selected for our study the SSI units financed by only one of the leading commercial banks in the public sector.

Hypotheses

On consideration of the several causes of sickness, internal and external, as revealed by the various studies, discussed in the foregoing pages, we have built two hypotheses for the research as under:

1. "That some small scale industrial (SSI) units become sick due to various internal factors like faulty selection and implementation of the projects, lack of managerial competence on the part of the small entrepreneurs in one or more of the functional

areas like marketing, finance, production and corporate management".

2. "That commercial banks can play a vital role in arresting the growing incidence of sickness in the small scale sector through prompt and realistic project appraisal, proper assessment and phased disbursement of loans (term loans and working capital advances), effective supervision and follow-up of the advances, and effective performance monitoring of the units, with a view to detecting early symptoms of sickness and initiating right remedial measures in right time so as to arrest the sickness at the incipient stage itself, and to rehabilitate the units, if they finally fall sick, by formulating and implementing suitable and comprehensive rehabilitation programmes in appropriate time".

If these parts of the hypotheses, on being put to test through the empirical study, are found to be true, then to suggest some positive orientation and approach on the part of the small entrepreneurs, and some modifications in the present systems and procedures being followed by the commercial banks such that

(i) Only viable projects are conceived, initiated and implemented by the entrepreneurs on healthy lines on an on-going basis; and

(ii) the commercial banks exercise due care and unceasing alterness right from the project appraisal stage to the assessment and disbursement of loans, supervision and follow-up of advances, and performance monitoring of the units at regular periodical intervals, with a view to arresting the growing incidence of sickness in the small scale sector.

Methodology

The research is based on the empirical study of the cases of sick small scale industrial (SSI) units, which are subjected primarily to qualitative analysis with a view to identifying the major causes of sickness in the SSI units and suggesting remedial measures for arresting the growing incidence of sickness in the small scale sector.

The methodology used in the research is the case method involving investigation of the records of the banks and personal interviews with the officers of the commercial banks and other financial institutions, the entrepreneurs of sick (viable and non-viable) SSI units and some successful entrepreneurs.

Besides, the technique of observation was also applied in a number of cases during the course of discussions between the entrepreneurs and the officers of the bank, both at the controlling offices and the branches concerned, involving negotiations for grant of further credit facilities and/or concessions for rehabilitation of the sick SSI units, etc.

Twenty-two cases of viable and non-viable sick SSI units of different constitutions, engaged in various manufacturing activities, and enjoying different quantum of credit facilities, ranging from over Rs.2 lakh to Rs.50 lakh, have been selected for the study on a random sampling basis. The units, included in the sample, have been financed by different categories of branches of the bank, falling under the administrative control of different regions, in different districts of Andhra Pradesh. The sample design has been discussed in the subsequent pages.

The primary data have been collected from the original records of the bank, identified for the study, available at its controlling offices and the branches concerned, including the correspondence between the borrowers and the Branch Managers, the Branch Managers and the Regional Managers, and bank's Zonal Offices and Head Office, and the conduct of the borrowers' bank accounts at the respective branches.

Besides, the officers of the bank, identified for the study, and other commercial banks, of different ranks, at the controlling offices (like the Chief General Manager, General Manager, Deputy General Manager, Regional Manager, Administrative Officer (Advances), Administrative Officer (Rehabilitation) and Desk Officer), at the branches (like the Branch Manager, Manager and Deputy Manager of the Small Scale and Small Business (SIB) Division, Field Officer, and Desk Officer), as also at the apex Colleges and Zonal Training Centres of the banks (like the Principal, Vice Principal and the Member of the Faculty), have been extensively interviewed by administering the semi-structured questionnaire placed at Appendix III.

The data, thus collected, were crosschecked by extensive interviews of :

(i) the officers of other financial institutions which mainly grant term loans to the small scale industries;
(ii) the entrepreneurs of sick (viable and non-viable) SSI units, and
(iii) the entrepreneurs of successful units;

by administering different sets of semi-structured questionnaire, suitably modified. The relative sets of the questionnaire are placed at Appendix IV, V and VI respectively.

Incidentally, we may mention that the different sets of the questionnaire were pre-tested before finalisation by conducting in-depth interviews of a few entrepreneurs, and officers of the banks and other financial institutions.

The interviews were conducted by the researcher himself with a view to maintaining uniformity in collection, collation and interpretation of the responses, and arriving at some conclusions regarding the main causes of sickness in SSI units.

The responses were tabulated as part of the rough work and only the final analyses, conclusions and interpretations have been incorporated in the study in a collective manner, with a view to limiting the size of the body of the book. Further, as most of the respondents preferred to remain anonymous and gave the information in strict confidence, their particulars have not been disclosed in the study.

While the bank records at the controlling offices and the branches, as also the various sets of questionnaire, personal interviews, discussions and observations provided the primary data for the research, the secondary data included:

1. Reserve Bank of India, Bombay, Report on Currency and Finance, Vol. I: *Economic Review*, 1978-79 to 1989-90.
2. Reserve Bank of India Bulletin, March 1991, (Supplement).
3. Reserve Bank of India, Bombay, Report on Trend and Progress of Banking in India, 1978-79 to 1986-87.
4. Reserve Bank of India Annual Reports, 1979-80 to 1989-90.
5. Small Scale Industries: Twenty-five years of Progress, Development Commissioner (SSI), New Delhi.
6. Hand Book of Statistics, 1989, Small Scale Industries in India, Development Commissioner (SSI), New Delhi.
7. Five Year Plan Documents (First to Seventh Plans).
8. Government of India, India 1990.
9. State Bank of India, Financing of Small Scale Industries: Report of the Study Team, Bombay, 1975.
10. State Bank of India Monthly Review, August 1981 to February 1991.

The secondary sources in regard to the industrial development and sickness, particularly in the samll scale sector, are wide and varied. Therefore, only a sample survey has been made in the study. Some of the secondary sources, however, form a part of the bibliography.

Sample Design and Data Base

The bank, identified by us for the study, had undertaken indepth viability studies of 100 sick SSI units, enjoying credit limits of over Rs. 2 lakh at its various branches in Hyderabad and five neighbouring districts during the period 1988-91. The district-wise break-up of these units is given in Table 1.5.

As may be observed from Table 1.5, out of the 100 units studied by the bank, 61 units pertained to District II. Further, among the 100 units, 39 units were found to be non-viable for rehabilitation, 48 units were found to be viable for rehabilitation, and the viability study of the remaining 13 units was still in progress.

Out of the 39 non-viable units, 29 or 74.36 per cent of the units belonged to District II and the remaining 10 or 25.64 per cent of the units were thinly spread over other districts. We have, therefore, randomly selected 12 or 41.38 per cent of the 29 non-viable units pertaining to District II.

Further, out of the 48 viable units brought under the bank's rehabilitation programme (Table 1.5), 29 or 60.42 per cent of the units pertained to District II, 16 or 33.33 per cent of the units belonged to District I, and the remaining 3 or 6.25 per cent of the units were situated in other districts – one unit in District V and 2 units in District VI. Districts III and IV, however, did not have any unit under the rehabilitation programme.

We have, therefore, randomly selected 6 viable units from District II, and 2 viable units from District I. Further, one of the two such units in District VI has also been included

TABLE 1.5: District-wise Break-up of 100 Sick SSI Units, Viability Study whereof was Undertaken by the Bank during the Period 1988-91

Districts	No. of units found non-viable for rehabilitation by the bank	No. of units found viable for rehabilitation by the bank	No. of units now under viability study or where the rehabilitation package was being finalised by the bank	Total
I	5	16	7	28
II	29	29	3	61
III	2	—	2	4
IV	3	—	1	4
V	—	1	—	1
VI	—	2	—	2
Total	39	48	13	100

in the sample. The single unit in District V has not been included in the sample inasmuch as while all the units included in the sample are manufacturing units, this unit only undertakes custom milling on behalf of the Food Corporation of India.

In this connection we may mention that out of the nine selected cases of viable SSI units being rehabilitated by the bank, the rehabilitation programme had so far been successful in seven cases and in the remaining two cases these had failed.

Further, out of the 13 sick SSI units, viability whereof was being examined by the bank the viability study in respect of one such unit in District II had been completed by December 1991. The unit has been found viable and the rehabilitation package was being finalised by the concerned

Regional Manager. This unit has, therefore, been included in our sample.

It would thus be observed that out of the 22 sick SSI units, randomly selected for the study, 19 or 86.36 per cent of the units pertain to District II, which has a concentration of a large number of SSI units, of different sizes, financed by the bank.

Further, out of the 19 units selected in the sample from District II, 11 units pertain to Branch No. 3, which is the largest and the only Category 'A' branch in the district and which has financed the largest number of SSI units in the district. As regards the remaining 8 units, while 4 units have been selected from Branch No. 4 (Category 'B' branch, which is the second largest branch in the district), two units have been selected from Branch No. 5 (the other Category 'B' branch in the district), and one unit each from Branch Nos. 6 and 7 (Category 'C' and Category 'D' branches respectively).

Further, the two units selected from District I comprise one unit each from Branch Nos 1 and 2 (Category 'A' and Category 'D' branches respectively). Besides, the only unit selected from District VI pertains to Branch No. 8 (Category 'D' branch).

It would, thus, be observed that the 22 units, included in the sample, have been financed by different categories of branches of the bank. While 12 units pertain to category 'A' branches and 6 units to Category 'B' branches, the remaining 4 units pertain to Category 'C' and 'D' branches – one unit from Category 'C' branch and 3 units from Category 'D' branches.

Further, 8 branches, of different categories, have contributed to the sample. While 2 branches each of the Categories 'A' and 'B' have contributed 12 and 6 units respectively to the sample, the remaining four units have been contributed by one Category 'C' branch and 3 category'D' branches - 'C' and 'D' category branches accounting for one unit each.

Further, the cases of the 22 sick SSI units, selected for the study, may broadly be classified as in Table 1.6.

TABLE 1.6: Classification of the Cases of the 22 Sick SSI Units included in the Sample

	Criteria	Category
1.	Units which were found non-viable for rehabilitation by the bank.	Category 1 (12 cases, Nos. 1 to 12)
2.	Units which were found viable for rehabilitation by the bank (10 cases) and	
	(i) where the rehabilitation programmes have been successful.	Category 2.1 (7 cases, Nos. 13 to 19)
	(ii) where the rehabilitation programmes have been unsuccessful.	Category 2.2 (2 cases, Nos. 20 & 21)
	(iii) where the rehabilitation programme was being finalised.	Category 2.3 (1 case, No. 22)

The Names of the Units and the Entrepreneurs used in the Cases are Pseudonyms

The branch-wise break-up, (under the respective districts), of the 22 sick SSI units, included in the sample, is given in Table 1.7.

These 22 units, included in the sample, are manufacturing 17 different products. The product-wise break-up of the sample units is given in Table 1.8.

The constitution of the 22 sick SSI units, included in the sample, varied from proprietary concerns and partnership firms to private limited companies. However, no public limited company happened to be included in the sample due to their rare presence in the small scale sector. The constitution-wise break-up of the units is given in Table 1.9.

TABLE 1.7: Branch-wise Break-up (Under the Respective Distrits) of the 22 Sick SSI Units, Included in the Sample

Branches [branch categories (A, B, C, D) in parentheses]	Number of units-category-wise*				
	Category 1	Category 2.1	Category 2.2	Category 2.3	Total
District I					
Branch No. 1 (A)	–	1	–	–	1
Branch No. 2 (D)	–	–	1	–	1
Total of District I	–	1	1	–	2
District II					
Branch No. 3 (A)	9	1	–	1	11
Branch No. 4 (B)	1	2	1	–	4
Branch No. 5 (B)	2	–	–	–	2
Branch No. 6 (C)	–	1	–	–	1
Branch No. 7 (D)	–	1	–	–	1
Total of District II	12	5	1	1	19
District VI					
Branch No. 8 (D)	–	1	–	–	1
Total of District VI	–	1	–	–	1
Grand Total of Districts I, II, & VI	12	7	2	1	22

* with reference to Table 1.6.

TABLE 1.8: Product-wise Break-up of the 22 Sick SSI Units included in the Sample

Sl. No.	Products manufactured	Case No – Category-wise*				
		Category 1	Cate gory 2.1	Category 2.2	Category 2.3	Total
1.	Plastic Moulding	1	–	–	–	1
2.	Carton & Printing of Labels	2	–	–	–	1
3.	Communication Items	3, 4	–	–	–	2
4.	Pharmaceuticals	5, 6,	17	–	–	3
5.	Mobile Cranes/Hydraulic Press	7	–	–	–	1
6.	Screen Printing & Dyeing 'Sarees'	8	–	21	–	2
7.	Machinery Components & Chemical Equipments	9	–	–	–	1
8.	Aluminium Utensils	10	–	–	–	1
9.	Metal Alloy	11	–	–	–	1
10.	Ceiling Fans & Fan Components	12	–	–	–	1
11.	Paint & Varnish	–	13	–	–	1
12.	Batteries	–	14	–	–	1
13.	Battery Boxes & Lavatory Pans	–	15	–	–	1
14.	Pumpsets	–	16	–	–	1
15.	Adhesive Gum Tape	–	18	–	–	1
16.	Electromagnetic Clutches/Clutch Assembly Units	–	19	–	22	2
17.	Biscuits	–	–	20	–	1
	Grand Total	12	7	2	1	22

* With reference to Table 1.6

The outstandings in the bank accounts of these 22 sample units range from over Rs. 2 lakh to Rs. 50 lakh. The

TABLE 1.9: Constitution-wise Break-up of the 22 Sick SSI Units included in the Sample

Sl. No.	Nature of the Constitution	Case No – Category-wise*				
		Category 1	Category 2.1	Category 2.2	Category 2.3	Total
1.	Proprietary Firm	2, 3, 4 8, 9, 11	18	21	22	9
2.	Partnership Firm	7, 10, 12	13, 16	–	–	5
3.	Private Limited Company	1, 5, 6	14, 15 17, 19	20	–	8
4.	Public Limited Company	–	–	–	–	–
	Grand Total	12	7	2	1	22

* With reference to Table 1.6.

distribution of the sample in terms of the size of the aggregate outstandings is given in Table 1.10.

For comparison, eight cases of healthy units have also been randomly selected for the study with a view to examining whether the healthy units also suffered from some of the major causative factors of sickness, but could avert or arrest the sickness at incipient stage, through effective management, or whether the major causes of sickness were conspicuously absent in the healthy units all through.

Further, based on the study of the cases of sick and healthy units, the profiles of successful and unsuccessful entrepreneurs have been broadly summarised in Chapter Five, Table 5.10, which may serve as a useful guide to the entrepreneurs (both present and prospective), the commercial banks and the other financial institutions.

Scheme of the Book

The book has been organised into six chapters. The intro-

TABLE 1.10: Distribution of the Sample of the 22 Sick SSI Units in Terms of the Size of Aggregate Outstandings

Sl. No.	Aggregate Outstanding	Case No – Category-wise*				
		Category 1	Category 2.1	Category 2.2	Category 2.3	Total
1.	Over Rs. 2 lakh and upto Rs. 5 lakh	8, 10	16	–	–	3
2.	Over Rs. 5 lakh and upto Rs. 10 lakh	11	18	20, 21	22	5
3.	Over Rs. 10 lakh and upto Rs. 20 lakh	2, 4 6, 9	14, 15 17, 19	–	–	8
4.	Over Rs. 20 lakh and upto Rs. 30 lakh	7	–	–	–	1
5.	Over Rs. 30 lakh and upto Rs. 40 lakh	3, 5 12	13	–	–	4
6.	Over Rs. 40 lakh and upto Rs. 50 lakh	1	–	–	–	1
	Grand Total	12	7	2	1	22

* With reference to Table 1.6

duction is followed by the second chapter which deals with the various definitions of sick small scale industrial units, the structural analysis of an industrial unit and the stages of sickness, the early symptoms of sickness and detection thereof, the viability study of sick of units, and the growing incidence of sickness in the small scale sector.

The third chapter presents the various causes of industrial sickness, as identified by other studies, and the summary of such causes, both internal and external. Chapter four has been subdivided into three parts, containing case studies of :

(i) non-viable sick units,
(ii) viable sick units, and
(iii) healthy units.

Chapter five contains the analysis and the inter-pretation of the data. The causes of sicknesss found in the case studies as also the factors which make the sick units non-viable or viable for rehabilitation by the banks, and which make the banks' rehabilitation programme a success or failure, have been discussed. Compartive profiles of successful and unsuccessful entrepreneurs have also been presented at the end of the chapter. Finally, the conclusions and suggestions are presented in the sixth chapter.

REFERENCES

1. Reserve Bank of India, Bombay, Report on Currency and Finance Vol. I: *Economic Review,* 1988-89, p. 73.
2. D. Nagaiya (Compiler), *Small Scale Industries in India: Hand Book of Statistics,* National Institute of Small Industry Extension Training (NISIET), Hyderabad, 1989, p. 11.
3. Government of India, India 1990, p. 303.
4. Report to the All India Congress Committee (AICC), Swaraj Bhawan, Allahabad, 1951.
5. Collected Works of Mahatma Gandhi, quoted by N. Raghunathan, former Development Commissioner (SSI), New Delhi, "Role and Performance of Small Scale Industries in the National Economy", the paper presented in the Seminar on 'Small Scale Industries and the National Economy', organised by the IIM, Bangalore, Nov. 27-29, 1988, p. 2
6. Small Scale Industries : Twenty-five Years of Progress, Development Commissioner (SSI), New Delhi, 1973, p. 7.
7. Reserve Bank of India, Bombay, Report on Currency and Finance, Vol. I: *Economic Review,* 1989-90, p. 70
8. Small Scale Industries: Twenty-five Years of Progress, Development Commissioner (SSI), New Delhi, 1973, p. 18.
9. Government of India, India 1990, p. 574.
10. Reserve Bank of India, Bombay, Report on Currency and Finance, Vol. I: *Economic Review,* 1989-90, p. 68.
11. R.R. Khan, *Management of Small Scale Industries,* S Chand & Company, New Delhi, 1979, pp. 2-3.

12. Hand Book of Statistics 1989, Small Scale Industries in India, Development Commissioner (SSI) New Delhi, p. 15 for all the changes in the definition of SSI in India from 1955 to 1985.
13. Reserve Bank of India, Bombay, Report on Currency and Finance, Vol. I: *Economic Review*, 1989-90, p. 70.
14. State Bank of India Monthly Review, Vol. 29, No. 6, June 1990, p. 297.
15. Government of India, India 1990, p. 517
16. Reserve Bank of India Bulletin, March 1991 (Supplement), p. 80.
17. Government of India, India 1990, p. 577.

2

SICKNESS IN SMALL SCALE INDUSTRIES

DEFINITION OF SICK SCALE INDUSTRIAL (SSI) UNITS

The authorities concerned have adopted different definitions or criteria for identifying a sick small scale industrial unit:

The State Bank of India

The study team of State Bank of India defined a sick SSI unit as one "which fails to generate internal surplus on a continuing basis, and depends for its survival on frequent infusion of external funds".[1]

The Reserve Bank of India

Refining this concept, the Reserve Bank of India advised all commercial banks, in November 1976, that "a unit may be considered as sick, if it had incurred cash loss for one year and, in the judgment of the bank, is likely to continue to incur cash losses for the current year as well as the following year and which has an imbalance in its financial structure, such as current ratio of less than 1:1 and worsening debt equity ratio (total outside liabilities to the net worth)".[2]

In February 1987, the Reserve Bank of India advised the revised definition of sick SSI units to all banks according to which "a SSI unit should be considered Sick' if it has —

(a) incurred cash loss in the previous accounting year and is likely to continue to incur cash loss in the current accounting year and has an erosion on account of cumulative cash losses to the extent of 50 per cent or more of its net worth, and/or

(b) continuously defaulted in meeting four consecutive quarterly instalments of interest or two half-yearly instalments of principal on term loans and there are persistent irregularities in the operations of its credit limits with the bank.

While both the conditions (a) and (b) should be satisfied in the case of larger SSI units, it would suffice if either alternative (a) or (b) is satisfied in case of the tiny and decentralised sector units".[3]

The definition of sick SSI units has further been modified by the Reserve Bank of India, in terms of its letter dated the 8th June 1989, addressed to all commercial banks, as under:

> "A small scale industrial unit should be considered as sick if it has, at the end of any accounting year, accumulated losses equal to or exceeding 50 per cent of its peak net worth in the immediately preceding five accounting years".[4]

Term Lending Institutions

Term lending institutions classify a unit as sick after taking into account any of the following symptoms:

(i) Continuous default in meeting four consecutive half-yearly instalments of interest or principal in respect of institutional loans.

(ii) Continuous cash losses for a period of two years or continued erosion in the net worth, say by 50 per cent.

(iii) Mounting arrears on account of statutory and other liabilities for, say, a period of one or two years.[5]

Government of India

With a view to encouraging amalgamation of sick industrial units with the healthy ones, by granting suitable tax incentives therefor, the Government of India, in the year 1977, classified a sick unit as one whose accumulated losses exceeded 50 per cent of its aggregate paid-up capital and reserves and the company was not financially viable.[6]

Deficiencies in the Definitions of Sick SSI Units

The officers of the banks and other financial institutions as also the researchers have expressed their dissatisfaction over the definitions propounded by the various authorities.

Viswanathan,[7] a practising banker, argues that while it was possible to objectively estimate the cash losses for the previous year, the estimates for the current and the following years may vary at the hands of an optimistic banker or otherwise. He, however, feels that "when in doubt, the banker would be well advised to adopt a conservative approach while determining the status of health of unit". He further opines that "if the unit is likely to incur cash losses for three years in a row, it is a sure sign of sickness", and the unit may be declared as such even though, in rare cases, the current ratio may be more than one.

Some financial analysts, however, feel that operating losses or net losses, and not cash losses, should be the criteria for determining the sickness in an industrial unit, inasmuch as it was technically possible for a unit to earn cash profits over a period but incur net losses throughout, i.e., after providing for adequate depreciation. "The banker should, therefore, be alert even if a company were to incur net losses for two years in a row", suggests Viswanathan.[8]

Pathak,[9] a bank officer, points out that, as per the latest (1989) definition of the Reserve Bank of India, the units, which may have genuinely fallen sick within the first five years of their existence, "can be categorised as sick earliest at the end of the sixth year", and by that time some units may "cross the stage of viability".

A similar view is expressed by Yadva[10] who feels that the cirterion of erosion of 50 per cent or more of the peak net worth for classifying a unit as sick is responsible for inordinately delaying the rehabilitation actions, and thereby adversely affecting the chances of its revival. He, therefore, suggests that the rehabilitaion programme may be initiated before the erosion of peak net worth crosses the 10-15 per cent limit.

Dholakia[11] also observes that thc criterion of recurring cash losses for identifying sick units results in such delays that by the time they are classified as sick, they become non-viable for rehabilitation.

Further, in some cases the definitions of sick SSI units have been interpreted, by the officers of the banks and other financial institutions, more in letter than in spirit.

There are cases where the term lending institutions like the State Financial Corporations had declared the SSI units as sick on the ground that they had failed to repay four consecutive half-yearly instalments of the principal or interest, as per the strict interpretation of the definition. But, in fact, in such cases, the State Financial Corporations had fixed thc due dates for the payment of the half-yearly instalments, calculated exactly after six months from the date of the disbursement of the loans, without considering the reasonable gestation period and the quantum and time of generation of internal surplus, based on the projected fund flow statements for the next few years.

Besides, there are cases of wilful defaulters who did not pay four consecutive half-yearly instalments, though their units were generating sufficient internal surplus to do so.

Such units may not justifiably be termed as sick, but these were declared as such by the term lending institutions. Similarly, it may not be justifiable for the bank officers to declare a unit as sick if it had to depend for its survival on frequent outside borrowings, because they had not fully met its genuine working capital requirements.

Operative Definition of Sick SSI Units

We do not want to enter into the controversy of the deficiencies in the different definitions, nor do we propose to suggest fault-free single definition of sick SSI units which may by uniformly acceptable and applicable to all concerned.

We have, however, adopted the definition of sick SSI units stipulated by the Reserve Bank of India in 1987, because

(a) all commercial banks follow the definition stipulated by the Reserve Bank of India, and
(b) all the sick SSI units covered under the study had fallen sick prior to the circulation of the Reserve Bank of India letter dated the 8th June, 1989, advising further modifications in the definition.

STRUCTURAL ANALYSIS OF AN INDUSTRIAL UNIT

While it is important to define a sick SSI unit to correctly identify a sick unit, it is far more important to detect the early symptoms of sickness with a view to initiating the required remedial measures in time to arrest and avert the sickness at the incipient stage itself. This way the prospect of restoring the unit back to health would be brighter and the quantum of cost involved would also be lesser, to the mutual advantage of the banks, the other financial institutions and the entrepreneurs concerned.

As we all know, an industrial unit, like a human being,

does not fall sick all of a sudden, but gradually, in stages. The banks, the other financial institutions and the entrepreneurs would, therefore, do well to bear this aspect in mind, and be sensitive enough to get alerted at the appearance of the early signals of sickness and to initiate the necessary corrective steps at the initial stage of the sickness, failing which even a minor ailment may gradually grow unabated, may become chronic and mostly may turn terminal.

"In order to have a better understanding of sickness, it is necessary to have a graphic insight into the anatomy of an industrial unit", maintain Bidani and Mitra.[12] They draw an analogy from the medical science and argue: "Before a pathologist learns about the nature, causes and remedies of a disease, he has to study the anatomy of the human being", so as to know about the "functioning of various organs, systems and sub-systems within the body". He also studies how the internal disorders or external bacteria or virus adversely affect the normal functioning of these systems or subsystems, "causing various diseases in the human body". Then he learns the different signals and symptoms of diseases for a proper diagnosis", and treatment.

Clinical Model of Anatomy of an Industrial Unit

Bidani and Mitra[13] have developed a clinical model of the anatomy of an industrial unit, (Figure 2.1), showing its various systems, and their critical elements by a circle divided into four quadrants which represent the four functional areas viz., finance production, marketing and personnel. There is also a core circle which indicates corporate management, responsible for coordinating these four functions.

Finance Quadrant

The finance quadrant represents the functional area responsible for all financial decisions relevant for the overall performance of the financial systems of the unit, viz., financial structure, financial planning and budgeting, utilisation of assets, working capital management, costing, pricing, accounting systems and procedures, etc.

Financial structure involves decisions regarding the most favourable sources of finance and the optimal level of debt equity ratio so as to maximise the wealth of the unit. Financial planning and budgeting includes foreseeing of the future financial requirements, formulation and settlement of the departmental budgets, and the performance appraisal and variance analysis in the various segments of the activity. Optimum capacity utilisation of plant and machinery, well above the break-even point, and efficient utilisation of current assets through effective working capital management are crucial for ensuring the profitability of the unit. Costing and pricing decisions are also important for minimising costs and maximising profits. Further, the proper system and procedure of accounting and an effective system of performance monitoring and control are necessary to assess and maintain the financial health of a unit on a day-to-day basis.

Production Quadrant

Production quadrant represents the decisions pertaining to the production area of the unit viz., selection of suitable site, choice of appropriate plant and machinery, product design, production planning and control, purchase policy and inventory control, maintenance management, quality control, research and development, etc.

The selection of the site of an industrial unit depends on various factors like availability of the necessary infrastructure (e.g. roads, railways, power-station, water supply, etc), availability of government subsidy and concessions (e.g., backward area subsidy, concessions in tax, power tariff etc. in the initial years of the unit), proximity to the sources of raw materials and markets, etc. While selecting the plant and machinery, their cost, size, installed capacity, operating

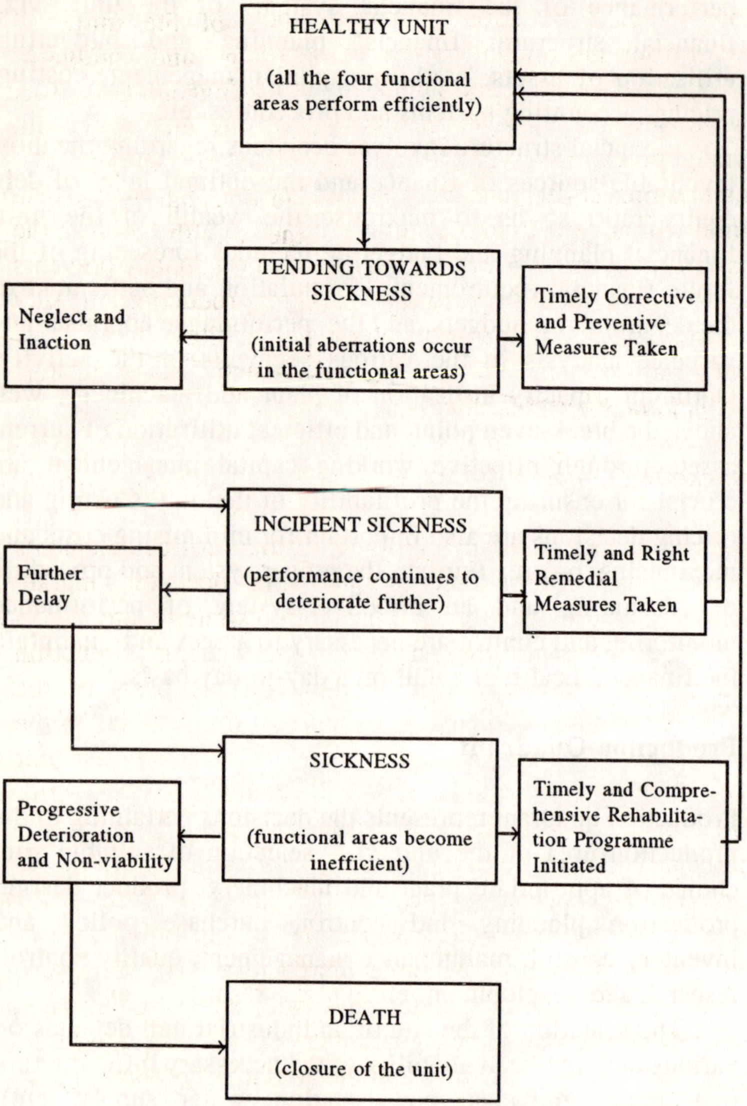

FIG. 2.1: Stages of Sickness and Recovery of an Industrial Unit

characteristic, market reputation, etc., are required to be considered. Production planning and control helps in controlling and regulating the process so as to achieve the budgeted level. Material management pertains to controlling the usage and wastage, quality and price, and above all, timely procurement of the all the required materials, (by maintaining sufficient safety stocks, depending on the lead time) with a view to maximising production and avoiding the risk of stock out. While maintenance management prevents break-downs and the resultant loss of production, quality control, and research and development facilitate innovations and improvement in the products, and guard against technological obsolescence.

Marketing Quadrant

The marketing quadrant involves various critical elements like demand forecasting, product mix decision, market segmentation, distribution and promotion strategy, etc.

Demand forecasting is necessary inasmuch as production and financial planning can be done on the basis of the estimated levels of demand and supply of the products in the market. By adopoting an appropriate product-mix, the unit can maximise its production, and its profitability therewith, with the available production capacity. The study of the market segments helps a unit to gain a better understanding of the attitudes and preferences of its consumers so as to suitably modify its products accordingly. This may also help the unit in adopting a suitable distribution and promotion policy, like providing better and widespread after sales service, offering increased guarantee period, with a view to improving the marketability and demand of its products.

Personnel Quadrant

The personnel quadrant pertains to the personnel functioning of an industrial unit which involves manpower planning, selection, recruitment and training of its personnel, wage and salary administration, labour relations, etc.

Manpower planning helps a unit in estimating its future manpower needs and the scope of its deployment and development. Recruiting the right type of people, placing the right people on the right job, training them to perform better in the present assignment and grooming them to schoulder higher responsibility in the near future, are some of the principles of pro-people policy, conducive for the organisational health of an industrial unit. A judicious approach regarding wage and salary, and constant endeavour to maintain good industrial relations with the employees and the officers, go a long way in increasing the productivity and profitability of the unit. As we work "with and through people", Peters and Waterman Junior[14] have rightly observed that "if you want productivity and the financial reward that goes with it, you must treat your workers as your most important asset.... Treat people as adults. Treat them as partners; treat them with dignity; treat them with respect". "The individual must be respected", is one of the three basic beliefs of the IBM's philosophy.[15]

Further, "caring for people" is the ethos in "A Passion for Excellence".[16] We may force people to work but may not force them to work well. We should, therefore, motivate and "help people reach their full potential" by catching them "doing something right" and praising them,[17] because the "people who feel good about themselves produce good results",[18] and the "people who produce good results feel good about themselves".[19] The healthy cycle thus goes on enabling the organisation to achieve excellence on an ongoing basis.

Corporate Management

Corporate management has been shown as a core circle in the

aforesaid model inasmuch as it enjoys a pivotal position in the management of an industrial unit and pervades through all the four functional areas. Its various critical elements include planning and organising, leading and motivating, monitoring and controlling, facilitating organisation development, etc.

Planning involves setting up of the objectives and goals of the organisation as a whole, and laying down the sub-goals, both quantitative and qualitative, for each functional areas. It establishes the policies and standards of performance, programmes and strategies, with a view to achieving the desired results at or above the budgeted levels.

Organising involves assignments of various roles and responsibilities to the different departments and people, and coordinating their inter-connected and inter-dependent activities, so as to optimise the productivity and profitability of the organisation. Leading and motivating people involve having a pro-people attitude, manifesting genuine concern for people, and sincerely endeavouring to meet their 'individual goals' along with the 'organisational goals'. By caring for our people, we may infuse into them a sense of belonging to their organisation. They would thus work hard and perform at the peak of their potentials, not because they 'have to' but because they 'love to'. They would thus work as a well-knit team, in an atmosphere of mutual trust and cooperation, conducive for the growth and prosperity of the organisation.

Performance monitoring and control involve periodical evaluation of the achievements of the budgeted levels of production, sales, etc., analysis of the adverse variances, if any, and initiation of corrective actions, wherever necessary.

Organisation development (OD) involves brining a planned chage in the oranisation, by carefully assessing its likely impact on the other inter-related functional areas of the organisation, to enable it to face the challenges of tommorrow.

STAGES OF SICKNESS IN AN INDUSTRIAL UNIT

We have so far discussed the various systems and sub-systems of an industrial unit and the functioning thereof. We have also observed that a unit does not fall sick all of a sudden but gradually, in stages. We would now discuss the various stages that a healthy industrial unit passes through, before it finally falls sick.

Western researchers have also found that there are various stages in an organisational decline and that very often the efforts for the revival of the units are made at a later stage when they prove to be ineffective. For example, Weitzel and Jonsson[20] have developed the following model of the stages of organisational decline and the corresponding organisational action:

Stages	Organisational Action
1. Blinded	Failure to anticipate or detect pressure toward entropy; decline begins.
2. Inaction	Failure to decide on corrective action; decline becomes noticeable.
3. Faulty Action	Faulty decisions; faulty implementation of decisions.
4. Crisis	Given faulty - action stage, and unforgiving environment, last chance for reversal. Given forgiving environment, slow erosion.
5. Dissolution	Given crisis stage and unforgiving environment, rapid demise. Given forgiving environment, slow demise.

In a comparative study of 57 large corporate failures and

a matched sample of survivors, Hambrick and D'Aveni[21] also observed different stages of sickness which they called the 'downward spiral' of the 57 failures. The various factors that finally led to the failure were both internal and external, viz., early weakness in performance, extreme and vacillating strategies, and abrupt environmental changes.

Indian researches and authors have also identified various stages of sickness in industrial units. For example, Bidani and Mitra[22] have indentified the following four stages of sickness before a healthy unit finally fails and closes down.

Healthy Unit

A healthy unit is one where all the systems and sub-systems, and all the functional areas like finance, production, marketing and personnel, are performing efficiently. That is, when a unit is earning sufficient profit, when its current ratio is more than one, when its tangible net worth is positive, and when its debt equity ratio is reasonable, it may be termed as healthy. Further, a healthy unit must also be capable of withstanding the everchanging external environment, as the anti-bodies in a healthy human being fight with the viral or bacterial infections.

Tending towards Sickness

When certain aberrations start taking place in any of the functional areas of a unit, due to some internal problems or external (environmental) constraints, it may be said to be tending towards sickness. The indicators of this stage may be the decline in the profit last year as compard to the previous year and the estimated losses in the current year.

At this stage, both the banker and the borrower would do well to carefully diagnose and analyse the various causes of the initial ailments and to take the necessary preventive measures so that the unit may be saved from falling sick.

Incipient Sickness

If the initial aberrations are not arrested in time, the position may deteriorate further and the actual sickness may set in. This stage may be termed as the incipient sickness stage of the unit, which may be determined by the following factors:

(a) The unit had incurred a cash loss during the last year and was expected to incur a cash loss even in the current year.
(b) Though the current ratio of the unit was more than one as at the end of its last financial year, it was expected to deteriorate to less than one during the current financial year.
(c) The tangible net worth (TNW) of the unit was expected to contract during the current financial year.
(d) The debt-equity ratio of the unit was expected to deteriorate during the current financial year.

The bank officers may be able to detect the incipient sickness in a unit in time through an effective system of supervision and follow-up of the advances. After having done so, they should promptly review the overall position of the unit, identify the area of deficiency, and initiate the necessary corrective steps, in full cooperation with the entrepreneurs, with a view to preventing the unit from falling sick.

Sickness

If the necessary corrective measures are not taken promptly at the incipient stage or are inadequate, the causal factors may continue to adversely affect the functional areas, gradually worsening the overall position of the unit, which may ultimately fall sick.

At this stage, the bank officers are expected to urgently undertake the detailed viability study of the sick unit. If the unit is considered viable, they should promptly formulate and implement a comprehensive rehabilitation programme with the close cooperation of the entrepreneurs, with a vew to bringing the unit back to health. Timely action is of essence in such matters because in undue delay may turn even a viable unit into a terminally sick unit. If the unit is, however, found to be non-viable for rehabilitation by the bank, the advance should be called up without delay so as to contain the losses of the bank and the borrowers.

Death or Closure of the Units

We have developled a model, (Fig. 2.1), showing the states of health and gradual sickness, and highlighting the stages of recovery back to health when timely remedial measures are taken at the early stages of sickness, and depicting the gradual deterioration in health or normal functioning of the unit, due to inaction or delayed action, culminating in death, i.e., the closure of the unit.

EARLY WARNING SIGNALS AND SYMPTOMS OF SICKNESS IN SMALL SCALE INDUSTRIAL (SSI) UNITS

We have so far seen that an industrial unit does not fall sick all of a sudden, but gradually, in distinct stages. We have also seen that if timely remedial measures are taken, at the various stages of sickness, the unit may be restored back to health, failing which its position may go on deteriorating further, and the unit may ultimately become non-viable for rehabilitation and may have to be closed down.

It is, therefore, important for the bank officers to be sufficiently sensitive and alert to pick up the early warning signals and symptoms of the sickness, at its various stages, through a system of periodical health check up by way of an effective performance monitoring system, with a view to initiating the necessary corrective steps at the early stages of the sickness and bringing the unit back to health.

Natarajan, Krishnamurthy and Rao'[23] studied one sick SSI unit in India and found the undernoted seven symptoms of sickness:

(a) Cumulative losses resulting in an erosion of capital.
(b) Negative net-working capital.
(c) Under-utilisation of installed capacity.
(d) Stoppage of production for a long period.
(e) Frequent interruptions in sales.
(f) Delay or default in paying the periodical instalments on term loan.
(g) Excessive and continuous dependence on external funds.

Other Indian studies have added declining business opportunities, outmoded facilities, low employee morale (Krishnan),[24] high employee turnover, absenteeism, accidents, and low level of trust (Dwivedi).[25]

The Western cases also showed similar symptoms. The most frequently mentioned symptoms are: cash losses and non-payment of dividends for four years at Olivetti (Turner),[26] high cost, low margin and inability to cope with competition at ICL (Marwood),[27] poor quality of goods and poor service at Woolworth (Rose),[28] ageing plant and machinery and demoralised people at Dunlop (Radford),[29] decline in market share at Asahi Breweries (Nakajo and Kono),[30] low margins, price cuts and credit incentives to effect sales and declining profits at MFI (Seabright),[31] low productivity and poor industrial relations at a distribution centre (Bamber & Lausbury),[32] and decline in sales and drop in capacity utilisation in a few West German cases (Muller).[33]

Most other models of predicting industrial sickness, however, rely heavily on internal factors, specially financial ratios. The ratios are subjected to trend analysis, discriminant analysis, etc., to determine the power of each ratio or some combination of them to predict sickness.[34]

As Manimala observes,[35] "the overall finding of such analyses is that financial ratios by themselves are not enough to predict sickness or turnaround, although they are very powerful indicators. The erosion of the capacity of the organisation for sustained growth and the regaining of it may show up through other indicators, such as strategic management practices, human resource management practices, organisation culture, and so on." Sharma[36] holds the view that "in a way, the health of a unit is reflected in the conduct of the account with the bank." He further adds that "the frequency of visits of the clients to the bank, the nature and type of request for accommodation and their frequency, the mode of withdrawal of money from the bank—self cheque or cash etc., —are some of the signals that bankers take as warning."

According to Yadav,[37] the early signals and symptoms of sickness include under-utilisation of capacity, irregular bank accounts, short-term liquidity problems, over-burden of debt, operating losses, adverse financial ratios, poor quality of products, poor labour relations, etc.

Some important symptoms of sickness, enlisted by Gangwal[38] are persistent shortage of cash or liquid assets, constantly worsening trend of current ratio, unsatisfactory debt equity ratio, default in payment to suppliers, employees, banks and financial institutions, and frequent requests for rescheduling the payment of the instalments.

Misra[39] has identified the important symptoms of industrial sickness as:

"(a) shortage of liquid funds to meet short-term financial and statutory obligations;

(b) growth of excessive inventory of raw materials, goods-in-process and finished goods;

(c) under-utilisation of capacity;

(d) declining return on investment falling below the prevailing rate of interest;

(e) falling financial ratios, like current ratio, capital-debt ratio, etc; and

(f) low morale of employees and their greater turnover, poor maintenance of plant and equipment and frequent work stoppage, etc."

According to Pal,[40] persistent irregularity in bank accounts, request for non-projected extra facility, bouncing of cheques and bills, non-receipt of information and accounts, non-payment of instalments and interest, are some of the important symptoms of sickness which "provide sufficient clues to the banker for having a deeper insight into the affairs of the constituent unit".

Viswanathan,[41] now Deputy Managing Director in the State Bank of India, categorises the symptoms of sickness under two broad categories, financial and non-financial, and holds the view that "usually, the non-financial symptoms precede the financial symptoms". According to him, while the financial symptoms incude irregularity in bank accounts, non-payment of interest on borrowings and instalments on term loans, inability to pay the creditors on time, etc., the non-financial symptoms include incapacity to produce according to schedule, inabilty to market the goods produced, fast turnover of executives, staff and labour, generally poor reputation in the market, etc.

Hingorani[42] is of the view that the state of health of a unit, ('good', 'not good' or 'bad') may be assessed on the following parameters:

(a) Bank transactions record, covering movement in the account (oscillation), credit-debt summations (velocity), drawing power, inventory norms, and information systems like submission of monthly stock statements and other financial statements;

(b) Financial information, covering current ratio debt: equity ratio, sales value growth, profit growth etc.; and

(c) Management abilities.

He, therefore, suggests that any adverse deviations in one or more of the aforesaid parameters may be early symptoms of sickness, which the banker may detect in time through an effective monitoring of bank accounts.

The various symptoms of sickness, according to Bhattacharya,[43] now the Managing Director, State Bank of Hyderabad, include continuous irregularity in bank accounts, downward trend in sales, stagnation or fall the profit, contraction in the market share, reduction in credit summation, failure to pay statutory liabilities, higher rate of rejection of goods, frequent return of bills, longer period of credit allowed on bills/book debts, failure to pay timely instalments of the principal and interest in respect of term loans, etc. non-submission of periodical financial data/stock statements, etc, on time, decrease in working capital due to increase in sundry debtors, decrese in creditors, piling up of inventories including slow or non-moving items, and diversion of funds, rapid turnover of key personnel etc. He, however, maintains, that 'the bank, by virtue of its close association with day-to-day dealings with an industrial unit, is perhaps the first outsider who could gauge the state of the unit's health and get an incling of impending calamity". He, therefore, opines that the bankers may be able to arrest to growing incidence of industrial sickness be picking up the various danger signals in good time and initiating appropriate remedial steps before the situation goes out of control.

DETECTION OF EARLY SYMPTOMS OF SICKNESS BY BANKS

We would now discuss the various sources and systems of information available with the bank officers, wherefrom they may pick up the early signals and symptoms of sickness with a view to arresting the sickness at the incipient stage itself by initiating the right remedial measures in right time.

The various sources of such signals and symptoms of sickness may broadly be classified as under:

1. Position and conduct of accounts.
2. Stock statements of the current assets charged to the bank.
3. Performance monitoring, and Management Information System.
4. Financial statements.
5. Miscellaneous information.

Position and Conduct of Accounts

The credit facilities enjoyed by the borrowers from the bank may be clsssified under four main categories of accounts, viz.

(i) Stock cash credit account.
(ii) Clean cash credit 'Bills' account.
(iii) Demand drafts purchased account.
(iv) Term loan account.

While the position of the accounts pertains to the level of utilisation of the credit limit on a particular day, the conduct of the accounts involves the behaviour of the accounts over a period.

Units facing financial problems find it difficult to manage their activities within their sanctioned limits. They, therefore, frequently request the bank for allowing temporary over-drawings on their accounts, and find it difficult to regularise the position of the accounts within a reasonable time.

The following features in the conduct of the various accounts may indicate the incipient sickness in the unit:

(i) *Stock Cash Credit Account*

(a) Frequent requests to the bank for allowing overdrawings on the account.
(b) Persistence of the irregularity for more then 3/4 weeks.
(c) Unsatisfactory turnover and fluctuations in the account i.e. low debit-credit summations, incommensurate with the level of sales, and almost stagnant level of outstandings in the account.

These factors may signify the undernoted unsatisfactory features in the conduct of the account:

(a) Unproductive expenditure and/or diversion of funds.
(b) Decline in production due to paucity of funds, etc.
(c) Poor turnover of stocks.
(d) Decline in sales due to poor quality of products, stiff competition in the market, poor marketing management, etc.
(e) Non-routing of the entire sale proceeds through the account.
(f) Depositing the sale proceeds with some other bank.

(ii) *Clean Cash Credit 'Bills' Account*

(a) Decrease in the number and amount of bills tendered with the bank, well below the sanctioned limit, signifying drop in the sales for the various aforesaid reasons.
(b) Frequent and high incidence of return of bills unpaid signifying

(i) lack of demand of the products in the market,
(ii) lack of acceptance of the unit's products in the market, and/or

(iii) payment of the bills by the buyers to the borrowers direct.

(iii) *Demand Drafts Purchased Account*

(a) Frequent return of cheques negotiated on the account for want of funds in the respective drawer's accounts.
(b) Frequent requests for negotiating cheques beyond the sanctioned limit.
(c) Frequent negotiation of cheques, drawn in round figures, suggesting that these may be accommodation bills, rather than genuine trade transactions.

(iv) *Term Loan Account*

(a) Undue delay or default in payment of the term loan instalments with interest.
(b) Frequent requests for re-scheduling of the repayment programme.

Stock Statements of Current Assets Charged to the Bank

The borrowers are required, as per the mutually agreed terms and conditions of the advance, to periodically submit the statement of stocks of raw materials, work-in-progress and finished goods, as also of the bills receivables charged to the bank. However, the obsolete items of inventory and the long outstanding bills, doubtful of recovery, are required to be excluded for the purpose of computing the drawing powers on the accounts. The stock statements, are required to be scrutinised by the bank officers followed by the physical verification of the stocks from the stock statements as also from the unit's books of accounts.

While scrutinising the stock statements and inspecting

the stocks of the unit, charged to the bank, the bank officers are expected to exercise due care to see whether any of the following symptoms of sickness of the unit surface at any stage, deserving, urgent attention and timely correction:

(a) Late submission or non-submission of the stock statements by the borrowers signalling reluctance on their part to do so due to depletion of stocks, holding of stocks of obsolete inventory, etc.
(b) Excess holding of finished goods, beyond the norms of sanction, indicating non-acceptance of their products in the market.
(c) Excess stocks of raw material, signifying avoidable blockage of funds, which may create financial difficulty and cause sickness in the unit.
(d) Inclusion of obsolete and non-moving old stocks of raw materials and finished goods in the stock statements with a view to obtaining more advances or to keep the account artificially regular.
(e) Over-valuation of the inventory by showing the materials of inferior quality as those of superior quality or by valuing the stocks of raw material, goods-in-process and finished goods, charged to the bank, at a higher rate than the actual cost of purchase or production. This way they may get higher drawing powers, allocated on their accounts, enabling them to make further drawings thereon or at least to make their accounts appear to be regular.

Performance Monitoring and Management Information System (MIS)

In terms of the recommendations of the Tandon Committee, subsequently modified by the Chore Committee, all the borrowers enjoying aggregate credit limits of Rs. 50 lakh or above are required to submit periodical statements to their bankers, on the proforma prescribed by the Reserve Bank of

India, comprising

(a) Projected levels of current assets and current liabilities (From I, Quarterly).
(b) Statement showing performance for the previous quarter (when compard with the current quarter) (Form II, Quarterly).
(c) Operating and fund flow statement (Form III, Half Yearly).[44]

The borrowers enjoying lower limits, however, submit such statements as per the follow-up information system of their respective bankers.

A careful scrutiny of these statements by the bank officers, besides giving them an overall view of the performance of the unit, may reveal to them the undernoted signals and symptoms of sickness:

(a) Production showing a significant negative variance from the budgeted level.
(b) Sales showing a significant negative variance from the budgeted level.
(c) Cost of the sales showing an increase as a percentage of net sales.
(d) Profitability showing a declining trend and falling short of the budgeted level.
(e) Sundry creditors showing an undue rise signifying lack of working fund.
(f) Sundry debtors showing an undue rise signifying inadequate credt policy and collection system, poor quality of goods, lack of demand for the products, etc.
(g) Undue accumulation of statutory liabilities.
(h) Declining trend in the net working capital (current assets-current liabilities).
(i) Diversion of short-term sources of funds for long-term uses as reflected in the fund flow statement.

(j) Miscellaneous problems and adverse features like:

(i) Non-availability of raw material.
(ii) Significant rise in the cost of raw materials not covered by the proportionate increase in the price structure.
(iii) Non-availability or short-supply of power.
(iv) Technical problems, frequent breakdowns, etc.
(v) Labour prolems, etc.

Financial Statements

A critical analysis of the financial statements like Balance Sheet, and Profit and Loss Account throw up some valuable indicators of sagging health of a unit. To take care of some possible factors of window-dressing in the balance sheet, the bank officers ask for some supple-mentary data and break-ups to correctly assess the financial position of the unit. Intra-firm comparison of the financial ratios, computed from the balance sheets of three to five years, may give a fair idea regarding the trend of the financial performance of the unit. An inter-firm comparison of these financial data, with those of the other similar units, may provide a deeper understanding regarding the functioning of the unit.

It would be desirable to prepare an unaudited proforma balance sheet at least half-yearly so that the unhealthy trend, if any, could be arrested at the initial stage itself.

A careful analysis and interpretation of the financial statements may reveal the undernoted signals and symptoms of sickness:

(i) Steady decline in sales.
(ii) Steady decline in profitability.
(iii) Continued occurence of cash losses and non-provision for depreciation.
(iv) Decline in tangible net worth.
(v) Worsening of current ratio or continued negative net

working capital.

(vi) Worsening debt-equity ratio.

(vii) Declining turnover of assets.

(viii) Accumulation of sundry creditors.

(ix) Accumulation of sundry debtors.

(x) Accumulation of statutory dues.

(xi) Diversion of funds. etc.

Miscellaneous Information

In addition to the aforesaid signals and symptoms, the following information may also provide the signals of sickness:

(i) Frequent requests for permitting overdrawings on the accounts or for granting ad hoc limits.

(ii) Non-adherence to the bank's financial discipline i.e., non-compliance of the terms and conditions of the advance.

(iii) Substantial fall in the percentage of the market share.

(iv) Frequent breakdown of plant and machinery.

(v) Unusual wastage of raw materials, etc.

VIABILITY STUDY OF SICK SSI UNITS: TECHNICAL FEASIBILITY AND ECONOMIC VIABILITY

We have so far examined the gradual stages of sickness in a small scale industrial unit, and the early warning signals and symptoms of sickness. If the bank officers exercise eternal vigilance, through an effective system of supervision and follow-up of advances and performance monitoring of the units, they may detect the sickness at the incipient stage itself. They may promptly initiate the necessary remedial measures and restore the units back of health within a reasonable time and with lesser cost and effort. However, despite taking such preventive care, some units may fall sick, all the same. At this stage, the bank officers are expected to identify the unit as sick and to examine whether the unit could be rehabilitated by giving additional funds, concessions and other relief, or the loan may have to be called up. This is a vital decision on the part of the bank and should not be delayed as the position may worsen further with the passage of the time to the mutual disadvantage of the bank and the borrower. For arriving at a decision, the bank officers conduct a detailed viability study of the unit to assess whether its surplus generation capacity may be improved by initiating some remedial measures.

Viability Study

Viability study involves a comprehensive investigation into the unit's various functional areas, viz., finance production, marketing, personnel, and corporate management, as also the study of the external environments influencing the unit in particular, and the industry in general.

The study covers the past and present performance of the unit, based on its working results, as also the projections of its performance in the coming years. This involves a realistic assessment of its capacity to generate sufficient internal surplus to service its debt within a reasonable time. The study also undertakes the SWOT (Strength, Weaknesses, Opportunities and Threats) analysis of the unit and recommends further course of action and special safeguards, if the unit is to be rehabilitated. A unit is considered potentially viable if it is expected to become capable of servicing its debt within a reasonable time, say in 5 to 7 years, at a reasonable, though concessional, rate of interest.

Internal and External Consultants

The study may be undertaken internally by the technical officers of the bank's consultancy services cell or it may be entrusted to some professional outside consultants. It is, however, generally felt that it would be better if the study is conducted internally by the bank officers (after imparting them the necessary training in the area, at the hands of some expert consulting agency, as has successfully been done by some banks) for various reasons given hereunder:

(a) They would be well conversant with the systems procedures and policies of the Bank and would, therefore, be able to undertake some meaningful indepth study.
(b) They would be more responsible and realistic in their approach with a view to safeguarding the interest of the bank.
(c) Their expertise would be available, in some serious and complicated cases, at the initial stages of rehabilitation, as also in the future, whenever required.
(d) They would refrain from giving unrealistic recommendations inasmuch as they may be held personally accountable by the bank.

Role of the Personnel conducting the Viability Study

The bank's internal consultants may, however, play safe sometimes to avoid the risk of being held personally accountable. They may, therefore, prefer to declare some marginal cases as non-viable for rehabilitation. Further, while recommending some cases as potentially viable for rehabilitation, they may stipulate several conditions and safeguards which the operating staff may usually find difficult to observe effectively.

It is in this context that the role and responsibility, approach and attitude of the personnel conducting the viability study assume great importance. As rightly suggested by Bidani and Mitra,[45] "an evaluator under-taking the viability study of a sick unit should act like a general physician. He should collect information by questions, inspecting, examining the sick unit, and recording his observations systematically. Then, he should study the data so collected critically to take out the relevant details for diagnosing and prescribing a treatment for restoring the sick unit to health". The bank officers, while writing the report, may bear in mind the "three cardinal rules" of "accuracy, brevity and clarity", as suggested by Bidani and Mitra,[46] and the reasoned recommendations should be based on the findings contained in the body of the report.

The recommendations, based on the viability study, may broadly be on the following lines:

(a) The unit is technically feasible and economically viable and, therefore, may be rehabilitated by giving some further financial assistance.

(b) The unit is potentially viable, though non-viable under the present conditions. That is, it may be made viable if some more items of machinery are financed and the installed capacity is increased, and/ or certain relief and concessions, by way of reduced margins on stocks, concessional rate of interest, etc., are given.

(c) The unit is potentially viable but the management lacks the required managerial capability.

(d) The unit is potentially viable but the integrity of the entrepreneurs is doubtful.

(e) The unit is considered non-viable for rehabilitation.

In the case (a) and (b) above, the bank should promptly formulate comprehensive rehabilitation pro- gramme and implement it, in close coordination with the entrepreneurs, with a view to bringing the unit back to health.

In regard to case, (c), the bank officers should objectively assess,

(a) whether the entrepreneurs have learnt from their

mistakes and developed some managerial capabilities by virtue of being in the line of the business for long, or

(b) whether some professional and/or technical people were joining the unit as Partners/Directors or employees.

On being satisfied of the managerial capabilities of the unit, the bank officers should decide to rehabilitate the unit. In cases (d) and (e), however, the bank should declare the unit as non-viable for rehabilitation and initiate the recovery proceedings.

Growing Incidence of Sickness in the Small Scale Sector

We have discussed in the foregoing pages that if the bank officers initiate the necessary corrective actions at the early stages of the sickness, the units may be restored back to health with lesser costs and efforts. If, despite such preventive measures, some units fall sick, the bank officers should undertake a detailed viability study of the units and, depending upon the findings of the study, they should formulate and implement comprehensive rehabilitation programmes for revival of viable units, or initiate the recovery proceedings in cases of non-viable units.

But the various studies have revealed that the incidence of sickness in the industrial units, specially in the small scale sector, has, of late, been steadily increasing. This has been a cause for great concern to the government and the Reserve Bank of India, to the commercial banks and other financial institutions, as also to the entrepreneurs – both present and prospective. This is so because the industrial sickness results in loss of employment, demotivation of the entrepreneurial talents, wastage of capital assets, loss of production, loss of income by way of interest and increase in the non-performing assets of the banks and other financial institutions, loss of revenue to the exchequer, etc.

Assuming an average yield of 14 per cent per annum on Rs. 1,797 crore (total bank credit outstanding in sick SSI units as on 31-12-1987: Table 2.1), the potent loss of income to the banks by way of interest component alone would be Rs. 251.58 crore from the small scale sector. Such potent loss of income on account of non-SSI sick/weak units with bank credit in such units at Rs. 4,459 crore as on 31-12-1987 (Table 2.1) at the average interest rate of 16 per cent per annum would be Rs. 713.44 crore. Besides the total potent loss of around Rs. 965 crore, the industrial sickness also means locking up of the bank's liquid funds to the tune of Rs. 6,256 crore in such non-performing assets, depriving the bank's of the opportunity of their profitable turnover, and the resultant net loss when a portion of the oustandings on sick industrial units has to be written off as bad debt.

Industrial sickness is not confined to developing countries alone. It is "all pervading...also in the developed countries", observes Manimala[47]. According to Bibeault[48] and Slatter[49] it is estimated that about 20 per cent of the large companies, listed on the stock exchanges in the U.S and U.K., are sick. Of these, only about one-third have chance of revival.

The spread of industrial sickness in India, in the industrial sector as a whole, may be assessed from the fact (Table 2.1) that the number of non-SSI and SSI units identified by banks as sick (including 720 non-SSI units identified as 'weak') increased by 57.80 per cent to 2,06,098 as at the end of December 1987 from 1,30,606 units as at the end of June 1986.[50] Bank credit oustanding against these units rose by 34.11 per cent to Rs. 6,256 crore (or 9.4 per cent of total bank advances) from Rs. 4,665 crore (or 8.4 per cent of total bank credit) during that period. It may, however, be observed that while the number of sick units in the small scale sector, is sabstantially large at 2,04,259 or over 99 per cent of the total number of sick industrial units at 2,06,098 as at the end of December, 1987 (Table 2.1), the total bank credit outstanding in sick SSI units at Rs. 1,797

TABLE 2.1 : Sick/Weak Non-SSI Units and Sick SSI Units as at the End of December 1987

Categories	Non-SSI units identified by banks as sick (as defined under SICA*)	Non-SSI units identified by banks as weak	SSI Units identified by banks as sick	Total
(a) Total No. of units	1,119	720	2,04,259	2,06,098
(b) Total bank credit outstanding in (a) above (Rs. in crore)	2,802	1,657	1,797	6,256
(c) Out of (a) above, No. of units considered by banks as viable	343	270	12,484	13,097
(d) Out of (c) above, No. of units put under rehabilitation programme by banks	223	158	8,470	8,851

Note : Outstanding aggregate bank credit to all sick/weak units as at the end of December 1987 amounted to Rs. 6,256 crore (or 9.4 per cent of total bank advnces).

* Sick Industrial Companies (Special Provisions) Act.

Source : Reserve Bank of India, Annual Report, 1988-89, pp. 128-29.

crore constitutes only 28.72 per cent of the toal outstanding bank credit in sick industrial units at Rs.6,256 crore. Thus, while the non-SSI Sector accounts for less than one per cent of the total number of sick industrial units, the bank credit outstanding in these units at Rs.4,459 crore constitutes 71.28 per cent of the aggregate bank credit outstanding in the total number of sick industrial units.

Extent of Viability and Rehabilitation of Sick Units

Let us now examine the extent of viability and rehabilitation of sick industrial units under the non-SSI and SSI sectors (Table 2.1).

Of the 1,119 sick non-SSI units, as on 31-12-1987, 343 units (or 30.65 per cent) were found viable and 223 units (or 19.93 per cent) were brought under rehabilitation programme by banks.

Further, of the 720 'weak' non-SSI unit, as on 31-12-1987, 270 units (or 37.50 per cent) were found viable and 158 units (or 21.94 per cent) were put under rehabilitation programme by banks.

In the small sector, however, the percentage of sick units found viable and brought under rehabilitation programme is even worse. Of the 2,04,259 sick SSI units, as on 31-12-1987, 12,484 units (or 6.11 per cent) were found viable and 8,470 units (or 4.15 per cent) were brought under rehabilitation programme by banks. Similar has been the position as at the end of June 1987 and June 1988, as contained in Table 2.2.

Conversely speaking, a much larger number and higher percentage of sick SSI units are identified by banks as non-viable. For example, as on 30.6.1987, 1,39,346 units, constituting 88.07 per cent of the total 1,58,226 sick SSI units, were considered non-viable for rehabilitation by banks (Table 2.3). Similar was the position as at the end of June 1988 (Table 2.4). Further, the banks had not decided the viability in respect of 6,818 SSI units as on 30-6-1987 (Table 2.3) and around 5,000 units (pertaining to public sector banks only) as on 30-6-1988 (Table 2.4). This is a matter of concern as an undue delay in the identification of a viable unit, and formulation and implementation of a comprehensive rehabilitation programme, may adversely affect the prospects of revival of potentially viable units and, with the passage of time, even these may become non-viable.

TABLE 2.2 : Sick SSI Units found Potentially Viable and Under Rehabilitation Programme by Banks

Categories	As on 30-6-1987	As on 31-12-1987	As on 30-6-1988
1, Total No. of SSI units identified by banks as sick	1,58,226	2,04,259	2,17,436
2. Out of the sick units total No. of units considered potentially viable by banks	12,062 (7.62% of No. 1)	12,484 (6.11% of No. 1)	12,959 (5.96% of No. 1)
3. Out of potentially viable units, units brought under rehabilitation programme by banks	4,980 (3.15% of No. 1)	8,470 (4.15% of No. 1)	8.347 (3.84% of No. 1)

Sources: (i) Reserve Bank of India, Annual Report, 1987-88, p. 88.
(ii) Reserve Bank of India, Annual Report, 1988-89. pp. 128-9.
(iii) Reserve Bank of India, Bombay, Report on Currency and Finance, Vol. I: *Economic Review*, 1989-90, p. 74.

Based on such unsatisfactory features, the Reserve Bank of India have observed that despite giving "comprehensive instructions to banks in the matter of rehabilitation of sick/weak industrial units,....there have been instances where banks have shown reluctance to assist the units although they were found to be potentially viable".[51] The Reserve Bank of India have, therefore, advised all banks that non-compliance of the instructions would be viewed seriously, with the hope that the position would improve.

Growing Incidence of Sickness in the SSI Sector

As would be observed from Table 2.5, there has been only marginal rise in the number of sick SSI units during the

TABLE 2.3 : Viability-wise Break up and Rehabilitation of Sick SSI Units by Banks as on 30-6-1987

Categories	No. of Units	Percentage of category item No. (1)
1. Small Scale Industrial (SSI) units identified by banks as sick	1,58,226	100%
2. Viability-wise break up of the sick SSI units as decided by banks:		
(i) Considered non-viable	1,39,346	88.07%
(ii) Viability not yet decided	6,818	4.31%
(iii) Considered potentially viable*	12,062	7.62%
* Out of potentially viable units the units brought under rehabilitation programme by banks	4,980	3.15%
	[41.29% of category 2 (iii)]	

Source : Reserve Bank of India, Annual Report, 1987-88, p. 88.

period September 1979 to June 1981 and even June 1982. But, as at the end of June 1983, the number of sick SSI units registered a steep rise at 64,388 from 26,973 as at the end of June 1982. The substantial increase in the number of sick SSI units has, however, been attributed to "a change in classification of sick units by the State Bank of India from the quarter ended September 1982 onwards".[52]

We further see that from the level of end June 1983, the number of sick SSI units has nearly doubled at 1,28,687 units as at the end of June 1986 and more than trebled at 2,17,436 units as at the end of June 1988, i.e. within a period of three years and five years respectively.

Similar trend has been observed in respect of bank credit outstanding against the sick SSI units during the period under review. While there has been a gradual rise in the bank credit outstanding against such accounts during the period

TABLE 2.4 : SSI Units Financed by Public Sector Banks with Details of Sick SSI Units as at the End of June 1988

Categories	No. of Units (in lakh)	Amount outstanding (Rs. in crore)
(i) Aggregate SSI units financed	23.15	10,798.43
(ii) Of which sick SSI units	2.15	1,901.77
(iii) Of the sick units those which are:		
(a) Potentially viable	0.13	429,28
(b) Non-viable	1.97	1,350.86
(iv) Viability not yet decided	0.05	121.63
(v) Of the potentially viable units, units under nursing programme	0.08	323.66

Note : Although in terms of number 9.3 per cent of the borrowing SSI units were sick, the amount locked up in these sick units formed 17.6 per cent of the aggregate advances to SSI sector.

Source : Reserve Bank of India Bulletin, March 1991, (Supplement), pp. 79-80.

September 1979 to June 1982, there has been a substantial rise from Rs. 393.67 crore as at the end the June 1982 to Rs.626.52 crore as at the end of June 1983, for the aforesaid reason. We, however, see that from the end of June 1983 level, the quantum of bank credit outstanding in sick SSI units has almost doubled at Rs.1,184.22 crore as on 30-6-1986 and has more than trebled at Rs. 1,979.85 crore as on 30-6-1988, i.e. within a period of three years and five years respectively.

The trend of growing sickness in small scale industries needs to be arrested. We would, therefore, proceed to study the various causes of sickness in the small scale sector so as to be able to suggest some remedial measures for arresting and averting sickness in SSI units as also for rehabilitation of sick units.

TABLE 2.5 : Position of the Incidence of Sickness in the Small Scale Sector and the Bank Credits Outstanding against such Accounts

Position as at the end of	No. of sick SSI Units	Bank/Credit outstanding against such accounts (Rs. in crore)
Sept. 1979	20,326	231.00
June 1980	22,355	295.43
June 1981	22,360	321.52
June 1982	26,973	393.67
June 1983	64,388	626.52
June 1984	81,647	788.00
June 1985	97,890	954.70
June 1986	1,28,687	1,184.22
June 1987	1,58,226	1,542.25
June 1988	2,17,436	1,979.85

Sources : (i) Reserve Bank of India, Annual Report, 1979-80 to 1989-90.
(ii) Reserve Bank of India, Bombay, Report on Currency and Finance, Vol. I : *Economic Review*, 1978-79 to 1989-90.
(iii) Reserve Bank of India, Bombay, Report on Trend and Progress of Banking in India, 1978-79 to 1986-87.

REFERENCES

1. State Bank of India, Financing of Small Scale Industries: Report of the Study Team, Bombay, 1975, p. 38.
2. R. Viswanathan, *Industrial Finance,* S Chand & Company, New Delhi, 1982, p. 255.
3. Reserve Bank of India, Bombay, Report on Currency and Finance, Vol. I: *Economic Review,* 1989-90, p. 77.
4. *Reserve Bank of India Bulletin,* March 1991 (Supplement), Bombay, p. 80.
5. V.K. Joshi, *Management of Industrial Sickness,* Kuber Associates, Jaipur, 1987, pp. 6-7.
6. R. Viswanathan, Industrial Finance, S Chand & Company, New Delhi, 1982, p. 255
7. *Ibid.,* p. 256

8. *Ibid.*
9. K. B. Pathak, "Rehabilitation of Sick SSI Units - Some Issues" State Bank of India Monthly Review, Vol. 29, No. 9, September 1990, p. 431.
10. R. A. Yadav, "Sick Industrial Companies Legislation – Remedy or Palliative", The Chartered Accountant, Vol. 35, No. 6, 1986, pp. 289-92.
11. B. H. Dholakia, "Industrial Sickness in India: Need for Comprehensive Identification Criteria", *Vikalpa*, Vol. 14, No. 2, 1989, pp. 19-24.
12. S.N. Bidani & P.K. Mitra, *Industrial Sickness: Identification and Rehabilitation,* Vision Books, New Delhi, 1982, p. 17.
13. *Ibid.*, pp. 17-19.
14. Thomas J. Peters & Robert H. Waterman Jr., *In Search of Excellence,* Harpers & Row, New York, 1982, p. 238.
15. F.G. "Buck" Rodgers & R.L. Shook, *The IBM Way,* Harper & Row, New York, 1986, pp. 9-15.
16. Tom Peters & Nancy Austin, *A Passion for Excellence,* Fontana Paperbacks, U.K., 1986, pp. 203-61.
17. Kenneth Blanchard & Spencer Johnson, *The One Minute Manager,* Fontana Paperbacks, U.K., April 1984, p. 39.
18. *Ibid.*, p. 19.
19. Kenneth Blanchard & Robert Lorber, *Putting the One Minute Manager to Work,* Fontana Paperbacks, U.K., 1984, p. 12.
20. W. Weitzel & E. Jonsson, Decline in organisations: A Literature Integration and Extension, *Administrative Science Quarterly,* Vol. 34, No. 1, (March 1989), p. 97.
21. D. C. Hambrick & R. A. D'Aveni, Large Corporate Failures and Downward Spirals, *Administrative Science Quarterly,* Vol. 33, No. 1, 1988, pp. 1-23.
22. S. N. Bidani & P. K. Mitra, *Industrial Sickness: Indentification and Rehabilitation,* Vision Books, New Delhi, 1982, pp. 31-33.
23. R. Natarajan, G. Krishnamurthy & K. V. J. Rao, Rehabilitation of Sick Units in SSI Sector through Marketing Strategy—A Case Study, *Indian Journal of Marketing,* Vol. 15, No. 7, 1985, pp. 13-16.
24. B. Krishnan, The Anatomy of a Sick Engineering Unit, *Indian Management,* Vol. 24, No. 5, 1985, pp. 18-22.
25. R. S. Dwivedi, On Becoming a Sick Enterprise – Diagnosis and Treatment, *Lok Udyog,* Vol. 17, No. 9, 1983, pp. 17-25.
26. G. Turner, Inside Europe's Giant Companies: Olivetti Goes Bear-Hunting, *Long Range Planning,* Vol. 19, No. 2, April 1986, pp. 13-20.
27. D.C.L. Marwood, ICL: Crisis and Swift Recovery, *Long Range Planning,* Vol. 18, No. 2, 1985, pp. 10-21.

28. D. Rose, Woolworth's Drive for Excellence, *Long Range Planning,* Vol. 22, No. 1, 1989, pp. 28-31.
29. G.D. Radford, How Sumitomo Transformed Dunlop Tyres, *Long Range Planning,* Vol. 22, No. 3, 1989, pp. 28-33.
30. T. Nakajo & T. Kono, Success Through Culture Change in a Japanese Brewery, *Long Range Planning,* Vol. 22, No. 6, 1989, pp. 29-37.
31. J.W. Seabright, Turnaround at MFI: From a Troubled Mail-Order Firm to a Leading Furniture Retailer, *Long Range Planning,* Vol. 18, No. 4, 1985, pp. 27-32.
32. G.J. Bamber & D. Lausbury, Management Strategy and New Technology in Retail Distribution: A Comparative Case Study, *Journal of Management Studies,* Vol. 25, No. 3, 1988, pp. 197-216.
33. R. Muller Corporate Crisis Management, *Long Range Planning,* Vol. 18, No. 5, 1985, pp. 38-48.
34. (i) E. I. Altman, Financial Ratios, Discriminant analysis and the Prediction of Corporate Bankruptcy, *Journal of Finance,* September 1968, pp. 589-609.
    (ii) V. Kumar, Prediction of Industrial Sickness—Need of the Hour, *The Chartered Accountant,* Vol. 30, No. 7, January 1982, pp. 427-34.
    (iii) J. Robertson & R. W. Mills, Company Failure or Company Health?—Techniques for Measuring Company Health, *Long Range Planning,* Vol. 21, No. 2, 1988, pp. 70-77.
    (iv) P.K. Sen, Trend Analysis of Financial Ratios and Forecast of Company Sickness, *Decision,* Vol. 6, No. 1, 1979, pp. 97-118.
    (v) S.S. Srivastava & R. K. Kumaria, Parametric Approach in Predicting Industrial Sickness, *Management in Government,* Vol. 12, No. 2, July - September 1980, pp. 123-32.
35. Mathew J. Manimala, Turnaround Management : Lessons from Successful Cases, *ASCI Journal of Management,* Vol. 20, No. 4, March 1991, p. 236.
36. Rattan K. Sharma, Industrial Sickness in India: An Analysis, *ASCI Journal of Management,* Vol. 15, No. 1, September 1985, p. 19.
37. R. A. Yadav, Assessment of Health of Small Scale Industries, A System Approach, *MDI Management Journal,* Vol. 3, No. 2, July 1990, pp. 104-5.
38. Subhash Gangwal, *New Dimensions in Industrial Sickness,* Sublime Publications, Jaipur, 1990, p. 34.
39. Banarsi Misra, *Monitoring of Industrial Sickness,* Deep & Deep Publications, New Delhi, 1990, p. 150.
40. D.K. Pal, Rehabilitation of Sick Industrial Units in the Small Scale Sector, *Chartered Secretary,* Vol. 14, No. 5, May 1984,

pp. 316-21.
41. R. Viswanathan, *Industrial Finance,* S. Chand & Company, New Delhi, 1982, pp. 257-58.
42. N.L. Hingorani, Towards Defining a Good Account, *Commerce,* Vol. 154, No. 3970, June 20 - 26, 1987, pp. 23-26.
43. A.K. Bhattacharya, Sickness in Medium and Large Industrial Undertakings, *State Bank of India Monthly Review,* Vol. 20, No. 8, August 1981, pp. 315-24.
44. S.N. Bidani & P. K. Mitra, *Industrial Sickness : Identification and Rehabilitation,* Vision Books, New Delhi, 1982, pp. 97-109.
45. S.N. Bidani & P. K. Mitra, *Industrial Sickness: Identification and Rehabilitation,* Vision Books, New Delhi, 1982, p. 64.
46. *Ibid.*
47. Mathew J. Manimala, Turnaround Management : Lessons from Successful Cases, *ASCI Journal of Management,* Vol. 20, No. 4, March 1991, p. 234.
48. D.B. Bibeault, *Corporate Turnaround: How Managers Turn Losers into Winners,* McGraw-Hill, New York, 1982.
49. S. Slatter, *Corporate Recovery: Successful Turnaround Strategies and Their Implementation,* Penguin, Harmondsworth, Middlesex, 1984.
50. (i) Reserve Bank of India, Bombay, Report on Trend and Progress of Banking in India, 1986-87, pp. 82-3.
(ii) Reserve Bank of India, Annual Report, 1988-89, pp. 128-29.
51. Reserve Bank of India, Bombay Report on Currency and Finance, Vol. I, *Economic Review,* 1989-90. p. 74.
52. Reserve Bank of India, Bombay, Report on Trend and Progress of Banking in India, 1983-84, p. 75.

3

CAUSES OF SICKNESS

CAUSES OF SICKNESS IN SMALL SCALE INDUSTRIAL (SSI) UNITS AS IDENTIFIED BY OTHER STUDIES

Causes of Sickness: A Major Determinant of Turn-around Strategies

It has been observed that the choice of strategy for rehabilitation of sick units largely depends on the perceived causes of sickness. For example, Schendel *et al.*[1], in their study of 54 turnaround cases, found that the causes of sickness were a major determinant of the strategies adopted for the turnaround of the companies. If the decline was caused by operating problems like production bottlenecks, labour troubles, etc., the remedial measures adopted were also of operating nature such as new cost control systems, modernisation of plant and machinery, and the like. Similarly, if the decline was due to strategic problems/factors such as obsolete products, new competitors, etc., the remedial measures adopted were also of strategic nature such as new products, redefining the business and so on.

Hofer's[2] analysis of 12 cases of poorly performing organisations also found support for the above hypothesis of strategic actions (doing different things) for strategic problems, and operating actions (doing things differently) for operating problems.

Frost[3] is also of the view that "the first step in 'curing' an organisation, of course, is recognising that a problem exists. But eliminating the symptoms will not cure the illness. An understanding of how the sickness came about, along with a willingness to dramatically alter a company's orientation, if necessary, is the only way to begin a cure".

Viswanathan,[4] a senior bank executive, also holds the view that "by locating the causes with a fair degree of accuracy, it will be easy to initiate such remedial measures as may be appropriate".

We would, therefore, proceed to survey the various causes of sickness as revealed by various studies of sick industrial units before we undertake the identification and analyses of the various causes of sickness in the specific cases, selected on random sample basis for the study, and endeavour to suggest some remedial measures for arresting the sickness in the small scale sector.

Causes of Sickness Reported by Western Cases

Nelson and Clutterbuck[5] have analysed the causes of sickness in twenty European companies. Based on these cases and some other case studies reported in various journals, Manimala[6] has analysed and summarised the major internal and external causes of industrial sickness.

He, however, feels that as these cases are brief, running into an average of 10 pages each, and the discussion on the causes is inadequate, the listing of the causes given below should not be taken as comprehensive and may serve only to give a general idea of the causes of sickness.

Internal Causes of Sickness

1. Continuance with "production orientation" even though changes in the environment call for a shift to "market orientation", resulting in poor quality of goods, poor customer service, wrong positioning of

products, excessive dependence upon one product, one region or one market.

2. Strategy of growing too fast through unrelated diversification, resulting in lack of synergy and cultural incompatibility.
3. Poor management of finances, resulting in high liverage, delays in collection, under-capitalisation, etc.
4. Wrong personnel policies resulting in overstaffing, poor employee relations, lack of adequate training of employees, and promotion and retention of incompetent managers.
5. Authoritarian and conservative attitudes of top management.
6. Technological obsolescence.
7. Uncontrolled and non-focussed R & D activities.
8. Poor management of inventories.
9. Structural inadequacies.
10. Inadequate information system.
11. Conflicts among stake-holders.

External Causes of Sickness

Among the external causes are changes in the particular industry, the economy as a whole and in the general environment. Manimala, however, observes that as these factors affect all the units, "the explanation for one unit getting sick should be sought within that unit as to why there was a deterioration in its capability to adapt to the changes in the environment. Hence, the distinction between external and internal causes does not seem to be relevant for turnaround decisions".

Causes of Sickness Reported by Indian Cases

Joshi[7] has classified the causes of sickness, based on the study of the sick units financed by Rajasthan State Financial Corporation, in five major groups:

1. Faulty project formulation like wrong product selection, poor technology, wrong location, absence of market analysis, false fixed investment decisions and low equity base.
2. Faulty project implementation like installation of defective machinery, entrepreneurs' failure to bring in the required margin money resulting in reduction of the qauntum of term loan adversely affecting the production, lack of coordination between the banks and the State Financial Corporation, and delayed disbursement of working capital advance by banks.
3. Faulty project operations like errors in marketing strategy, low-key market development efforts, defects in production planning and other arrangements, inadequate or late sanction or working capital assistance by banks, inept working capital management, heavy personal withdrawals and excessive overhead expenditure.
4. Unfavourable environmental factors like changes in government policies, shortage of raw materials, power, coal, skilled labour, and delayed payment of bills.
5. Entrepreneurial incompetence in the various functional areas of management like production, marketing, finance and personnel, lack of cost and budgetary control and management information system, dissensions among partners or promoters, and lack of integrity and commitment on the part of the entrepreneurs.

Further, Joshi has identified the ten most widely prevalent individual causes of sickness, ranked in the descending order of their presence, as under:

(i) Inadequate working capital,
(ii) Entrepreneurial incompetence,
(iii) Errors in marketing,
(iv) Incohesive partnership/Board,
(v) Doubtful integrity,
(vi) Low-key market development effort,
(vii) Low equity base,
(viii) Faulty product selection,
(ix) Poor technical assessment,
(x) Critical shortages of raw materials, power, etc.

Gangwal[8] analysed the causes of 119 sample sick SSI units, financed by the Rajasthan State Financial Corporation and found that the broad reasons of sickness were delay in project implementation, the problems pertaining to the management of the functional areas of production, marketing, finance and personnel, and external problems.

Jyothi Rani[9] studied eleven joint venture units of the Andhra Pradesh Small Scale Industries Development Corporation (APSSIDC), selected on deliberate sampling basis, and found that the main causes of sickness in these units were under-utilisation of the installed capacity, shortage of raw materials and power, problems of marketing, delayed payments by government and large scale industries, shortage of working capital, improper government policies relating to taxation, production, pricing, distribution, etc., and managerial deficiency like improper planning, wrong cost estimation, diversion of funds, personnel deficiencies, and poor marketing and financial management.

Udaya Shanker and Rao[10] studied the cases of 13 sick SSI units in the states of Orissa and Andhra Pradesh during 1984 and 1987 respectively, and identified the various causes of sickness as under:

(i) Lack of technical and managerial skills.
(ii) Unplanned diversification.

(iii) Heavy investment in building.
(iv) Improper machinery.
(v) Improper product planning,
(vi) Over-dependence on a single buyer, including government department,
(vii) Labour problem,
(viii) Differences among partners,
(ix) Sickness in the parent unit,
(x) Shortage of raw materials, power, transport, etc.,
(xi) Lack of coordination between banks and other financial institutions,
(xii) Changes in government policy.

Reddy[11] studied 11 cases of sick units in the small scale sector in the Visakhapatnam and Vijayawada regions and came to the conclusion that the units had fallen sick largely due to the following reasons:

(a) Inadequate finance, particularly working capital.
(b) Shortage of raw materials.
(c) Managerial deficiency.
(d) Poor and inadequate marketing avenues.
(e) Bureaucratic delays both from the government and financial agencies resulting in cost escalation and delay in starting the production.

Shanmugham[12] studied 50 cases of engineering units in the SSI sector in Coimbatore, started by relatively young entrepreneurs, and found that mainly the following problems affected the small entrepreneurs:

(i) Poor financial planning and management,
(ii) Poor collection of receivables (54 per cent),
(iii) Exessive stock level (10 per cent),
(iv) High Competition,
(v) Power cuts,

(vi) Lack of sufficient orders,

(vii) Erratic supply of raw materials, and

(viii) High incidence of sales tax and excise duty.

The study frther revealed that the majority of the entrepreneurs (72 per cent) had not problem in obtaining a loan, while the remaining 28 per cent pointed out the delay, procedural formalities and expenses as some of the problems. It was, however, found that there was an extensive use of borrowed fund in the capital structure.

A recent study by Khandwalla,[13] however, has identified financial institutions' own procedures and practices as an important cause of industrial sickness along with mis-management, already identified by several earlier studies as a major case of sickness.

Naidu and Padmavathi[14] made a study of 31 cases of sick small scale industrial units in the Chittoor district of Andhra Pradesh in 1986 and found that nearly two-third of the total 31 sick SSI units in the district or 63.7 per cent units were sick due to two main reasons, viz., lack of finance (36.4 per cent) and lack of marketing facilities (27.3 per cent). The remaining 36.3 per cent units became sick due to lack of raw materials (18.3 per cent) lack of skilled labour (9.0 per cent) and mismanagement (9.0 per cent).

Hejmadi[15] studied the industrial health of 273 SSI units, in the Dakshina Kannada district of Karnataka, in relation to the level of education of the entrepreneurs and found that the graduates were faring better than the non-graduates, and even post-graduates, in keeping the small industry healthy. He, however, suggests "to bring the entrepreneurial movement to the doors of these educated unemployed youths, keeping in view the eradication of the growing unemployment problem and contributing to the industrial development of the backward areas of the district".

The study conducted by the Indian Council of Small Industries, cited by Bidani and Mitra[16], has identified the undernoted reasons for sickness in small scale industries:

(i) Faulty planning and incorrect appraisal of projects.

(ii) Limited loss sustainig capacity.

(iii) Delayed payments by large scale industries and the government undertakings.

(iv) Stringency in working finance in several cases whereby the units come to grief due to temporary phases of holdovers and the bank's hesitation in giving timely temporary assistance for a short period, delay in getting the expected cash incentive in respect of exports, revision of prices of raw materials (purchased by small industry) by the government canalising agency with retrospective effect, etc.

(v) Delay in implementation of the projects due to shortage of controlled items of raw materials: cases are identified wherein buildings were not completed, water and electricity were not available in time but the commercial banks started enforcing the recoveries and charging interest even at penal rate.

(vi) Shortage or non-availability of raw materials at controlled price at the right time.

(vii) Disputes and labour trouble. In some cases even though the products were good, market was attractive and profits were more than adequate, the small units came to grief due to internal disputes and labour troubles.

(viii) Longer gestation period either at the initial stage or during the stage of expansion. The gestation period can be cut short by timely assistance from the banks.

(ix) Lack of marketing efforts and unexpected competition from the large units.

(x) Temporary phases of material shortages.

(xi) Unit's failure due to wrong product or wrong choice

of area or placing.

Internal and External Causes of Sickness in Indian Cases

Most of the Indian authors and researchers have classified the various causes of industrial sickness under two broad categories:

1. *Internal causes*, pertaining to the factors within the control of the management;
2. *External causes*, pertaining to the factors beyond the control of the management.

Bidani and Mitra [17] have enlisted the various internal and external causes of sickness separately under the four functional areas like finance, production, marketing and personnel, besides the corporate management in general.

Internal causes of sickness, arising due to internal disorders in these areas, as identified by them, are:

1. Finance functions including weak equity base, poor utilisation of assets, inefficient working capital management, absence of costing and pricing, absence of financial planning and budgeting, and inappropriate utilisation or diversion of funds.
2. Production functions including wrong selection of site, inappropriate plant and machinery, inadequate materials control, inadequate maintenance of plant and machinery, lack of quality control, and lack of emphasis on research and development.
3. Marketing functions including inaccurate demand forecasting, selection of inappropriate product-mix, absence of product planning, dependence on a few buyers, lack of market research and inappropriate sales promotions.
4. Personnel functions including inappropriate wage and salary administration, bad labour relations, lack

of behavioural approach cuasing dissatis-faction among the personnel, and absence of manpower planning.

5. Corporate management including improper corporate planning, lack of coordination and control, resistance to change, strife and lack of integrity in top management.

External causes of sickness, arising from the changes in the environment, adversely affecting the four functional areas, as identified by them, are:

1. Financial constraints due to credit restraint policy, delay in disbursement of loans, unfavourable investment climate and fear of nationalisation.
2. Production constraints due to shortage of raw materials, power, fuel and such other essential inputs, and import restrictions on essential inputs.
3. Marketing constraints due to liberal licensing policy, restraint on purchases by bulk purchasers, change in international market scene, excessive taxation policy of the government, and market recession.
4. Personnel constraints like non-availability of skilled manpower, wage disparity in similar industry, general labour unrest in the areas, and inter-union rivalry.

They further observe that "the first and foremost reason for sickness is the improper project planning and appraisal", particularly in the small scale sector. They also maintain that while the aforesaid causes of sickness are applicable to the small scale sector, too, "the prime reasons of sickness among small units is faulty disbursement of bank finance".

According to Viswanathan,[18] now the Deputy Managing Director in the State Bank of India, the major internal causes include low productivity of labour, high cost of labour, obsolete plant and equipment, obsolete technology, weak marketing department, inefficient and/or dihonest management, and poor financial planning resulting in high debt/equity ratio and/or low net working capital and current ratio. Among the major external causes of sickness, identified by him, are non-availability or high cost of raw materials, non-availability of power, water, etc., marketing difficulties and non-availability of finance.

According to Misra,[19] "the internal causes may be attributed to managerial sickness, lack of proper reporting system of accounting data, poor production, marketing, financial and personnel management, while the external causes may be attributed to changes in the environment resulting from economic, social, political, international or legislative changes which, in turn, cause financial, production, marketing and personnel constraints for industrial enterprises".

Internal causes of sickness, according to Agarwal,[20] include factors like choice of wrong location, under-estimation of capital cost, over-estimation of demand, delay in implementation of the projects and cost acceleration, lack of financial management and cost control, and managerial deficiency. The external factors causing industrial sickness include the government policy, lack of raw materials, power, transport, etc., recession in demand, shortage of finance and working capital, improper product-mix, poor collection of bills receivable, diversification of funds and poor funds management, etc.

Further, Agarwal is of the view that "among the agencies which are engaged in the process of nursing and rehabilitation package, banks have to play the most important role". He further suggests that "the banks should streamline their lending criteria with an active coordination of other agencies involved in the process", should rehabilitate only potentially viable units and the "purely non-viable (units) should be allowed to die".

According to Pal,[21] the internal factors, "which are

within the control of management,...... include choice of wrong location, delay in implementation of the project, management deficiency or even unscrupulousness, lack of planning in layout, information system, cost control system, repair and replacement of plant and machinery, lack of control on working capital, and current assets management, etc."

The external factors, "over which the unit has hardly any control", relate to changes in government policy, demand recession, non-availability of essential raw materials and stores, adverse labour relations, paucity of working capital, power crisis, transport bottlenecks, etc.

He further adds that "sickness can originate right from the state of conception to the state of crystallisation of the concept and/or implementation of the project". He stresses the need for prevention of sickness at the incipient stage and suggests that "by an effective monitoring, commercial banks may identify the insidious ailment of the unit, before the damage is deep-rooted", making the exercise of rehabilitation costlier.

According to Rao,[22] the main internal causes of sickness in the small scale sector are lack of finance and marketing, improper layout, machinery breakdown, high material waste and lack of production planning. The main external factors responsible for sickness in small units, according to him, are (faulty) government policy, recession in demand, shortage of raw materials and power, and obsolescence of the product. He is, however, of the view that the "sickness may be prevented through early detection and timely action".

Bagchi,[23] on the basis of his study of the Bengal Chemical and Pharmaceuticals Limited (BCPL), also concludes that the "primary attention of the management should be to identify sickness at the incipient stage. Once that is done, steps for nursing could be suitably taken". He, however, points out that in the case of BCPL, "the sickness was remotely identified at a late stage" due to which the remedial steps taken "proved abortive".

According to Sood,[24] "among the internal factors the single most important factor for industrial sickness is management inefficiency". The external factors of sickness, according to him, include recession and competition in industry, frequent changes in government policies, inadequate and delayed financial assistance provided by banks and other financial institutions, erratic availability of raw materials, power, etc.

Sood[25] further maintains that in many a case the "rehabilitation package fails to yield results due to considerable time-lag between its conception and implementation" due to bureaucratic procedures and delays. "The situation", according to him, "demands quick decision making and toning up of the administration".

According to Devendra Babu,[26] the industrial units fall sick due to internal and external factors like inexperienced entrepreneurs, corruption and mismanagement, lack of demand for the products, shortage of raw materials, etc. He suggests that "as the Board for Industrial and Financial Reconstruction (BIFR) has no jurisdiction over the small and ancillary units, a similar type of Board should be set up to tackle the problems of sickness which is widespread in small scale sector also".

According to Rai and Brahmanandam,[27] while the internal causes are concerned with the choice of location, understimation of cost of capital, over-estimation of demand, mismanagement, failure to introduce proper control techniques and tools, poor maintenance of machines and equipments and poor public relations, the external causes relate to changes in government policies, shortage of raw materials, power, transport, etc., non-availability of adequate and timely finance for working capital requirements, absence of industrial peace and mounting inflation.

Ratnam[28] has examined the effect of inflation as a cause for sickness of the ageing units and traced a path to avoid sickness caused by inflationary effects.

Meena[29] enlists the various causes of sickness in

industrial units (not exhaustive), identified by banks (including the RBI), as

(a) environmental (scarcity and uneconomic price of quality raw materials, disturbed industrial relations, etc.).
(b) managerial (lack of technical and managerial expertise, etc.,
(c) operational (lack of market penetration, etc.), and
(d) financial (lack of proper financial planning and control).

According to Joshi,[30] industrial sickness is largely a phenomenon of dwindling financial viability in suh a way that the structure cn neither stand on its own feet nor can it be made to stand by help from outside agencies". Besides enlisting the various internal and external causes of industrial sickness, he mentions about certain causes of sickness in the small scale sector, as pinpointed by the Reserve Bank of India, like lack of managerial and technical competence, decline in demand for their products from the medium and large scale industries, and the overall demand recession, delay in payment of bills by government departments and large units, lack of quality consciousness, poor marketing strategy etc.

While discussing the causes of industrial sickness, Nadkarni[31] former Chairman of State Bank of India, adopts Shakespeare's well known dictum and says that "some industries are born sick, some achieve sickness and some have sickness thrust upon them."

Industries born sick are those which are destined for disaster right from their conception due to one or more factors like lack of experience, faulty planning, lack of capital, delay in project commissioning, wrong location, flawed financial planning, too much capital going into fixed assets, obsolete technology, and incomplete market surveys.

Industries which achieve sickness are those which fail

after becoming operational due to internal causes like bad management, unplanned expansion, stock mismanagement, diversion of funds, avoidable expenses and personal extravagance, failure to follow-up receivables, faulty purchasing methods, poor maintenance, failure to modernise, labour problems, etc.

The third category of sick units include those which have collapsed from extenal causes and problems, not of their own making, like shortage of raw materials and power, changes in government policies, delays in disbursement of loans by banks and financial institutions, etc.

The external causes of industrial sickness, as identified separately by Agarwal,[32] Prasad,[33] Rajagopal,[34] Ramaswamy,[35] and Sharma,[36] are transition from sellers' market to byuers' market, inflation, excise duties, taxaion policies and import-export policies of the government, slow economic growth, recession and lack of demand, shortage of raw materials and power, change in inter-national market conditions, technological changes, depression in capital market and delays caused by financial institutions.

According to Ramesh,[37] the main factors adversely affecting the health of small scale industries are: promoter's limited capacity to raise equity, problems in raising institutional funds, delayed and insufficient working capital loans by banks, competition from multi-nationals and large scale industries, wild fluctuations in prices of raw materials, sub-optimal capacity utilisation, fall in finished goods prices, severe labour turnover, scarcity of skilled work-force, poor maintenance management, lack of cooperation and understanding by the revenue collecting authorities, utimely and sudden seizures and closure of units by financial institutions.

Some of the major causes of sickness, as revealed by several studies/surveys, have been summarised by Reddy[38] as under:

1. Delay in the implementation of the project due to

vaious sanctions/approvals required by different government agencies;

2. Long delays and inadequate financing by the financial institutions;
3. Obtaining term loan for creating fixed assets and under-utilisation thereof;
4. Problems relating to shortage of working capital funds, raw materials and power supply, and lack of marketing efforts/skills/channels.

Reddy is of the view that "there is definitely a case for a detailed study into the role of banks/finance corporations to bring about more efficient performance of these institutions." He further observes that "the two major areas of weakness in the small industrial sector are Management of Marketing and Financing Functions."

Mismanagement as the Major Cause of Sickness

Various Indian studies have revealed that lack of managerial effectiveness on the part of the entrepreneurs, in one or more of the functional areas, has been the major cause of industrial sickness specially in the small scale sector.

The vital role of managerial acumen in the performance of a unit is well recognised in the Western literature, too. Penrose[39] identified three basic constraints to the growth of firms, viz., "managerial ability; product or factor markets; and uncertainty and risk." All considered, he concluded, that "the fundamental limit to the productive opportunity of the firm cannot be found in external supply and demand conditions; we must look within the firm itself." Likewise, Morris[40] considered the growth of a firm as a managerial objective. Bosewell[41] analysed the rise and decline of 64 small firms in U.K. (all employing less than 500 persons) out of which 28 or 44 per cent were found to be in decline. Among the main causes of the decline like market and technological factors and limitation of inheritor management the management factor appeared to be more important.

According to a Reserve Bank of India study, based on the data furnished by the commercial banks (quoted by Agarwal,[42] Mehta,[43] Nair,[44] Ramaswamy,[45] Sandesara,[46] Sharma[47]) out of the 378 sick industrial undertakings enjoying credit limits of over Rs. one crore each from the banking system as on December 31, 1979.

197 units, or 52 per cent of the reported units, had fallen sick due to mismanagement/management deficiencies (including diversion of funds, infighting, lack of marketing strategy). Further, 86 units (23 per cent) had fallen sick due to market recession, 52 units (14 per cent) due to faulty initial planning and other technical drawbacks, 34 units (9 per cent) due to power cut, shortage of raw materials and other necessary inputs in time, and 9 units (2 per cent) due to labour trouble.

The RBI study, thus, revealed that the most vital cause of sickness was mismanagement of units, which alone contributed 52 per cent or more than half. Faulty initial planning and other technical drawbacks, which contributed 14 per cent of the sick units were also related to mismanagement or incompetent management. Even the market recession that contributed 32 per cent of the cases may be due to lack of proper planning and forecasting on the part of the management. Thus we see that 89 per cent of the reported units fell sick due to mismanagement. Further, the shortage of raw materials, power etc., and labour trouble, which are often said to be the major causes of sickness, contributed only 11 per cent of the cases.

Other empirical studies by the RBI, (quoted by Sandesara,[48] Mehta[49]) like the analysis of causes of sickness in 341 sick industrial units and the case studies by RBI of 18 and 15 units, cited in the Tiwari Committee Report (1984), also confirmed the earlier conclusions that mismanagement was the most widespread cause of industrial sickness. The RBI study revealed that out of the 341 sick units, 222 or 65 per cent of the units had fallen sick due to management deficiency, mismanagement or management dissensions. According to Tiwari Committee, appointed by RBI as a follow-up of its aforesaid studies, mismanagement "may take the form of poor production management, poor labour management, poor resource management, lack of professionalism, dissensions within the management, or even dishonest management." Further, according to the Committee, the management deficiency (may be classified broadly in two distinct stages of a project:

1. sickness arising at the time of planning and during implementation; and
2. sickness arising after implementation".

The report of the State Bank of India Study Team (1975)[50] popularly known as the Varshneya Commettee Report, analysed the performance of the selected 120 small scale industrial (SSI) units financed by the bank, (100 in the unsatisfactory group and 20 in the success group) with aggregate advances of Rs. 2 lack and above and identified the industrial sickness as the "lack of working funds" due to "drop in internal cash generation", caused by various factors. The report has categorised such factors or causes of sickness under three broad heads:

1. Poor Cash and Working Capital Management
2. Drop in Production
3. Increased Cost of Production

Poor Cash and Working Capital Management: include deliberate diversion of funds, unplanned diversification, poor collections, unplanned payment to creditors, high inventory, and unproductive and flamboyant expenditure.

Drop in Production: may occur due to:

(a) Problems in production like frequent machine

breakdowns, poor maintenance, poor quality of raw materials, poor labour productivity, power shortage, lack of production planning and quality control, delayed supplies from sub-contractors, poor industrial relations, and transportation bottlenecks.

(b) Lack of orders caused by competition, recession, low quality of products, due to technical incompetence and/or poor quality control, irregular deliveries, poor marketing effort, dependence on one buyer/few buyers, products obsolescence, power shortage, wrong distribution policy or methods and government policies.

(e) Lack of raw materials resulting from national or regional shortage or high cost, overdue payment to suppliers, poor quality, uncertain supplies and lack of planning.

Increased cost of production may be due to:

(a) Increased cost of raw material, increased cost not recovered in selling prices due to faulty costing, large order book at fixed prices in an inflationary market, high material wastage and high inventory costs.

(b) Increased overhead costs due to inefficient production, unutilised capacity, heavy borrowings involving higher interest charges, increased administration of selling costs, unplanned capital expenditure and new product development or diversification.

It would thus be observed that except for a few external factors (beyond the control of the management), like shortage of raw materials and power, delayed supplies from sub-contractors, and changes in the government policies, the rest of the causes of sickness, identified by the SBI study, fall in the category of internal factors (within the control of the management) which, in a way, pertain to lack of managerial and/or technical competence on the part of the entrepreneurs.

In a study (quoted by Rao and Reddy[51]) of the 23 medium and small scale industries, largely financed by the Andhra Pradesh Industrial Development Corporation (APIDC) and the Andhra Pradesh State Financial Corporation (APSFC), inefficient management emerged as the main cause of sickness. For example, while improper project planning and management, and inefficient operations were found in 12 or 52.17 per cent of the units covered by the study, financial problems were found in 9 or 39.13 per cent, and defective corporate management in 8 or 34.78 per cent of the units. Further, external factors accounted for sickness in 7 or 30.43 per cent, and problems of technology in 6 or 26.09 per cent of the units. Interestingly enough, labour problems were found to be present in only 1 or 4.35 per cent of the units.

Likewise, in another study (quoted by Rao and Reddy)[52] conducted by the Andhra Pradesh State Financial Corporation (APSFC) in November/December 1976, covering 618 assisted units spread over the entire State, found that while 94 units were limping, 108 units were sick. Further, 56 or 51.85 per cent of the 108 sick units had fallen sick due to managerial problems, disputes or lack of interest among the partners. The remaining 52 or 48.15 per cent of the units had fallen sick due to various other reasons: 20 or 18.52 per cent units due to production problems, lack of raw materials, shortage of power etc., 18 or 16.67 per cent units due to financial problems and lack of margin money for working capital coupled with inadequate bank finance for working capital, and 14 or 12.96 per cent units due to lack of market.

According to the Federation of Indian Chambers of Commerce and Industries (FICCI) study of sick small scale units (February 1988), quoted by Mehta,[53] basic cause of sickness in small units is the imbalance in the investment and financial structure of the units, higher investment in fixed assets and less importance given to working capital. Thus, as Mehta rightly puts it, "the management is the single most important factor identified for success or failure of a unit."

Besides the studies conducted by RBI, SBI, APIDC, APSFC and FICCI, the Indian researchers and writers are almost unanimous that the major cause of industrial sickness is management failure, also termed as mis-management, or inappropriate or indifferent management. They have mentioned a few other causes such as dishonesty of entrepreneurs, dissensions among the entrepreneurs, surplus workforce, faulty production programmes, and such other areas of mismanagement.[54]

Srivastava[55] studied over 200 new projects, whose term loans were in default between June 1970 and December 1980 and, while analysing their main weaknesses, found that 22.19 per cent units had suffered due to lack of good management, 21.70 per cent due to poor implementation, 15.81 per cent due to marketing problems and 5.74 per cent due to labour trouble. Thus, as 65.44 per cent units suffered, in a way, due to lack of good management, he concluded that "normally sickness is caused by internal factors which mostly relate with the mismanagement in various areas." The balance 34.56 per cent factors constituted non-availability of raw materials (13.45 per cent), shortfall of working capital (7.20 per cent), technical/operational problems (5.55 per cent) and miscellaneous factors (8.36 per cent).

According to Singh,[56] 30 per cent of the small scale industrial units fall sick due to inefficient working capital management, 22 per cent due to inefficient raw materials management, 13 per cent due to lack of demand for the products (indicating inefficient marketing management), 10 per cent due to inefficient management and the balance 25 per cent due to miscellaneous reasons. It may thus be observed that while 75 per cent of the SSI units fall sick, in a way, due to lack of managerial efficiency, the other reasons (external factors) taken together account for sickness in just 25 per cent units.

Mukherjee[57] the cases of an engineering industrial unit and, on analysing the sequence of events and causes of sickness, came to the conclusion that "the very crux of the problems begets with faulty management decisions and/or indecisions." He also observes that "a good proportion of the colossal problem of industrial sickness may be averted if the 'aborigine' unviable projects are duly censured before these are launched."

According to Prithpal Singh,[58] "a review of the various studies made to determine causes of sickness in small scale industry highlights lack of management expertise as the most important factor responsible for extensive sickness."

Aswathappa and Ratnam[59] observe that the main reasons due to which a company becomes sick may be classified as:

> Shrinking of market share due to inadequate product – "market mix, choice of an improper technology, technological obsolescence, cost-overruns, diversion of short term funds for long term requirements, pile up of inventory and build-up of debtors, ineffective materials management, poor industrial relations", and "a thorough mis-management" which "could be downright incompetency or total inexperience or utter dishonesty." Further, according to Economic Survey 1984-85 also, "the management fleeces and mismanages the unit to the point of making it permanently sick and unviable and looks forward to government take over of the sick industrial company".

Keeping in view the growing sickness in the small scale sector, mainly due to lack of managerial efficiency in the entrepreneurs, Reddy *et al.*[60] have suggested that the problem may be tackled urgently on three fronts such as (i) preparation of viable projects, (ii) completion of projects according to schedules, and (iii) professionalisation of management.

Role of Commercial Banks and other Financial Institutions in Arresting the Growing Incidence of Sickness

According to Yadav,[61] "one of the basic causes of the growing sickness in industry on which there is a fairly wide consensus is the poor management, coupled with inadequate information and reporting systems, resulting in poor monitoring, both during the implementation and operational phases of projects." He, therefore, emphasises the "need to evolve a more effective monitoring system" and the "importance of detection of sickness at the incipient stage as also the need for proper coordination between commercial banks and term lending institutions in formulation and implementation of rehabilitation packages.

Sharma[62] observes that sickness in industry is mainly caused by management deficiency. He, therefore, argues that "the management should be the first to take steps to prevent the sickness" at the incipient stage. "Next to management", he feels, "thc onus to identify the potentially sick units rests more with the commercial banks than with any other external party like term-lending institutions, governments, etc" as they deal with their borrowers on a day-to-day basis.

Gangwal[63] also feels that "commercial banks can detect first warning signal of sickness and, thus, take suitable and timely action to prevent the incidence of sickness."

Dholakia[64] also maintains that "in the light of growing incidence of industrial sickness and also the increasing proportion of non-viable units among the identified sick units, it is obvious that the financial institutions will have to play a major role in detecting and preventing sickness at the earliest possible stage."

Role of Employees' Cooperation in Arresting Sickness and Revival of Sick Units

Researchers have observed that mismanagement of the

personnel functions are commonly found in Indian companies. Most of the entrepreneurs fail to treat their employees as partners in progress,[65] resulting in low level of trust in their employees[66] and poor productivity of their labour.[67]

Citing the case of Jaipur Metals and Electricals Limited (JMEL), Mittal[68] argues that human relations are more important in turn-around than financial strategies. He maintains that "the motivation and active support provided by the management enabled the employees to virtually own the company which they revived in a short time by their hard work", and thus the company became "a living example.... of the success of participative management." Further, based on the case studies of five public sector enterprises and four private sector enterprises, Khandwalla[69] has found that "by and large, successful turn-arounds seem to be characterised by a management style that emphasises openness, participative decision making, resourcefulness, result orientation, professionalism, and selective use of management tools." Ruwe and Skinner[70] also observe that a successful company "requires the support not only of management but also of hourly workers."

Vittal, [71] based on his experience in Gujarat Narmada Auto Limited, has come to the conclusion that with the "determination and commitment of people", and the "cooperation from all concerned", including the financial institutions, government and people, even a sick unit may be revived and put on the path of progress. He further opines that "perhaps Iaccoca's formula is valid universally – people, product, profit, in that order".

Mehta[72] while empasising the need to make "labour also a partner", argues that "in the present framework labour can provide the greatest bulwark against industrial sickness." To vindicate his point, he cites the cases of success of Jaipur Metals, Gujarat Tractors and Kamani Tubes "where labour has been able to turn-around the sick units", as also those of the failure of National Textile Corporation, State Textile

Corporations and other units, "taken over by the government without involving labour fully."

Mukherjee[73] also studied the processes of sickness and revival of the aforesaid three turn-around cases (Jaipur Metals and Electricals Limited (JMEL), Gujarat Tractors Corporation Limited (GTCL), and Kamani Tubes Limited (KTL). He observes : "The findings of the case studies confirm the widely held view that efficiency of management or, so to say, mismanagement is the most important cause of sickness of industrial units." He further points out : "To this may be added the corrupt management practices as indicated particularly in the cases of JMEL and KTL." Highlighting the "key-role" played by the workers in reviving the three sick units, he stresses on the point that "removal of industrial sickness calls for .... a closer involvement of labour, management as well as government." Likewise, Cherian[74] observes that, for revival of sick industries, "workers' cooperation is a viable proposition for the small and medium sized units."

Summary of the Causes of Industrial Sickness as Identified by other Studies

The major causes of industrial sickness, particularly in the small scale sector, as revealed in various Indian researches, reports and literature, may be summarised as in Table 3.1.

TABLE 3.1: Summary of the Causes of Industrial Sickness as Identified by other Studies

I. Relating to Project		
	Internal	External
	1	2
a	Faulty project selection and planning and delay in implementation of the project	Faulty project appraisal by commercial banks and other Financial institutions

TABLE 3.1 : *Contd.*

	1	2
b	Wrong selection of site	Delay in sanctions/approvals pertaining to the project, by different government agencies concerned
c	Inappropriate plant and machinery	
d	Under-estimation of capital cost	
e	Over-estimation of demand	
f	Over-estimation of profit	

II. Relating to Finance

	Internal	External
	1	2
a	Weak equity base	Delayed disbursement of loans
b	Poor utilisation of current assets and under-utilisation of installed capacity	Inadequate disbursement of loans
c	Inefficient working capital, management particularly high inventory and poor collection of bills receivable	Delay in payment of bills by government departments and large industries
d	Unplanned payment to creditors	Credit restraint policy
e	Absence of costing and pricing	Unfavourable investment climate
f	Lack of cost control	Inflation
g	Absence of financial planning, budgeting and control	
h	Inappropriate utilisation or diversion of funds	
i	Unplanned expansion/diversification	
j	Unproductive and flamboyant expenditure	

TABLE 3.1 : *Contd.*

1	2
k Lack of proper management information system (MIS)	
l Large order book at fixed prices in an inflationary market	
m Inability to raise price with the increase in cost due to competition	
n Heavy outside borrowings involving higher interest charges	

III. Relating to Production

Internal	External
1	2
a Inadequate materials control	Shortage of raw materials, power, fuel, water, transport, and such other essential inputs
b Lack of production planning and control	Import restrictions on essential inputs
c Inadequate maintenance of plant and machinery	Delayed supplies from subcontractors
d High material wastage	
e Lack of quality control	
f Lack of emphasis on research and development	
g Obsolete plant and machinery and technology	

IV. Relating to Marketing

Internal	External
1	2
a Inaccurate demand forecasting	Market recession and competition

TABLE 3.1 : *Contd.*

	1	2
b	Inappropriate product-mix	Restraint on purchases by bulk purchasers
c	Lack of product planning	Excessive taxation policy
d	Poor quality of products or product obsolescence	Liberal licensing policy
e	Dependence on one buyer or very few buyers	Change in international market scene
f	Irregular deliveries	
g	Lack of market research	
h	Inappropriate sales promotion	
i	Poor public relations	

V. Relating to Personnel

	Internal	External
	1	2
a	Lack of behavioural approach causing dissatisfaction among the personnel	Non-availability of skilled manpower
b	Poor industrial relations	Inter-union rivalry
c	Low productivity of labour	General labour unrest in the area
d	Absence of manpower planning	Wage disparity in similar industry
e	High cost of labour	
f	Inappropriate wage and salary administration	

TABLE 3.1 : *Contd.*

VI. Relating to Corporate Management	
Internal	External
1	2
a Lack of professionalism in management	
b Improper corporate planning	
c Lack of coordination and control	
d Resistance to change	
e Strife and lack of integrity in top management	
f Unplanned expansion	
g Failure to treat employees as partners in progress	

REFERENCES

1. D.E. Schendel, G. R. Patton & J. Riggs, Corporate Turnaround Strategies: A Study of Profit Decline and Recovery, *Journal of General Management,* Vol. 3, No. 3, 1976, pp. 3-11.
2. C. Hofer, Turnaround Strategies, *Journal of Business Strategy*, Vol. 1, No. 1, 1980, pp. 19-31.
3. T. F. Frost, *The Sick Organisation,* Part I: Neurotic, Psychotic, Sociopathic, Personnel, Vol. 62, No. 5, May 1985, pp. 40-44.
4. R. Viswanathan, *Industrial Finance,* S. Chand & Company, New Delhi, 1982, p. 258.
5. R. Nelson & D. Clutterbuck (eds), *Turnaround: How Twenty Well-known Companies Came Back from the Brink,* Mercury Books, Division of W.H. Allen & Company, London, 1988.
6. Mathew J. Manimala, Turnaround Management: Lessons from Successful Cases, *ASCI Journal of Management,* Vol. 20, No. 4, March 1991, pp. 238-40.
7. V.K. Joshi, *Management of Industrial Sickness,* Kuber Associates & Publishers, Jaipur, 1987, pp. 32-59.

8. Subhash Gangwal, *New Dimensions in Industrial Sickness,* Sublime Publications, Jaipur, 1990, p. 115.
9. T. Jyothi Rani, *Sickness in Small Scale Industrial Sector,* Sandeep Publishing House, Warangal (A.P.), 1985.
10. P. Udaya Shanker & G.U.K. Rao, Sickness in Small Industry - Some Cases, *SEDME,* Vol. 17, June 1990, (Published by NISIET, Hyderabad) pp. 63-82.
11. K.C. Reddy, Sickness in Small Industry - Case Studies, in K.C. Reddy (ed), *Sickness in Small Scale Industries,* Ashish Publishing House, New Delhi, 1988, pp. 95-121.
12. R. Shanmugham, Entrepreneurship in Small Scale Industry: A Case Study, *Indian Management,* Vol. 29, Nos. 11&12, Nov. & Dec. 1990, pp. 13-15.
13. P.N. Khandwalla, What Can Financial Institutions Do to Prevent Corporate Sickness?, *Vikalpa,* Vol. 13, No. 2, April-June 1988, pp. 11-23.
14. L.K. Naidu & A. Padmavathi, Why This Growing Sickness in Small Scale Units? (A Case Study), *Yojana,* Sept. 1-15, 1987, pp. 14-17.
15. Madhava Hejmadi, Entrepreneurship in Small Industries, *Indian Management,* Vol. 29, Nos. 11&12, Nov.& Dec. 1990, pp. 17-21.
16. S. N. Bidani & P. K. Mitra, *Industrial Sickness: Identification and Rehabilitation,* Vision Books, New Delhi, 1982, pp. 116-17.
17. S.N. Bidani & P. K. Mitra, *Industrial Sickness: Identification and Rehabilitation,* Vision Books, New Delhi, 1982, pp. 47-60 & 116.
18. R. Viswanathan, *Industrial Finance,* S Chand & Company, New Delhi, 1982, pp. 258-59.
19. Banarsi Misra, *Monitoring of Industrial Sickness,* Deep & Deep Publications, New Delhi, 1990, pp. 150-51.
20. V.K. Agarwal, What Do We Need to Tackle Industrial Sickness, *Yojana,* July 1-15, 1987, pp. 15-18.
21. D.K. Pal, Rehabilitation of Sick Industrial Units in the Small Scale Sector, *Chartered Secretary,* Vol. 14, No. 5, May 1984, pp. 316-21.
22. A.V.V.S.K. Rao, Industrial Sickness in Indian Economy, *Facts For You,* Vol. 9, No. 12, June 1988 (Annual Number-1988-89), pp. 22-26.
23. D. Bagchi, Industrial Sickness: A Growing Phenomenon, *Lok Udyog,* Vol. 18, No. 3, June 1984, pp. 43-55.
24. G.S. Sood, Industrial Sickness: Some Issues, *Yojana,* September 1-15, 1987, pp. 4-7.
25. G.S. Sood, Rehabilitating the Sick Industrial Units, *Yojana,* September 16-30, 1987, pp. 24-29.
26. M. Devendra Babu, Sick Industries: Task Before BIFR, *Yojana,* September 1-15, 1987, pp. 18-21 & 27.
27. H.L. Rai & G.N. Brahmanandam, Sickness in Small Industry – A Disgnostic View, *Indian Journal of Marketing,* Vol. 15, Nos. 2 & 3, October & November 1984, pp. 25-28.
28. M.V. Ratnam, Sickness in Industry – How to Avoid it? *The Management Accountant,* Vol. 19, No. 6, June 1984, pp. 308-09.

29. K.P. Meena, Industrial Sickness, *Yojana*, Vol. 33, No. 18, Oct. 1-15, 1989, p. 5.
30. N.C. Joshi, Solving Industrial Sickness on War Footing, *The Journal of the Indian Institute of Bankers,* Vol. 54, No. 4, Oct-Dec. 1983, pp. 184-91.
31. V.N. Nadkarni, Sickness in Industry and its Effect on Banking, *State Bank of India, Monthly Review,* Vol. 22, No. 6, June 1983, pp. 245-55.
32. B.K. Agarwal, Sickness in Indian Industry, *Decision,* Vol. 6, No. 1, 1979, pp. 65-73.
33. N.S. Prasad, Curing Sickness in Industries, *Indian Journal of Marketing,* Vol. 13, No. 3, 1982, pp. 19-22.
34. S. Rajagopal, Preventing Corporate Sickness: Improving the Working of Financial Institutions, *Vikalpa,* Vol. 14, No. 1, 1989, pp. 65ff.
35. C.S. Ramaswamy, Credit System and Industrial Sickness, *Mainstream,* Vol. 19, No. 46, 1981, pp. 15-17.
36. D.R. Sharma, Industrial Sickness: Case Study of Small Units in Kumaun Region, *Indian Journal of Marketing,* Vol. 13, No. 8, 1983, pp. 15-18.
37. T. Ramesh, Problems of Small Scale Industries, *The Chartered Accountant,* Vol. 39, No. 7, Jan. 1991, pp. 557-59.
38. V.R. Reddy, Problems of Small Industries in India, *Indian Management,* Vol. 29, Nos. 11 & 12, Nov. & Dec. 1990, pp. 43-46.
39. E.T. Penrose, *The Theory of the Growth of the Firm,* Basil Blackwell, London, 1980, pp. 43-44.
40. R.L. Morris, The Economic Theory of Managerial Capitalism, MacMillan, London, 1964.
41. J. Boswell, The Rise and Decline of Small Firms, George Allen & Unwin, London, 1973.
42. V.K. Agarwal, What Do We Need to Tackle Industrial Sickness, *Yojana,* July 1-15, 1987, pp. 15-18.
43. S.S. Mehta, Sick Industry Syndrome in India: Some Aspects, *Decision,* Vol. 15, Nos. 3 & 4, July & Oct. 1988, pp. 179-90.
44. N.P. Nair, Two Studies on Industrial Sickness (Editorial), *Indian Manager,* Vol. 13, No. 1, Jan-March 1983, pp. 5-12 (b).
45. C.S. Ramaswamy, Credit System and Industrial Sickness, *Mainstream,* Vol. 19, No. 46, 1981, pp. 15-17.
46. J.C. Sandersara, Industrial Sickness in India, *Decision,* Vol. 15, Nos. 3 & 4, July & Oct. 1988, pp. 161-65.
47. R.K. Sharma, Industrial Sickness in India: An Analysis, *ASCI Journal of Management,* Vol. 15, No. 1, September 1985, p. 15.
48. J.C. Sandesara, Industrial Sickness in India, *Decision,* Vol. 15, Nos. 3 & 4, July & Oct. 1988, pp. 161-65.
49. S.S. Mehta, Sick Industry Syndrome in India : Some Aspects, *Decision,* Vol. 15, Nos. 3 & 4, July & Oct. 1988, pp. 179-90.
50. State Bank of India, Financing of Small Scale Industries, *Report of the Study Team,* Bombay, 1975, pp. 6-9, 89 & 91.

51. P.B. Appa Rao & T. Subbi Reddy, Sickness in Small Industry in Andhra Pradesh, *Decision,* Vol. 15, Nos. 3 & 4, July & Oct. 1988, pp. 235-45.
52. *Ibid.*
53. S.S. Mehta, Sick Industry Syndrome in India: Some Aspects, *Decision,* Vol. 15, Nos 3 & 4, July & Oct. 1988, pp. 179-90.
54. (i) D.R. Sharma, Industrial Sickness: Case Study of Small Units in Kumaun Region, *Indian Journal of Marketing,* Vol. 13, No. 8, 1983, pp. 15--18.
(ii) M. Hegde, Western and Indian Models of Turnaround Management, *Vikalpa*, Vol. 7, No. 4, 1982, pp. 289-303.
(iii) B. Krishnan, The Anatomy of a Sick Engineering Unit, *Indian Management,* Vol. 24, No. 5, 1985, pp. 18-22.
55. S.S. Srivastava, Management of Industrial Sickness, *Productivity,* Vol. 24, No. 3, Oct-Dec. 1983, pp. 367-73.
56. Anil Pratap Singh, Diagnosing and Treating Industrial Sickness, *Yojana,* July 1-15, 1987, pp. 11-14.
57. B. Mukherjee, Industrial Sickness: Propensities and Prevention, *The Journal of the Indian Institute of Bankers*, Vol. 53, No. 2, April-June 1982, pp. 77-82.
58. Prithpal Singh, The Small Scale Sector and Issues of Management, *Indian Management,* Vol. 29, Nos. 11 & 12, Nov. & Dec. 1990, pp. 32-37.
59. K. Aswathappa & V.G. Ratnam, Turnaround Strategy in a Competitive Environment, *Indian Management,* Vol. 29, No. 9, September 1990, pp. 34-36.
60. B. Bhargava Reddy, A.R. Reddy & B. Krishna Reddy, Three Pronged Attack on Sickness in Small Scale Industries, *Yojana,* September 1-15, 1987, pp. 8-11 & 17.
61. R.A. Yadav, Designing Management Information System for Monitoring Industrial Health, *ASCI Journal of Management,* Vol. 20, No. 1, June 1990, pp. 1-13.
62. R.K. Sharma, Industrial Sickness in India: An Analysis, *ASCI Journal of Management,* Vol. 15, No. 1, September 1985, pp. 15-18.
63. S. Gangwal, New Dimensions in Industrial Sickness, Sublime Publications, Jaipur, 1990, pp. 144-45.
64. B.H. Dholakia, Industrial Sickness in India: Magnitude and Identification Criteria, *Decision,* Vol. 15, Nos. 3 & 4, July & Oct. 1988, pp. 149-59.
65. P.D. Agarwal, Organisational Sickness: Causes and Cures – A Case Study of the Banking Industry in India, *Prajnan,* Vol. 6, No. 2, 1977, pp. 173-204.
66. R.S. Dwivedi, On Becoming a Sick Enterprise: Diagnosis & Treatment, *Lok Udyog,* Vol. 17, No. 9, December 1983, pp. 17-25.
67. A.R. Mukherjee, Sickness in Indian Engineering Industries, *The Management Accountant,* Vol. 18, No. 11, Nov. 1983, pp. 467-70.

68. B.B. Mittal, Revival of a Sick Unit: A Case Study, *The Chartered Accountant,* Vol. 36, No. 5, Nov. 1987, pp. 432-35.
69. P.N. Khandwalla, Strategy for Turning Around Complex Sick Organisations. *Vikalpa,* Vol. 6, Nos. 3 & 4, July & October 1981, pp. 143-65.
70. D.M. Ruwe & W. Skinner, Reviving a Rust Belt Factory, Harvard Business Review, Vol. 65, No. 3, May-June 1987, pp. 70-76.
71. N. Vittal, The Unusual Story of Gujarat Narmada Auto Ltd. – A Case Study, *Management in Government,* Vol. 20, No. 4, Jan.-March 1989, pp. 339-48.
72. S.S. Mehta, Guest Editorial Note, *Decision,* Vol. 15, Nos. 3 & 4, July & October, 1988, pp. 147-48.
73. S. Mookherjee, Industrial Sickness and Revival: A Study of Selected Organisations, *Decision,* Vol. 15, Nos. 3 & 4, July & Oct., 1988, pp. 213-33.
74. Samuel Cherian, Industrial Sickness in India: The Case of West Bengal, *Decision,* Vol. 15, Nos. 3 & 4, July & Oct., 1988, pp. 191-212.

4

CASE STUDIES OF NON-VIABLE SICK UNITS, VIABLE SICK UNITS AND HEALTHY UNITS

I

NON-VIABLE SICK UNITS

1. PENTAGON PLASTICS

Five young enthusiastic entrepreneurs, Sarvashri Akash, Alok, Vikas, Vivek and Trilok had formed a private limited company named *Pentagon Plastics (Private) Limited* in January 1985 for manufacturing injection moulded plastic items for domestic and industrial uses.

They had started with an equity base of Rs. 4.50 lakh, which was subsequently raised to Rs. 5.60 lakh. They had obtained a working capital limit of Rs. 19 lakh (including Bank Guarantee limit of Rs. 5 lakh) from the bank. They had also been sanctioned and disbursed a term loan of Rs. 19.40 lakh (including a soft loan of Rs. 2 lakh) from the State Financial Corporation for land, building, plant and machinery (including moulds). The Small Scale Industrial Development Corporation (SSIDC) had also loaned a sum of Rs. 2 lakh by way of quasi-equity participation. Thus, the total outside liabilities of the unit, to begin with, amounted to Rs. 40.40 lakh and the total capital employed (with the equity-base of

Rs. 5.60 lakh) worked out to Rs. 46 lakh.

The factory was located in a backward area with a view to availing of the concessions and incentives attached therewith. But the source of supply of raw materials and the market for their finished products were located in the city, situated at a distance of about 80 kms from the factory.

The company commenced its commercial production in right earnest. But its products could not pick up in the market mainly due to poor quality and lack of quality control. There was high incidence of return of goods due to sub-standard supplies. About 70% of its goods supplied to one of its prime purchasers were returned on this count. The value of such returned goods in the year 1990 alone amounted to Rs. 5.69 lakh. Thus, the level of inventory of their finished goods, including returned goods, kept on rising. Further, these goods could not even be recycled as raw material, and had to be disposed of as scraps at a throw away price, resulting in substantial loss to the unit. The unit was finding it difficult to improve upon the quality of its products, even subsequently. The level of its sundry debtors, including unpaid bills, disputed bills and returned bills, also kept on rising.

With the loss of reputation of the company's products, its level of sales started coming down, steadily. There was a consequential drop in its production activity. It was operating well below its installed capacity and even below the break-even point, resulting in accumulated losses. There was mounting pressure from the sundry creditors. The company was in real financial difficulties.

Despite all this, the directors' extravagant expenses, including frequent (avoidable) visits to Bombay and Delhi, went on unabated. They were also drawing remunerations to the tune of Rs. 2.56 lakh per year. Further, the office premises in a posh market place in the city (in addition to the spacious factory premises) was costing the company an annual rental of Rs. 60,000 without serving much useful purpose and adding to the overheads, instead. The unit had also indulged in an irrational and deliberate diversion of funds – by applying the short term sources of funds (working capital loan) for long term uses. It had mis-utilised the entire working capital loan of the bank, and even more, (i.e. Rs. 18.17 lakh as against the sanctioned limit of Rs. 14.00 lakh) for purchase of moulds and dies worth Rs. 10.87 lakh and for repayment of instalments of Rs. 7.30 lakh on the term loan obtained from the State Financial Corporation (SFC).

Further, the company had incorporated yet another sister concern in the year 1988-89, and had even started some construction work, by diverting the short term sources, in anticipation of sanction and disbursement of yet another term loan by the SFC. It was with this end in view that the company had repaid the initial instalments to the SFC, though it had not generated any cash surplus.

The unit soon faced the problem of scarcity of raw materials. To keep the wheels of production moving, it had to purchase the raw materials from the SSIDC at a higher price. But the unit could not increase the price of its products proportionately, due to stiff competition in the market.

Thus, the financial hardship of the unit was getting further hardened. The bank came to its rescue and enhanced the working capital limit from Rs. 14 lakh to Rs. 26.70 lakh in December 1989. But this could not help much and for long. The unit did not show any sign of improvement. The outstandings and irregularity on the bank accounts went on increasing, instead which is evident from the position of the accounts in February 1991, as given hereunder.

It would thus be observed that while the total irregularity on the three accounts was to the extent of Rs. 42.19 lakh, the Cash Credit (Hyp) account itself was irregular by Rs. 30.93 lakh, i.e., to the extent of 250% of the sanctioned limit. It is not clear to us how the bank could allow drawings on the account to the extent of about 300% of the sanctioned limit.

The bank was now no longer permitting further irregularities on the account. To circumvent this, the company stopped routing its sale proceeds through these

(Rs. in lakh)

Sl. No.	Type of Facility	Limit	Drawing power	Outstandings	Irregularity
1.	Cash Credit (Hypothecation)	12.70	3.70	34.63	30.93
2.	Cash Credit (Bills)	11.00	Nil	9.76	9.76
3.	Working Capital Term Loan	3.00			1.50
	Total	26.70	3.70	44.39	42.19

accounts. It had opened a collection account, in March 1991, with another local bank for the purpose. This did alert the bank. But now it was too late. The company was incurring losses since inception which, at the end of the last five years, had got accumulated to Rs. 23 lakh (excluding depreciation). The bank had, by now, lost the faith in the company. And, the growing dissension among the five directors came as the final blow, making the revival of the unit well nigh impossible.

Despite all this, the bank had not given up all hopes. It was still prepared to undertake the rehabilitation of the unit provided the directors of the company could bring in a further capital of Rs. 20 lakh so as to adjust at least 50% of the irregularity on the accounts. The directors were further required to meet the 25% margin on the additional working capital limit, to be sanctioned to the unit, from their own resources.

As these conditions were well beyond the capacity of the company to comply with, the loan was finally called up and legal proceedings were initiated against the company by the bank for recovery of its dues.

Comments

The main cause of sinckness of the unit was the poor quality of its products and lack of quality control, emanating from lack of technical competence on the part of the directors and even dirth of technically qualified personnel in the company.

It had further ramifications like huge return of goods, disputed and outstanding bills, high sundry debtors and poor collections, loss of reputation and lower level of sales, sub-optimal level of production activity and resultant losses on a continuous basis, and so on. These facts speak of lack of managerial skills on the part of the directors in the areas of financial management, production management and marketing management.

The diversion of funds and unplanned expansion and diversification, extravagant and avoidable expenses and overheads, heavy withdrawals by the directors despite continuous losses since inception, are also indicative of poor planning and lack of financial management skills.

The decision to locate the factory in the backward area, 80 kms away from the city, also proved to be ill-conceived because the cost of transportation of the raw materials and finished goods had outweighed the marginal benefits available in backward areas. The cost-benefit analysis was apparently not done.

The technical non-feasibility and economic non-viability of the unit, all through, are indicative of ill-conceived project on the part of the young entrepreneurs and faulty project appraisal on the parts of the bank and the State Financial Corporation.

The entrepreneurs could have well been counselled by the bank and the other financial institutions to start the venture on a much smaller scale than Rs. 46 lakh, as also to commence commercial production only after some successful trial runs. This way they could have been able to set right the technical defects in their products, and would have taken the meagre initial losses in their stride, and thereby may have gained sufficient experience and expertise in the management of the activity. And only then they should have thought in terms of expansion and diversi-fication. But the possibility of the young entrepreneurs trying to borrow as much as possible under the entrepreneur scheme, and the bankers and other financial institutions also endeavouring to lend as much as permissible under the scheme, so as to achieve the pre-fixed target of disbursement of loans, may not be ruled out, either.

There was lack of performance monitoring and supervision and follow-up on the part of the bank which is evidenced from the indiscriminate overdrawings allowed in the account, far in excess of the sanctioned limit. Further, no sincere and serious attempt was made by the bank to diagnose the real causes of sickness of the unit, so as to initiate some suitable remedial measures in a systematic and comprehensive manner. Merely enhancing the working capital limit by Rs. 12.70 lakh was no remedy.

While the unit was incurring losses on a continuing basis and various other unsatisfactory and unhealthy features were attached with the working of the unit, right from the inception, the unit was declared sick by the bank after four years in 1989, and the loan was called up in 1991.

2. CUTE CARTONS – LOVELY LABELS

Mr. Karim had established a proprietary concern named *Cute Cartons - Lovely Labels* in 1977 for manufacturing cartons and printing labels. The firm was sanctioned a working capital limit of Rs. 1.92 lakh by the bank in October 1978. The State Financial Corporation had also granted a term loan of Rs. 3.23 lakh for the required items of machinery.

Well before the unit could stabilise its position, Mr Karim purchased a car on loan and appropriated a portion of the bank's working capital finance to provide the margin thereon as also for payment of the periodical instalments. Such diversion of funds caused the cash crunch, adversely affecting the day-to-day operations of the unit.

The financial constraints of the unit got further accentuated as its sundry debtors kept on mounting. Its bills aggregating Rs. 2.10 lakh were long outstanding. Besides poor realisation mechanism, Mr Karim's poor marketing ability also started surfacing. The firm's sundry creditors were pressing hard for payment. Its level of sales started showing a declining trend. Consequently, its production activities came down to a sub-optimal level, well below the break-even point, resulting in continuous losses. The unit also suffered due to lack of skilled labour and frequent breakdowns of machines.

Mr Karim ultimately requested the bank to enhance the working capital limit so that he could overcome the financial difficulty. The limit was accordingly enhanced to Rs. 4.02 lakh, in December 1981.

But this did not prove to be of much help. The unit's accmulated cash losses went on steadily increasing from Rs. 6.45 lakh in 1986 to Rs. 8.38 lakh in 1987, Rs. 9.83 lakh in 1988 and Rs. 11.45 lakh in 1989.

Such state of affairs had made the unit over-dependent on the bank finance. It, therefore, resorted to frequent overdrawings on its bank accounts which it could not repay or even reduce due to continuous losses

By the year 1984 the unit's cash credit accounts with the bank were irregular by Rs. 2.14 lakh. But the irregularity kept on rising unabated so much so that by May 1990 it had increased to Rs. 16.26 lakh, that is over four times the sanctioned limit of Rs. 4.02 lakh, and that too, against the drawing power standing at "nil", inasmuch as the entire stocks of raw materials and finished goods had got gradually depleted and the unit had not submitted the stock statements since October 1988. Since early 1988 the unit had stopped routing its bills and sale proceeds through the bank. Mr Karim had, however, admitted to the bank that, of late, the production of cartons had been given up and the work pertaining to printing of labels only was being undertaken.

By now the bank had put its foot down and was prepared to consider the rehabilitation proposal of the unit only after Mr Karim could bring in a further capital of at least Rs. 10 lakh towards reduction of the irregularity of Rs. 16.26 lakh on the accounts. But it was not within the means of Mr Karim to meet the bank's requirements. The bank, therefore, ultimately declared the unit as non-viable for rehabilitation, called up the loan and filed a civil suit for recovery of its dues.

Comments

The diversion of funds was the first step towards the sickness of the unit. High sundry debtors and long outstanding bills as also pressing sundry creditors had further aggravated the unit's financial difficulties adversely affecting its day-to-day operations. These are indicative of poor cash management, poor credit policy and collection mechanism, in particular, and lack of financial management skills, in general.

Further, the lower level of sales and poor marketing ability suggest that Mr Karim faltered on the marketing management side also.

Besides, the sub-optimal level of production, well below the break-even point, lack of skilled labour and frequent break-down of machines speak adversely of the production management and maintenance management of the unit, too.

The cost-volume-profit (CVP) analysis was obviously not done at the project stage itself by the borrower, the bank and the State Financial Corporation. It is, thus, a case of faulty project appraisal by the bank and the State Financial Corporation.

The gradual reduction in the unit's activity, both on production and sales fronts, was well reflected in the lower levels of debit/credit summations on its bank accounts, right from its inception. But the bank had failed to detect the early signals of sickness and to initiate some corrective steps in time. The unit was operating well below the break-even point, all through, resulting in substantial losses on a continuing basis. The unit had not submitted the stock statements since October 1988, as its stocks had got completely depleted over the years. It is not clear how the bank's officials were conducting even the physical verification of stocks, leave alone the monitoring of the various activity levels of the unit. The act of allowing unrestricted overdrawings on the account over a period of time, well above the sanctioned limit and against 'nil' drawing power, is in itself a matter of concern. The aforesaid facts are indicative of the lack of performance monitoring of the unit and supervision and follow-up of the advance by the bank. The early warning signals of sickness of the unit were not taken serious note of by the branch staff. No sincere efforts seem to have been made to identify the various factors leading to the sickness of the unit with a view to taking some remedial steps in time. The enhancement of the working capital limit was, at best, an *ad-hoc* step and not a real remedy.

3. RAJHANS ENTERPRISES

Mr Raj Kumar had established a proprietary concern named *Rajhans Enterprises* in 1978 for undertaking communication contracts from the Posts and Telegraphs Department and the Railways Department.

The unit was working well during the first few years. It had received various awards viz. *Best Import Substitution Award* in 1984 from the Government of India for manufacturing cable terminal boxes as also *Udyog Patra* in 1985 and *Udyog Ratna* in 1986.

But it experienced an initial setback in 1984 when the P & T Department took a policy decision to stop expansion of manned exchanges and to convert the existing ones into auto-exchanges. Consequently, the unit's order book started showing a declining trend. To tide over the difficulty, Mr Raj Kumar established two sister concerns with a view to procuring the maximum possible orders from the P & T Department, by submitting competitive tenders/quotations in the names of all the three concerns. The two sister concerns, however, were existing only on paper inasmuch as they neither had any stocks or machinery of their own nor were engaged in any production activity.

The P & T Department somehow came to know of the 'strategy' of Mr Raj Kumar. They, therefore, decided in 1987 not to place any further orders with any of the three firms. A great chunk of business was thus lost to the unit, though, in the meantime, the P & T Department had reversed their earlier decision and had since revived their expansion programme in regard to the manned exchanges.

The decision of the P & T Department had further ramifications. The level of sales of the unit had drastically dropped, adversely affecting its profitability. The level of inventory of finished goods, specifically manufactured for the P & T Department, had got piled up for lack of market therefor. The creditors were pressing hard for payment. The level of sundry debtors was also steadily rising specially because, while the P & T Department were making full payment of the bill on the supply of the materials, the Railways Department were retaining 20% of the payment till the completion of the labour work. All these factors had caused liquidity problem to the unit adversely affecting its production activity.

The unit had, however, been able to procure orders from the Railways Department to the tune of Rs. 100 lakh during the year 1987-88 and had repaid a sum of Rs. 6 lakh (including interest) in its bank account. But the year 1988-89 happened to be a lull period. Besides, the unit was not able to withstand the severe jolt received by way of complete stoppage of orders from the P & T Department. Its production activity had sharply come down by March 1989.

A further setback came to Mr Raj Kumar when his wife suffered a severe heart attack and had to be taken to the United States for treatment resulting in heavy expenses. The unit, therefore, could not execute the orders of the Railways Department in time whereby they also dis-continued giving further orders to the unit. The unit was now in deep trouble.

The unit's account with the bank was running irregular since June 1987. And, due to frequent over-drawings allowed on the account over a period of time the irregularity thereon was steadily going up so much so that as on the 10th February 1991 it stood at Rs. 33.40 lakh as against the limit of Rs. 20.30 lakh and the drawing power reduced to 'nil'.

The bank had sanctioned working capital limits of Rs. 5 lakh each to both the fictitious sister concerns of the unit despite the fact that they did not have any stocks or machinery of their own. And the irregularities on these two accounts together amounted to Rs. 12 lakh as on the 10th February 1991 as against 'nil' drawing power, in the absence of stocks since inception.

Thus, the total irregularity on all the three accounts amounted to Rs. 45.40 lakh as against 'nil'drawing power. Further, the stoppage orders, both from P&T and the Railways departments, the only two customers of the units, had rendered all of them non-viable beyond rehabilitation. Besides, the integrity of Mr Raj Kumar was also being questioned. Under the circumstances, the bank called up the loans and filed civil suits against all the three firms for recovery of its dues.

Comments

In the initial stage the unit performed well. It had the requisite technical competence which was further evidenced by the three awards that it had received during the period 1984 to 1986. But it received a setback in 1984 with the change in the government policy resulting in some loss of business from the P & T Department. And its dubious designs resulted in a total loss of business from them (P & T Department). Subsequently, the Railways Department had also stopped placing orders with the unit. The unit was thus left with no market. Over-dependence on only two bulk buyers had proved to be an unsound marketing strategy, even suicidal to the unit. The serious sickness of Mrs Raj Kumar had further accentuated the problems of the unit. The frequent over-drawings on the accounts and gradual depletion of stocks indicate lack of financial discipline and financial management on the part of Mr Raj Kumar. Above all, his integrity was also being doubted by the bank. All the three units were, therefore, declared non-viable and the loans were called up.

The over-drawings allowed on the accounts, from time to time, beyond the sanctioned limits and against 'nil' drawing powers, due to gradual depletion of stocks, indicate some laxity somewhere in regard to the effective supervision and follow-up of the advances by the bank. Further, the act of sanctioning the working capital limits to the two sister concerns of the unit, in the absence of any stocks or machinery, also suggests some flaw in the pre-sanction survey and credit appraisal by the officers of the bank.

It is for consideration whether at the project appraisal stage the bank officers could possibly caution the entrepreneurs against the imminent pitfalls connected with over-dependence on one or a few bulk buyers, as in the instant case, and counsel them to simultaneously explore some alternative broad-based market also to fall back upon.

The unit had started showing early signs of sickness in June 1987 but no sincere efforts seem to have been made by the bank and the borrowers to revive the units and regularise the position of the accounts. The position worsened further and ultimately the loans were called up after four years in 1991.

4. ARVIND ENTERPRISES

Sri Arvind had established a proprietary firm named *Arvind Enterprises* in 1980 for manufacturing telecommunication line materials exclusively for the Department of Telecommunications. The unit was sanctioned a working capital limit of Rs. 21 lakh by the bank in 1981.

The unit was working satisfactorily for the first five years. But it received a serious setback in the year 1986 due to the change in the government policy to switch over to advanced technology in the area of telecommunication. This resulted in a sudden stoppage of orders from the Telecom. Department. The goods worth Rs. 4.20 lakh, already produced exclusively for the department, were not picked up by them, either. These had, therefore, to be disposed of as scraps at a throw away price for lack of an alternative market therefor. This resulted in a heavy loss to the unit. Due to the stoppage of orders from the Telecom.Department, the unit was compelled to stop its production activity in the absence of any alternative line of production to cater to the open market. The unit had, however, attempted to change its line of production to PVC coiling of G.I. wire for supply to the P & T Department. But the relative samples were not approved by the department. The accumulated losses were steadily increasing due to overhead costs, etc. Besides, the payment of supply bills aggregating Rs. 4.15 lakh, pertaining to the period 1985-86, were not forthcoming from the Telecom. Department resulting in severe financial hardship to the unit.

The drawing power on the account was reduced to 'nil' as the stocks of raw materials had got depleted over a period of time and the stocks of finished goods, not lifted by the Telecom. Department, were worth scraps only. The account of the unit was thus running irregular since 1986 and the unit had, in fact, fallen sick then itself. And, Shri Arvind did not seem to be sincere in rehabilitating the unit, as he was not furnishing the bank with the information and financial data required in this regard. But the unit was declared non-viable and the loan was called up by the bank in July 1991 by when the irregularity on the account had gradually risen to Rs. 19.16 lakh against 'nil' drawing power.

Comments

The unit had fallen sick mainly because it was exclusively

dependent upon one single purchaser, so much so that the moment the Telecom. Department stopped placing orders with the unit, due to change in the government policy, its production activity came to a sudden halt and the unit became sick. Its products were so specific to the requirement of the Telecom. Department that these could not be sold out elsewhere in the open market, even at a concessional rate, and had to be disposed of as a scrap. Besides the change in the government policy, the non-payment of the bills had further worsened the financial position of the unit.

The unit could have foreseen the imminent difficulty connected with exclusively depending upon a single purchaser and that too a government department. It could have, at the project stage itself, thought of an alternative line of manufacture also, to fall back upon or to run concurrently, even if this would have involved some additional items of machinery or some minor additions/alterations in the existing ones. The bank could as well have forewarned and counselled the unit accordingly, at the project appraisal stage itself.

The unit had attempted to change its line of activity but had failed because its products could not pass the test of quality. This goes to suggest some lack of technical competence on the part of Shri Arvind in the new venture.

The fact that the stocks of raw materials had got depleted over a period of time and the irregulairty on the account had gradually risen, due to frequent overdrawings, go to suggest that there had been some lacuna in the periodical inspection of stocks and effective supervision and performance monitoring of the unit by the bank. The unit had fallen sick in the year 1986 but it was declared non-viable by the bank in July 1991.

5. POPULAR PHARMACEUTICALS

Popular Pharmaceuticals (Private) Limited was incorporated in June 1974 with Sri Pravin and Sri Kamalesh as the Managing Director and Director respectively, for manufacturing biological and pharmaceutical products, and liver extract. The company was sanctioned a working capital limit of Rs. 9 lakh by the bank in June 1975. It was facing difficulty, *ab initio*, as its products could not pick up in the market due to poor quality. To tide over the financial difficulty of the unit, its limit was enhanced to Rs. 19 lakh in 1986, on an *ad-hoc* basis, pending finalisation of the nursing programme. But the unit could not show any sign of improvement even thereafter. It subsequently stopped routing its sale proceeds through the bank. Besides, the unit had arranged concurrent borrowings from some other bank without the knowledge of the previous bank. It had diversified into production of veterinary drugs before consolidating its earlier activity. The statutory dues had got accumulated. meanwhile, some dispute had also cropped up between the two directors, adversely affecting the business of the company and stoppage of production since July 1988.

The company had not submitted the stock statement since long despite reminders as the entire stocks had got depleted over a period of time. The drawing power on the account was, therefore, reduced to 'nil'. The account was running irregular since September 1988. Due to frequent overdrawings, the irregularity on the account had risen to Rs. 39.60 lakh as on 31.5.1991 as against the sanctioned limit of Rs.19 lakh. The directors had stopped cooperating with the bank and were not coming forward for discussions with the bank officers regarding the rehabilitation package for reviving the unit. They were also reluctant to renew the documents which were getting time-barred shortly.

The bank, therefore, declared the unit as non-viable for rehabilitation in September 1991, called up the loan and filed civil suit for recovery of its dues.

Comments

The fact that the unit was facing marketing problems, right from the beginning, speaks adversely on its marketing skills as also technical competence evidenced by the sub-standard quality of its products. Tnese aspects do not seem to have been considered by the unit thoroughly at the project stage itself. Market survey, or even a quick market census, do not seem to have been conducted, either. High irregularity on the account, depletion of the entire stocks and unplanned diversion into veterinary drugs, suggest lack of financial management skills. Resorting to concurrent borrowings, without the knowledge of the bank, was a breach of trust and the integrity of the borrowers was being questioned. Reluctance on the part of the directors to discuss the rehabilitation package with the bank as also to renew the documents made the bank believe that they were not serious about the revival of the unit. The loan was, therefore, called up.

The fact that the company's products had not picked up in the market, at any stage, go to suggest that the economic viability and technical feasibility of the project were not studied thoroughly by the bank at the project appraisal stage. Even later, the early signals of sickness in the unit could not alert the bank to initiate the necessary corrective steps in time, based on the detailed scrutiny of the various causal factors, to revive the unit. Mere enhancement of the limit, on an *ad-hoc* basis, without detailed viability study, does not seem justifiable. The depletion of the entire stocks and high irregularity on the account, over twice the sanctioned limit, go to suggest lack of periodical inspection of stocks and effective supervision and follow up of the advance by the bank.

The unit was not working on sound lines, right from the beginning, and its account was running irregular since September 1988. But the loan was called up by the bank after three years in September 1991.

6. IDEAL PHARMACEUTICALS

Ideal Pharmaceuticals (Private) Limited, established in 1985, was manufacturing pharmaceutical formulations, viz. tablets, capsules, injections, ointment and liquid preparations. Sri Krishna and Sri Sachdeva were the Managing Director and Director of the company respectively.

The company had projected its annual sales at Rs. 100 lakh. It was sanctioned a working capital limit of Rs. 20.50 lakh by the bank in January 1986 and a term loan of Rs. 11.04 lakh by the State Financial Corporation for purchase of plant and machinery.

But, due to tough competition from the multi-nationals and other established units, the unit was suffering from lack of orders since its inception. The unit was, therefore, operating at well below the break-even point, resulting in losses right from the beginning. It was later undertaking only job work from other SSI units which was quite insufficient to cover the overhead costs. Though the unit had been able to procure a substantial export order for some tablet preparations, it was subsequently cancelled as the products had failed to pass the test of quality.

The entire stocks of the company, charged to the bank, had got depleted over a period of time. The company was, therefore, not submitting the stock statements to the bank. The drawing power on the account was, accordingly, reduced to 'nil'. The account had become irregular in early 1987 but, due to frequent overdrawings on the account, the irregularity had risen to Rs. 18.90 lakh by July 1991.

The directors did not seem to be serious about the rehabilitation of the unit as they were not coming forward with any viable proposal. They were not submitting the required data/information to the bank in this regard.

The bank, therefore, declared the unit as non-viable for rehabilitation in September 1991, called up the loan and filed civil suit for recovery of its dues.

Comments

The estimated annual sales at Rs. 100 lakh proved to be over-ambitious. The market survey or a quick market scanning does not seem to have been done by the company at the project stage. The extent of competition from multi-national companies and other established concerns was not assessed properly, either. The fact that the samples, relating to the export order, could not pass the test of quality suggests lack of technical competence and quality control on the part of the entrepreneurs. These vital factors, pertaining to economic viability and technical feasibility of the unit, do not seem to have been objectively examined by the bank and the State Financial Corporation at the project appraisal stage.

The gradual depletion of the entire stocks, charged to the bank, goes to suggest some lacuna in the effective periodical inspection of stocks by the bank. The high irregularity on the account, allowed, by the bank over a period of time, as against 'nil' drawing power, suggests lack of effective supervision and performance monitoring of the unit by the bank. The unit was suffering from serious marketing problems, right from the beginning. But the bank does not seem to have undertaken a timely study of the problems of the unit, on various fronts, so as to initiate the required remedial steps to revive the unit at the early stage of its sickness.

The unit was running on unsound lines, *ab initio*, and its bank account had become irregular in 1987, that is within two years of its inception. But the unit was declared non-viable and the loan was called up by the bank after four years in September 1991.

7. S.N. FABRICATION WORKS

Sri Shekhar and Sri Nagendra had established a partnership firm named *S.N. Fabrication Works* in 1971 for manufacturing mobile cranes for supply to BHEL and Indo-Nippon. The firm was sanctioned a term loan by the bank in August 1971 for the purchase of machinery. It had commenced production the same year and was selling its products to the aforesaid two companies only. But, after some time, due to some delay in the execution of orders as also for some technical defects in the products, both the aforenamed companies returned the sub-standard goods and stopped giving fresh orders to the unit. This had caused a major setback to the unit. Its production level had thus gone down, well below the break-even point, resulting in accumulated losses.

The unit had, therefore, changed the line of its activity to the manufacturing of hydraulic presses. It was sanctioned a working capital limit of Rs.8.35 lakh by the bank in August 1982. But the new product also suffered from some technical defects in the fabrication work which adversely affected the reputation of the product in the market and resulted in the loss of business to the unit. The unit had been able to procure some export order which, too, was subsequently cancelled due to some manufacturing defects.

The unit had become almost defunct by the year 1986. It was only doing some job work which was hardly sufficient to meet the high overhead costs. Its accumulated losses were, therefore, steadily rising. It was not submitting the stock statement to the bank as its stocks had got completely depleted over a period of time. The drawing power on the account was, therefore, reduced to 'nil'. But, due to frequent over-drawings allowed by the bank, the irregularity on the account had gradually risen to Rs. 22.10 lakh by July 1991, that is, about three times the sanctioned limit of Rs.8.35 lakh. The firm was not coming forward with any concrete proposal for reduction of the irregularity on the account and to revive the unit.

Under the aforesaid circumstances, the unit was declared non-viable by the bank in September 1991 and the loan was subsequently called up and legal action initiated against the firm for recovery of the bank's dues.

Comments

The unit had suffered the initial setback due to

overdependence on a couple of buyers only. It had, however, been able to change the line of production. But the new product could not pick up in the market, and the export order was also cancelled, due to technical and manufacturing defects. These facts suggest some lack of technical competence as also marketing skills on the part of the entrepreneurs. These aspects do not seem to have been duly considered by the bank, either, at the project appraisal stage.

The stocks had got depleted over a period of time whereby the drawing power on the account was reduced to 'nil'. The irregularity on the account had also gradually risen to about three times the sanctioned limit. These facts indicate some lack of effective periodical inspection of stocks as also proper supervision and performance monitoring of the unit by the bank.

The unit had become almost defunct by the year 1986 and the irregularity on the account was steadily rising. The partners were not showing interest in the revival of the unit since the beginning. But the unit was declared non-viable by the bank after five years in September 1991.

8. ALPANA ARTS

Ms Alpana had established a proprietary firm named *Alpana Arts* in May 1985. The line of activity of the unit was graphic arts and screen printing. The firm was sanctioned a working capital limit of Rs. 2.60 lakh by the bank in July 1985. It, however, diverted a portion of the bank finance for purchase of some fixed assets like flame treatment equipment. This had created some liquidity problem for the unit. Besides, the payment of its bills were not forthcoming and the level of its sundry debtors, including bad debts, was steadily rising. Its production activity, therefore, got adversely affected. Its stocks had also gradually got depleted. There was no activity in the unit since 1987. It had continuously been incurring losses. In the meantime, Ms Alpana got married, leaving the business in the hands of her brother, Sri Vikas. But, due to lack of experience, he could not manage the affairs of the unit. And, by July 1991 the irregularity on the account had risen to Rs. 4.30 lakh as against the sanctioned limit of Rs. 2.60 lakh and the drawing power reduced to 'nil', for want of stocks. Besides, the guarantors were reluctant to renew the documents which were soon getting time-barred. The bank, therefore, declared in the unit as non-viable for rehabilitation in July 1991, called up the loan and filed civil suit for recovery of its dues.

Comments

The unit experienced the initial setback due to diversion of funds. Poor collections, resulting in high sundry debtors, including bad debts, had increased the financial difficulties of the unit. The stocks had also gradually got depleted and the irregularity on the account was steadily rising due to frequent over-drawings allowed on the account. These factors suggest some lack of financial management, including credit management, on the part of the entrepreneur.

After the marriage of Ms. Alpana, the proprietor, there was none to take care of the unit. The second line of management could have been conceived initially and developed gradually.

Due to frequent overdrawings allowed on the account, besides application of interest, the irregularity thereon had risen well above the sanctioned limit. The drawing power on the account was also reduced to 'nil', as there was no stocks left. These circumstances, and the bank records, show some lack of effective supervision and follow-up of the advance on the part of the bank staff. The unit had become defunct in 1987, and there was no sign of its recovery, specially after the marriage of Ms. Alpana. But the unit was declared non-viable and the loan was called up by the bank after four years in 1991.

9. S.P. INDUSTRIES

Sri Satya Prakash had established a proprietary firm named *S.P. Industries* in 1971, for manufacturing machinery components and chemical equipments. The firm was selling its products to a single bulk buyer Messrs Magnum Machinery Limited, in the large scale sector. The arrangement had worked satisfactorily for quite some time. But, by the year 1985, the firm started receiving complaints from the Company regarding manufacturing defects in the products. Accordingly, the company withheld the payment of the bills of the unit pertaining to the goods under dispute. substantial fund of the unit thus got blocked in the sundry debtors. The Company had also invoked the bank guarantee of Rs. 4 lakh which had made the liquidity position of the unit still worse. The Company ultimately cancelled all its previous orders and stopped giving fresh orders to the unit. The production activity of the unit thus got severely affected.

The unit was, thereafter, taking up job work only which was quite insufficient to cover its overhead costs. For example, in the year 1990 the job work undertaken by the unit worth Rs. 4.40 lakh had yielded a profit of Rs. 43,000. The unit was thus operating at well below the break-even point and its accumulated losses were steadily increasing. After some time the unit started receiving complaints in regard to the job work also which, in some cases, resulted in litigation.

The unit's bank account was running irregular since January 1987. The stocks charged to the bank had got depleted over a period of time whereby the bank had reduced the drawing power to 'nil'. Besides, due to frequent overdrawings, the irregularity on the account had risen to Rs. 18.70 lakh by July 1991 which was about two and a half times the sanctioned limit of Rs. 7.80 lakh.

Sri Satya Prakash was not coming forward with any reasonable proposal for the rehabilitation of the unit. Besides, a sister concern of the unit, financed by another local branch of the bank, had also fallen sick and legal action was being initiated against it. The unit was, therefore, declared non-viable by the bank in July 1991 and legal proceedings were initiated against it for recovery of the dues.

Comments

The unit had fallen sick mainly due to inadequate quality control of its products and even job work. Besides, over-dependence on a single bulk buyer had accentuated the problem. Poor quality of job work and the widespread dissatisfaction among its customers had adversely affected its reputation in the market. The high sundry debtors had made the unit financially weak.

The stocks of the unit, charged to the bank, had got completely depleted over a period of time, suggesting some lack of effective periodical inspection of stocks by the bank. The increasing irregularity on the account, due to frequent over-drawings, indicated some lack of effective supervision and follow-up of the advance, and periodical performance monitoring of the unit by the bank.

The account of the unit was running irregular since January 1987, and the unit had started showing signs of sickness even earlier. But the bank declared the unit as non-viable and initiated legal proceedings against it after over four years in July 1991.

10. ANURAG ENTERPRISES

Sri Anupam and Sri Raghuvir established a partnership firm named *Anurag Enterprises* in 1983 for manufacturing aluminium utensils. The unit was sanctioned a working capital limit of Rs. 3.90 lakh by the bank in March 1985.

The unit had commenced commercial production soon thereafter but the whole lot of goods, supplied by the unit to the Government Department, under the 'mid-day meal' scheme, was rejected, due to sub-standard quality. The rejected goods were not found saleable in the open market and, therefore, had to be disposed of as scraps at a throw away price. This resulted in a heavy loss to the unit. Its reputation in the market was also adversely affected. It was not able to procure fresh orders either from the Government Department or from the open market. Its production activities, therefore, came to a sudden halt resulting in heavy accumulated losses.

The stocks of raw materials, charged to the bank, had got depleted completely over a period of time. The unit was, therefore, not submitting stock statements to the bank and the drawing power on the account was reduced to 'nil'. The irregularity on the account rose to Rs. 4.90 lakh by August 1991.

The unit was depositing its sale proceeds with some other bank. The two sister concerns of the unit were also reported to have defaulted with other two banks who had filed civil suits against them. Sarvashri Anupam and Raghuvir were not coming forward with any reasonable proposal for the rehabilitation of the unit. Their integrity was also being questioned.

Under the circumstances, the bank declared the unit as non-viable in August 1991, called up the loan and initiated legal proceedings against it for recovery of its dues.

Comments

The unit had suffered mainly due to over dependence on one bulk purchaser viz. the Government Department. Further, the unit should have first got some samples approved by the department, before going into bulk production. The bank somehow could not counsel the unit on these lines at the project appraisal stage.

The entire stocks of the unit had got depleted and it was depositing the sale proceeds with some other bank. Besides, its two sister concerns had also defaulted with other two banks. Under the circumstances, the integrity of the promoters was also being questioned.

The gradual depletion of the entire stocks, charged to the bank, indicated some lack of effective periodical stock inspection by the bank. The steady rise in the irregularity on the account also indicated some lack of supervision and follow-up of the advance.

The unit's working was unsatisfactory right from the beginning and its account became irregular in June 1986. But, the unit was declared non-viable by the bank after about five years in 1991.

11. MASTER METAL WORKS

Sri Vikram established a proprietary firm named *Master Metal Works* in 1985 for manufacturing zinc and non-ferrous metal alloys.

The unit suffered an initial, set-back with the change in the government policy imposing strict restrictions on the production of LPG cylinders. This resulted in a substantial loss of business to the unit. The scarcity of raw materials and non-allotment of quota therefor in time adversely affected its production activity. It was, therefore, operating at well below the break-even point. The machines were almost lying idle. Most of its stocks had become slow moving or even non-moving, resulting in their deterioration in quality and value. Under the circumstances, its accumulated losses were steadily rising. The unit was undertaking some job work which was quite insufficient to meet the over-head costs. Its bank account had become irregular since June 1986. Due to depletion of stocks as also loss in the value thereof the drawing power on the account was reduced by the bank to 'nil'. The irregularity on the account had gradually risen to Rs.9.50 lakh as on 27-2-1991.

Sri Vikram was not showing any interest in the rehabilitation of the unit and was reluctant to renew the documents which were about to get time-barred shortly.

The unit was, therefore, declared non-viable by the bank and the loan was called up in 1991.

Comments

The main causes of sickness of the unit had been the change in the government policy and scarcity of raw materials, which had seriously affected the production activity, marketability and profitability of the unit. The non-moving and slow moving items of stocks could have better been disposed of by the unit, even at a discount, well before the deterioration in their quality and value. The bank officers could as well have counselled the unit on such lines during the periodical inspection of the stocks. The steady rise in the irregularity on the account also suggests some lack of effective supervision and follow-up of the advance.

The account had been running irregular since June 1986 and the unit had started showing signs of sickness even earlier. But the unit was declared non-viable by the bank after about five years in 1991.

12. WINDY FANS

Sri Ram Chandran and Sri Krishna Kumar, own brothers, had established a partnership firm named *Windy Fans* in August 1985 for manufacturing ceiling fans and fan components. The unit had commenced commercial production on 8-2-1986 and was selling the ceiling fans under the brand name *Windy*. It was enjoying working capital limits from the bank aggregating Rs. 37.50 lakh (against stocks - Rs. 12.50 lakh and against outward bills - Rs. 25.00 lakh).

Unfortunately, on the 3rd July 1991, Sri Ram Chandran, the Managing Partner, expired. The firm, therefore, stood dissolved. Consequently, the operation on the unit's cash credit account was stopped by the bank, pending reconstitution of the firm. A new partnership firm was constituted on 26-7-1991, under the same name, with Sri

Krishna Kumar, the surviving partner, as the Managing Partner, and Smt Prabha Devi, wife of Late Sri Ram Chandran, as the Partner.

It was at this stage that the branch submitted a detailed report to the controlling office in regard to the unit whereby several unsatisfactory features connected with the advance came to the knowledge of the controlling authority for the first time.

The outstandings on the stock cash credit account stood at Rs. 34.91 lakh as on 23-8-1991, as against the limit of Rs. 12.50 lakh and the drawing power reduced to 'nil'. The unit, in fact, had stocks worth Rs. 6.40 lakh charged to the bank. But, the sundry creditors for stocks stood at Rs. 23.50 lakh. Thus, as the stocks were not paid for, the bank did not allow any drawing power thereon.

The outstandings on the unit's cash credit account against outward bills stood at Rs. 26.10 lakh as on 23-8-1991, as against the drawing power of Rs. 16.60 lakh. The account was thus irregular by Rs. 9.50 lakh. And the total irregularity on both the accounts stood at Rs. 44.41 lakh.

In fact, a substantial amount of Rs. 70.67 lakh was locked up in the sundry debtors as on 23-8-1991. But the bank had allowed drawing power only on such bills which were outstanding for 90 days or less, aggregating Rs. 28.62 lakh. The age-wise break-up of the balance (overdue) bills aggregating Rs. 42.05 lakh is given hereunder:

91 days to 180 days	-	Rs. 19.69 lakh
181 days to 1 year	-	Rs. 14.72 lakh
1 year to 2 years	-	Rs. 7.50 lakh
Over 2 years	-	Rs. 0.14 lakh

The unit had, however, been able to realise bills worth Rs. 4.39 lakh during the month of August 1991. But the payment of bills worth Rs. 3.25 lakh was considered doubtful and the bills worth Rs. 10,000 were to be written off as bad debts.

The total sales and net profit figures of the unit for the last three years are given hereunder:

(Rs. in lakh)

	31-7-1988	31-3-1990	31-3-1991
Total Sales	27.94	78.68	136.68
Net Profit	0.88	2.65	1.29
Net Profit/Sales(%)	3.14 %	3.37 %	0.94 %

The net profit to sales thus stood at a very low level, at around 3%, which came further down to less than 1% in the year 1991, mainly due to the production at sub-optimal level, heavy expenditure on advertisement (Rs. 4.71 lakh), conveyance and transport (Rs. 1.42 lakh), donations (Rs. 0.46 lakh), etc. The break-even point now stood at Rs. 177 lakh, mainly due to heavy interest burden on account of high sundry debtors and outstandings on the bank accounts.

A personal interview with both the partners of the unit revealed that late Sri Ram Chandran was rather over-ambitious. He wanted to out-smart other fan manufacturing companies of repute and, therefore, resorted to wide publicity, advertisement and public relations activities, incommensurate with the level of activity of the unit. Besides, he preferred to manage all the activities of the unit himself and did not pay the desired attention towards recovery of the over-due bills, whereby the level of sundry debtors kept on rising. The other partner, Sri Krishna Kumar, was asked to look after the production work only and, therefore, he was not aware of the other facets of the business.

The own stake (Tangible Net Worth) of the unit, as compared to the total outside liabilities, had gradually got substantially reduced to around 4%.

The detailed stock verification had revealed the undernoted unsatisfactory features:

(i) No records were maintained for finished goods.
(ii) Finished goods were over-valued at the selling price, which included profit, taxes, etc., instead of at the cost price.
(iii) The level of sundry creditors was higher than the level of stocks of raw materials.

As per the present arrangement, the bank was releasing 25% of the realised amount of the outstanding bills to enable the unit to continue its production activity. The balance 75% of the amount deposited with the bank was being appropriated towards adjustment of the irregularity on the account. The position was, however, to be reviewed by the bank after three months.

A personal interview with the bank officers revealed that, in view of the aforesaid unsatisfactory features connected with the advance, the unit was not considered viable for rehabilitation. But the loan was not being called up, for the time being, with a view to recovering the maximum possible amount from the unit under the aforesaid arrangement.

Comments

The frequent overdrawings permitted by the bank on the stock cash credit account, to the extent of about three times the sanctioned limit, indicated some lack of control over the conduct of the account. The fact that the drawing power was allowed on the stocks obtained from the suppliers on credit also speaks adversely on the effectiveness of the periodical inspection of stocks and conduct of the advance by the bank staff.

Though the controlling office had sanctioned the working capital limits to the unit, there was some lack of effective monitoring and control of the conduct of the advance on their part, too. This became evident from the fact that the controlling office could come to know of the unsatisfactory features connected with the advance, only after the Branch Manager submitted a detailed report to them, after the demise of Sri Ram Chandran. The control functions at the administrative office of the bank, specially in regard to high value SSI advances, deserved to be geared up, through effective monitoring of the various control returns/ statements, required to be submitted by the branches at regular monthly/quarterly intervals, coupled with the visits to the branches by the Regional Managers and/or other officers, whenever considered necessary.

The level of sundry debtors at Rs. 70.67 lakh, as against the annual sales of Rs. 78.68 lakh in 1990 and Rs. 136.68 lakh in 1991, was on the high side. The substantial amount locked up in overdue bills, outstanding for over 90 days and even upto two years and over, had severely affected the liquidity position of the firm. It is also indicative of poor collection machinery on the part of the unit. As revealed by the personal discussions with both the partners of the reconstituted firm, the unit was a one-man show by Sri Ram Chandran (deceased), so much so that the ever worsening position of the overdue bills was not known to Sri Krishna Kumar during the life time of Sri Ram Chandran. It was also revealed by the partners that Late Sri Ram Chandran had spent huge amount to the tune of Rs.25/Rs. 30 lakh, (well above the officially reported figures), in advertisements, including on TV, which the unit could hardly afford.

II

VIABLE SICK UNITS

13. RAINBOW PAINTS

Rainbow Paints, a partnership concern, with Sri Ravi and Sri

Alok as partners, was established in February 1979 for manufacturing paints, varnish and thinner. It had obtained a working capital limit of Rs. 8.50 lakh from the bank in 1980, which was subsequently enhanced to Rs. 20 lakh.

The unit had initially started working satisfactorily, but subsequently its account began to show some unsatisfactory features, mainly because it had stopped routing its entire sale proceeds through the bank account. It had, instead, opened a collection account with some other bank. Thus, by the year 1985, its cash credit account with the bank had become irregular by Rs. 12 lakh, as the outstandings on the account stood at Rs. 23 lakh as against the drawing power of Rs. 11 lakh. By August 1985, the unit had started incurring cash losses. In view of the persistent irregularity on the account, the bank declared the unit as sick in 1986.

But the unit was still considered viable by the bank, keeping in view the following factors:

(i) The unit was continuing its production and sales activities to the tune of Rs. 45 lakh each in the years 1987 and 1988, though the sale proceeds were not being deposited in the bank account. The firm was, however, willing to route its entire sale proceeds through its bank account henceforth, provided the bank agreed not to impound the entire sale proceeds so deposited towards the adjustment of the irregularity, but only to retain a certain percentage thereof, so that the irregularity on the account could be adjusted gradually, and the unit could continue its production activities, too, without any financial hardship. This reasonable request of the borrower was readily acceded to by the bank.

(ii) The unit was continuing its production and sales on profitable lines and its turnover was also, of late, showing a gradual rise. Besides, there was a declining trend in regard to its losses, year after year, as per the details given hereunder:

	1987	1988
Loss	Rs. 52,000	Rs. 32,000
Cash Losses	Rs. 27,000	Rs. 3,000

And, at this rate, the unit was expected to come out of the red in the next couple of years.

(iii) During the course of time, the entire capital of the firm had got eroded and its Tangible Net Worth (TNW) had become negative and stood at (-) Rs. 8.04 lakh. Despite the aforesaid unsatisfactory feature, the undernoted strengths of the borrowers prompted the bank to take a positive attitude towards rehabilitation of the unit:

(a) The integrity of the borrowers was satisfactory.
(b) They were able to procure orders and execute them satisfactorily. They already had firm orders to the tune of Rs. 6.75 lakh from various companies of repute.
(c) They were, of late, extending their full cooperation to the bank.
(d) They were showing keen interest in rehabilitating the unit and were sincerely striving therefor.

The bank examined, in detail, the various causes of sickness of the unit as also the strategies adopted by the unit to guard against them. These are discussed hereunder:

	Causes of Sickness	Strategies adopted
i.	The unit was facing stiff competition from large scale industries and thus was selling its products at a lower price	The entrepreneurs brought in some fruitful changes in the product mix and developed some new products like

Causes of Sickness	Strategies adopted
whereby its margin of profit was reduced	decorative paints, industrial resistant paints, and the paints to be used in fan industry which had good market in Andhra Pradesh and Kerala. They also introduced 'sealing compound', a product solely developed by them, which was an import substitute and in great demand by reputed companies viz. M/s. Lohia Machines Ltd. M/s. Maharashtra Scooters and M/s Bajaj Auto. The unit expected substantial business in this product.
ii. Though the cost of raw materials had gone up, the large scale industries did not increase the price of their products so as to oust the SSI units from the market. Thus the unit also could not increase the price and consequently the margin of its profit got further reduced.	With the experience gained by the entrepreneurs in the line of activity, they were able to reduce the cost of production and thereby increase the margin of profit as also sustain the competition.
iii. The entrepreneurs had accepted tenders of large amount on a contract basis for a fixed period and so they could not increase the price of the products, despite the increase in the cost of raw materials.	The entrepreneurs had since stopped accepting tenders on such losing terms. They were instead, securing floating orders and had entered into new market areas. As the quality of their products was good, they had captured the market. Their order book was steadily satisfactory and their bills were being paid usually within 90 days.
iv. In 1985 the State Government had increased the	The anomaly in the sales tax structure was removed

	Causes of Sickness	Strategies adopted
	rate of sales tax from 6.5% to 11.7%. The cost of products of local SSI units, therefore, went up. As against this, the large scale industries were required to pay the sales tax @ 4% on production of the Form 'C'. This factor adversely affected the unit.	by the government in 1987 by stipulating a uniform rate of 4% on local sales. This favourable development benefited the unit to a substantial extent.
v.	The unit had opened an office in Cochin also, to tap the growing market of Kerala. But it meant an increased establishment cost and overheads.	This investment, however, was considered necessary to tap and retain the new market potentials of Kerala. And this strategy had paid rich dividend in the long run.
vi.	The unit had, in the formative years, suffered from lack of experience and expertise on the part of the entrepreneurs, particularly in the areas of financial and marketing management.	With the passage of time, the entrepreneurs had gained sufficient experience, expertise and confidence to run the business on sound lines.

Keeping in view the aforesaid positive factors, the unit was brought under the rehabilitation programme by the bank in February 1990. In the rehabilitation package no enhancement of limit was proposed as the existing limit of Rs. 20 lakh was considered sufficient. The only facility that was given to the unit was that the irregularity on the account to the tune of Rs. 15.66 lakh, comprising amount of interest for the period of sickness, was converted into an interest free clean term loan, repayable in instalments.

The unit worked sincerely with the close cooperation and coordination of the bank, and the rehabilitation programme, initiated in February 1990, proved a success which was evident from the position of the account of the firm as on the 14th September 1991 given hereunder:

(a) All the account of the firm were regular.
(b) A sum of Rs. 8.60 lakh had so far been repaid by the firm towards instalments on the clean term loan account.
(c) The turnover of the unit during the last five months stood at Rs. 53.33 lakh as against the projected turnover of Rs. 37.50 lakh. That is, there was a positive variance of Rs.15.83 lakh or 42% over the budgeted level.
(d) The current ratio worked out to 1.28.

In view of the aforesaid circumstances, the unit's performance was rated by the bank as "Excellent".

Comments

An in-depth study of the case and personal interview with the bank officers revealed that the following factors facilitated the successful rehabilitation of the unit:

(i) The bank officers had thoroughly examined the various causes of sickness of the unit as also the strategies adopted by the entrepreneurs to guard against them.
(ii) The borrowers were honest and hard working, sincerely striving to bring the unit back to health. They had learnt from their mistakes and had also

earned sufficient experience and expertise in the line of the business.

(iii) The bank officers were extending their full cooperation and helping hands to the unit.

(iv) The bank officers, both at the branch and the controlling office, were meaningfully monitoring the performance and progress of the unit, on a regular monthly basis.

14. SUNRISE BATTERIES

Sunrise Batteries (Private) Limited, incorporated in November 1978, with Sri Arvind and Sri Prakash as the Managing Director and Director respectively, was manufacturing lead acid storage batteries for automobiles and stationary applications. The unit was sanctioned a working capital limit of Rs. 3 lakh by the bank in 1980. The commercial production, however, commenced in December 1981.

Initially, the unit was largely depending on the Andhra Pradesh State Road Transport Corporation (APSRTC) for the bulk purchase of its products. But the corporation had taken about two years in issuing the necessary test certificate confirming the standard of the product. And, due to stiff competition, the company's products were not yet established in the market.

Under the foregoing circumstances, the unit was incurring cash losses right from its inception. While upto the year 1984, its accumulated cash losses were contained within Rs. 1.00 lakh, these had gone up to Rs. 1.50 lakh and Rs. 2.35 lakh respectively in the next two years. But the company still continued its production activity and its sales showed a steady rise from Rs. 3.20 lakh in 1985 to Rs. 10.40 lakh in 1986 and Rs. 11.10 lakh in 1987. Further, by the year 1987 its losses had come down to Rs. 1.10 lakh. But the Company's cash credit account with the bank was still irregular by Rs. 11 lakh, including the amount of interest at Rs. 6.3 lakh as on

1-1-1988. However, by this time, the company had reached the desired standard of quality and was issued the ISI certification. Its products were now well received in the market and were also approved by the undernamed public sector undertakings for bulk purchases :

(i) Andhra Pradesh State Road Transport Corporation (APSRTC)
(ii) Andhra Pradesh State Electricity Board (APSEB)
(iii) Andhra Pradesh Electronic Development Corporation (APEL) (for solar energy battery system)
(iv) Indian Oil Corporation (IOC)
(v) Central Power Research Institute
(vi) Central Institute of Road Transport (CIRT)
(vii) Electronic Testing and Development Corporation

While the company had recently executed orders worth Rs. 8.5 lakh, further firm orders worth Rs.24 lakh – from APSRTC (Rs.12.5 lakh), APEL (Rs.9.5 lakh) and IOC (Rs.2 lakh) – were already in hand for execution during the next 6/8 months. The company was expecting substantial orders from other corporations also. Enquiries were flowing in from the open market, too. Its products had passed the test of standard and quality of the Russian Laboratories, and so some export orders were also expected.

The necessary raw materials were available locally at a competitive price and the company was maintaining good rapport with its sundry creditors for supply of goods. Both the directors of the company were full time directors. While Sri Arvind looked after production, Sri Prakash looked after marketing, planning and realisation of bills.

The unit had a viable expansion and diversification plan, viz:

(i) Solar Photovoltaic System (for solar batteries) which was in great demand with the emphasis on rural electrification;

(ii) Uninterrupted Power Supply System.

Keeping in view the aforesaid positive factors, the bank considered the unit as economically viable with potentials to succeed. The unit was, therefore, brought under the bank's rehabilitation programme in June 1988. The company also worked hard in close coordination with the bank. By August 1991, its cash credit account was regularised. Besides, the company was paying the periodical instalments on its clean term loan account regularly and, by August 1991, it had deposited a sum of Rs. 2.40 lakh therein. The conduct of the company's account was, therefore, rated by the bank as "Excellent".

Comments

The unit suffered the initial setback mainly because of its over-dependence on one bulk purchaser, viz., APSRTC. Besides, its products had not picked up well in the market for the first two years. But, the unit had soon improved the quality of its products, got the ISI certificate and established itself in the market. Availability of raw materials at competitive price and good rapport maintained with the sundry creditors had ensured uninterrupted production.

The two directors had good understanding and sufficient role clarity amongst themselves. They had gradually developed sufficient experience and skills in marketing management, production management and financial management. They had a viable expansion and diversification plan and were quality-conscious.

The entrepreneurs had never given up the production activity. The bank officers had also extended the required financial help and guidance in time, after thoroughly studying the technical feasibility and economic viability of the unit. Moreover, they were effectively monitoring the performance of the unit at regular monthly intervals. The directors of the company were also working hard and were extending full cooperation to the bank.

15. V.R. INDUSTRIES

V.R. Industries (Private) Limited, incorporated in June 1982 with Sri Vinod and Sri Ramesh as Managing Director and Director respectively, was manufacturing window sills and window guides exclusively for the Railways for the second class compartments.

The company had started the venture with an equity base of Rs.6.37 lakh. It was sanctioned a medium term loan of Rs. 2.68 lakh (for the purchase of plant and machinery and metal moulds and dies) and a working capital limit of Rs. 10.27 lakh by the bank in December 1982. The company had commenced commercial production in February 1983. But soon thereafter, the Railways had changed the design of the window, rendering all the existing metal moulds and dies of the unit redundant. The company, therefore, purchased a fresh set of moulds and dies. But these new moulds started giving some trouble after only 7000 pieces had been manufactured. The company promptly took up the matter with the suppliers concerned who ultimately refunded the cost of the defective moulds.

Thus, the deal with the Railways proved to be a losing proposition for the company. The stocks of semi-finished goods and finished goods, rendered obsolete with the change in the design of the window, had got piled up and were ultimately disposed of as scraps. This had resulted in substantial loss and financial hardship to the company. The amount of interest on bank loans had got accumulated to Rs. 11 lakh. Besides, the fixed cost and other establishment costs were further increasing the financial burden of the unit.

The company, therefore, changed the line of its activity in 1986 and started manufacturing bathroom fittings, like lavatory pans, cisterns, bath tubs, etc., as also battery boxes for solar energy products. It, therefore, disposed of the entire set of machinery and moulds, since rendered superfluous, and deposited the sale proceeds with the bank in the term loan account.

The unit's products soon attained the desired level of quality with wide acceptability in the market. The company was effecting strict quality control in its own testing laboratory. It thus obtained the ISI certification, too.

The company's main item of production was lavatory pans, for the supply whereof it had entered into rate contracts with various departments of the State Government, viz., the Public Health Department, the Panchayat Raj Department and the State Housing Corporation. The total requirement of the State Government was estimated at Rs. 150 lakh and the company expected to get orders worth Rs. 20 lakh, as the ISI mark had given it an added advantage.

The company was also negotiating with EID Parry Limited for orders worth Rs.4 lakh per month in respect of the 'low level flushing cistern', and the deal was expected to be finalised shortly.

Besides, the company had received firm orders worth Rs. 4.50 lakh in respect of its other product, viz., battery boxes for solar energy products. Keeping in view the increasing popularity of the non-conventional sources of energy, the sale of this product was expected to go up in the near future.

On an overall assessment of the viability of the unit, as revealed by the aforesaid satisfactory features, the bank brought the unit under its rehabilitation programme in April 1990. And since then the unit's performance, on various parameters, was being closely and effectively monitored by the bank, both at the branch and the controlling office levels, in close coordination with the entrepreneurs, at regular monthly intervals.

Within 18 months, i.e., by August 1991, the irregularity on the account was brought down to Rs. 3.25 lakh as the company had geared up its bills collection machinery by resorting to timely reminders and effective follow-up.

Further, the aforesaid irregularity was on account of withdrawal of government supply bills from the drawing power, as the payment was not forthcoming from the respective government departments, and the currency period stipulated by the bank for such bills had expired.

Besides, the unit had deposited a sum of Rs.5.76 lakh in its term loan account during the period April 1990 to August 1991. All considered, the unit was now working satisfactorily.

Comments

The main cause of the sickness of the unit was its overdependence on one single bulk buyer viz., the Railways. The unit soon realised the disadvantages and risks attached with such over-dependence, and changed the line of its activity, with a broad-based clientele system. It could make a dent in the market in the line of its new activity as it was producing quality products with ISI mark. Due to quality control, the unit's products earned a good reputation in the market whereby its order book was steadily showing a rising trend.

The entrepreneurs had, by now, acquired good marketing skills, as was evident from the firm orders obtained from the government departments, EID Parry Limited, etc.

The undue delay in the payment of the bills, aggregating Rs. 3.25 lakh, by the government departments, had caused financial constraint on the company. However, the gearing up of the collection machinery and effective follow-up by the company was a healthy sign of financial management.

It goes to the credit of the entrepreneurs that they withstood the initial setback, switched over to another line of activity, and stabilised their position. The bank's timely decision to rehabilitate the unit, after conducting the detailed viability study, and the effective and close performance monitoring of the unit, at regular monthly intervals, in close coordination with the entrepreneurs, could bring the unit back to health.

16. DURABLE PUMPS

A partnership firm, named *Durable Pumps & Company,* was established in 1986, with Sarvashri Abhay, Vikas, Trilok and Pravin as partners, for manufacturing submersible pumpsets to draw water from bore wells for irrigation and drinking purposes. There was a good demand for the product from the agriculturists for irrigation purposes, and from the government departments for providing drinking water in the villages. Sri Trilok, one of the partners of the firm, had the requisite technical expertise to ensure good quality of the product. The bank thus found the unit to be technically feasible and economically viable, and sanctioned a working capital limit of Rs. 1 lakh in 1986. The unit commenced the production soon thereafter, and its products were gradually picking up in the market. Its performance, during the initial couple of years, was satisfactory.

But, by the year 1989, deep dissension developed amongst the partners. Sri Trilok, the only technically competent partner, could not take it any more and severed his connections with the firm. This caused a great setback to the unit. The quality of the product was the first casualty which had far reaching remifications. The firm's sales were steadily dropping and its reputation in the market was adversely affected. There was high rejection of the goods due to sub-standard quality. The stocks of semi-finished goods had also got piled up. The high sundry debtors, to the tune of Rs. 2 lakh, further increased the financial constraint of the unit.

By the end of September 1989, the irregularity on the firm's account with the bank had increased to Rs. 4.50 lakh. The stocks, charged to the bank, had gradually got depleted substantially. Besides, the partners, due to their differences, were reluctant to renew the documents, which were getting time barred shortly. The bank, therefore, filed a civil suit against the firm in October 1989, well before the documents could become time barred. Further, consequent upon several defaults committed by the firm, the State Financial Corporation (SFC) had seized the factory premises of the unit on 21-12-1989.

The unit had run into trouble mainly due to the sharp differences among its partners, the lack of technical expertise adversely affecting the quality of its products, and the chain reactions connected therewith.

Sarvashri Vikas and Pravin, the two partners of the firm, were, however, still maintaining good understanding and congenial relations amongst themselves. They were seriously contemplating to revive the unit. With this end in view, they reconstituted the firm in December 1989, with Sarvashri Ajay and Vinod as the two new partners.

The new firm started working sincerely in close coordination and mutual understanding among all its partners. It employed a technically qualified person so as to ensure the standard of the quality of its products. It had set up a testing lab and obtained the ISI certification. Its production gradually started picking up in the market.

The unit finalised the rate contract with the Panchayat Raj Department and Irrigation Development Department, and expected good orders from them under the scheme to provide drinking water in all the villages. The unit had obtained an immediate order for 50 pumpsets and was confident of getting more orders in the near future.

The entrepreneurs were men of high integrity and were sincere in the rehabilitation of the unit so much so that they had requested the bank to withdraw the civil suit, and had agreed to reimburse the bank with the amount of the court fee.

All the partners were working hand in hand and were keenly pursuing the steps required for the rehabilitation of the unit, in close coordination and cooperation with the bank.

Keeping in view the aforesaid points of strength, and the sincerity of purpose on the part of the entrepreneurs, the bank withdrew the civil suit and brought the unit under the rehabilitation programme in July 1990.

The unit was now working satisfactorily in strict adherence to the bank's financial discipline. By August 1991, it had adjusted the irregularities on all its accounts and had deposited a sum of Rs.1.16 lakh in its clean term loan account.

Comments

The unit fell sick mainly due to the dissensions among the partners. The partners of the reconstituted firm were, however, working in close cooperation with each other. They were sincere, honest and hard working. They had adopted sound strategies for reviving the unit. They were also having the required managerial skills, technical competence, quality consciousness and marketing ability.

The bank officers had conducted a detailed viability study of the unit and had evolved the rehabilitation package in consultation with the entrepreneurs. They were effectively monitoring the progress and performance of the unit at regular monthly intervals, both at the branch and the controlling office, in close coordination with the entrepreneurs.

17. PIONEER PHARMACEUTICALS

Pioneer Pharmaceuticals (Private) Limited was in-corporated on 26-10-1985, with Sri Dinesh and Sri Prashant as the Managing Director and Director respectively, for manufacturing bulk drugs (Ibuprofen B.P.).

The company was sanctioned a term loan of Rs. 39.90 lakh by the State Financial Corporation, for the purchase of plant and machinery, a seed capital loan of Rs. 5 lakh by the Industrial Development Bank of India (IDBI), and a suitable working capital limit by the bank in 1988. The company commenced its commercial production in February 1989 and was working satisfactorily.

But, unfortunately, a fire accident took place in the

unit's factory on 6-12-1989 when most of its stocks of goods and plant and machinery got severely damaged or destroyed. It was a serious setback to the unit. Its production activity came to a sudden halt, but its overheads, like salary and wages, interest, etc., kept on increasing. Due to the destruction of the stocks in the fire, the drawing power was substantially reduced by the bank, resulting in heavy irregularity in the account.

The company's stocks and plant and machinery were not insured against fire risk for full value thereof. Besides, the insurance company had raised some technical points regarding the storage of goods, warranty, etc. Under the circumstances, the insurance company had settled the claim on 8-3-1990 for Rs. 2.87 lakh for stocks and Rs. 22.10 lakh for plant and machinery, (total Rs. 24.97 lakh), as against the claims submitted for Rs. 15 lakh and Rs. 30 lakh respectively. Thus, there was a net shortfall of about Rs. 20 lakh. The matter was, however, under negotiation with the insurance company.

The unit, being in real difficulties, approached the bank for help. In view of the satisfactory performance of the unit in the past, the bank took a positive and helpful attitude in the matter. It thoroughly studied and assessed the detailed plan of action, including financing of new items of machinery and such other related issues, in close coordination with Sri Dinesh and Sri Prashant. The unit was brought under the bank's rehabilitation programme in August 1990 and was now working satisfactorily.

Comments

The main cause of the sickness of the unit was the fire accident and its ramifications. The bank had adopted a helpful and positive attitude towards the rehabilitation of the unit, as the latter had conducted its account satisfactorily and had adhered to the bank's financial discipline in the past. The bank considered the various facets of the problem and finalised the rehabilitation package within nine months from the date of the fire accident. The company had, by now, realised that it would be prudent to get the goods and the plant and machinery insured against fire risk for their full value.

18. AMAR ADHESIVE

Sri Amar Krishna established a proprietary firm named *Amar Adhesive* in 1981 for manufacturing adhesive gum tapes. The firm was sanctioned a working capital limit of Rs. 1.85 lakh and a medium term loan (for purchase of items of machinery) of Rs. 1.64 lakh by the bank in 1981.

The unit started working satisfactorily. Its products, being of good quality, picked up well in the market. The unit was awarded a gold medal in the Transworld Fare held at Hyderabad in 1987.

The firm was initially selling its products at a lower price so as to establish itself in the market. It was also giving commission at a higher rate of 15% to its sales agents. Besides, its bills aggregating Rs. 40,000 could not be realised from its commission agents. The payment of its other bills aggregating Rs.1.40 lakh was over-delayed and the level of its sundry debtors was steadily rising, adversely affecting its production activity. It resorted to frequent over-drawings on its bank account and could not pay a single instalment on its term loan account.

The unit incurred cash losses during the initial years which got accumulated to Rs. 1.40 lakh by the year 1985. Subsequently, however, it could make marginal profits of Rs. 28,000, Rs. 21,000 and Rs. 12,000 in the years 1986, 1987 and 1988 respectively. The profit was showing a declining trend as the sales were gradually going down from Rs. 8 lakh in 1986 to Rs. 7 lakh in 1987 and Rs. 6.25 lakh in 1988. And, during the year 1989 the sales substantially declined to Rs. 1.87 lakh, resulting in a loss of Rs. 1.84 lakh. The production activity of the unit was adversely affected due to the lack of working capital caused by the high level of sundry debtors. The bank also imposed restrictions on the over-drawings as the firm's accounts had become substantially irregular, as is revealed by the position of the accounts as on 31-5-1989 as given below:

(Rs. in lakh)

Facility	Limit	Drawing Power	Outstandings	Irregularity
Stock Cash Credit	0.90	0.30	3.28	2.98
Clean Cash Credit (Bills)	0.95	nil	0.46	0.46
Medium Term Loan	1.64	nil	1.83	1.83
Total	3.49	0.30	5.57	5.27

But Sri Amar Krishna did not give up and was, instead, prepared to face the difficulties with courage and determination. He continued his production activity, of course, on a limited scale. He procured firm orders worth Rs. 2 lakh which were of a repeat nature. But he was not able to execute these orders for want of funds, though all the items of machinery were in good working order and the necessary infrastructure facilities were available in a reasonable measure. Sri Amar Krishna was also confident of recovering his over-due bills of Rs. 1.40 lakh on resumption of the supply of goods to his sundry debtors. He, therefore, approached the bank for rehabilitating the unit by releasing further funds and extending other permissible concessions to the sick unit. He, on his part, was prepared to bring in additional funds of Rs. 21,000 by raising interest-free loans from his friends and relatives, not to be withdrawn during the currency of the advance.

The bank conducted a detailed study regarding the technical feasibility and economic viability of the unit. Keeping in view the sincerity and perseverance of Sri Amar Krishna, his technical competence and marketing ability (in producing quality goods and obtaining firm orders of repeat nature), the satisfactory working conditions of the machinery and the availability of the necessary infrastructure, the bank's controlling office finalised the rehabilitation package in June 1959, well within one month of the receipt of the reasoned recommendations from the branch dated the 31st May 1989.

The undernoted rehabilitation programme was implemented at the branch on 11-8-1989:

(i) The amount of interest on all the three accounts aggregating Rs. 1 lakh since 1-4-1988 (i.e., the financial year since when the unit had started incurring cash losses) was transferred to an interest-free Funded Interest Term Loan account.

(ii) The amount of irregularity on the accounts to the tune of Rs. 2.90 lakh was transferred to the Working Capital Term Loan account at a concessional rate of interest of 10% p.a.

(iii) The working capital limit was enhanced to Rs. 2.72 lakh [stock cash credit - Rs. 1.10 lakh and clean cash credit (bills) - Rs. 1.62 lakh] based on the projected level of sales at Rs. 9.70 lakh, which seemed to be realistic, keeping in view the firm orders of Rs. 2 lakh in hand, which were of a repeat nature, and the sales level of Rs. 8 lakh that the unit had achieved in the past in 1986.

(iv) The repayment of the term loan of Rs. 1.83 lakh was rephased and made payable, with interest, in 5 years with a cushion period of 2 years provided for contingencies, keeping in view the position of profitability and cash flow worked out for the next 7 years.

(v) Further, the activity of the unit was brought under a rigorous system of performance monitoring and review, both at the branch and controlling office levels, at regular monthly intervals, in close coordination with the entrepreneur, through a joint free and frank discussions, based on the perusal of the relevant statements and the books of accounts.

The conduct of the account of the unit, after the implementation of the rehabilitation prgramme, had been satisfactory. The position had substantially improved in a period of about one year inasmuch as both the cash credit accounts were running regular as on 20-9-1990. There was, however, a marginal irregularity of Rs. 53,000 in the term loan accounts taken together, which was expected to be wiped off shortly. Besides, the unit had achieved the projected sales of Rs. 9.70 lakh.

The bank sanctioned yet another clean term loan of Rs. 55,000 in November 1990 to enable the unit to pay the sales tax dues for the years 1985 to 1988, which was not provided for at the time of formulating the rehabilitation package.

The unit, however, again faced some financial hardship as the payment of its bills aggregating Rs. 70,000 (long overdue for over 2 years) was not forthcoming and the other bills amounting to Rs. 1 lakh were withdrawn by the bank from the cover. These resulted in lack of working fund causing substantial drop in production to Rs. 29,000, as against the anticipated monthly production of Rs. 1.10 lakh. The entrepreneur was not able to bring in any further cash in the venture. The firm was, therefore, reconstituted into a partnership in September 1991 and the new partner, Sri Laxman Das, brought in Rs. 1.79 lakh in the business. The unit also sold a piece of its land for Rs. 1 lakh and deposited the sale proceeds in the term loan accounts. The unit was now working satisfactorily and all its accounts were running regular as on the 10th October 1991.

Comments

The unit had fallen sick mainly due to the faulty pricing and credit policy, and blockage of substantial funds in sundry debtors, adversely affecting its production and profitability, culminating in cash losses. The unit did not adhere to the financial discipline of the bank and resorted to frequent over-drawings on the accounts. The gradual depletion of stocks and steadily increasing irregularity on the accounts speak adversely of the bank's effective supervision and follow-up.

The unit could be revived mainly due to the sincerity and determination of Sri Amar Krishna. The bank also acted promptly in conducting the detailed viability study of the unit and in preparing and implementing the rehabilitation programme, followed by an effective monitoring of the performance of the unit. Besides, the bank was having a considerate and helpful attitude towards the unit, all through.

During the course of rehabilitation, the unit had faced some financial problems, over again, which were also tackled by Sri Amar Krishna with patience, perseverance and pragmatic approach, by reconstituting the firm into a partnership and by selling a piece of surplus land, whereby the much needed fund could be brought into the venture.

19. MODERN ENGINEERING

Modern Engineering (Private) Limited was established in 1987, by Sri Ram Kumar as the Managing Director and Ms. Madhu Kumari (Wife) as the Director, for manufacturing clutch assembly units for the two wheelers, as an ancillary unit to Bharat Scooters Limited.

Sri Ram Kumar was a Mechanical Engineer and had worked with Messrs Sundaram Clayton Limited and the Larsvin Group of Companies for over 20 years, whereby he had gained sufficient experience and expertise in the manufacturing of auto parts. Besides, the required infrastructural facilities like power, fuel, water, etc., were available to the unit in the industrial area.

Sri Ram Kumar, along with his wife, started the venture with a paid-up capital of Rs. 4.20 lakh (authorised capital Rs. 5.00 lakh). The unit was sanctioned a working capital limit of Rs. 10.50 lakh by the bank, a term loan of Rs. 25.50 lakh by the State Financial Corporation and the seed capital assistance of Rs. 2 lakh by the Industrial Development Bank of India (IDBI). The company had, however, availed of the term loan to the extent of Rs. 18.21 lakh.

The company first conducted trial-runs of its products and when the samples were approved by the parent company it commenced commercial production in December 1987. But the two-wheelers produced by the parent company could not pick up in the market and consequently it fell sick by the end of the year 1988, adversely affecting the production activities of its ancillary units.

Due to the failure of the parent company, the unit was operating below the break-even point, resulting in cash losses. The statutory liabilities, wage bills and other overheads were gradually raising the level of its accumulated losses, so much so that the company's tangible net worth ultimately got completely eroded. Its bills worth Rs. 8.20 lakh were long over-due for payment by its parent company which had created liquidity problems, adversely affecting its production activities.

The irregularity on its bank account was steadily rising which stood at Rs. 12.52 lakh as on 1-6-1990 (limit Rs. 10.50 lakh, drawing power Rs. 3.05 lakh, outstandings Rs. 15.57 lakh). The bank, therefore, restricted further over-drawings on the account. Besides, the unit had not paid any instalment to the State Financial Corporation on its term loan account.

But Sri Ram Kumar did not give up. He was confident of his technical competence and marketing ability. He was still continuing his production activity, of course, on a lower scale. Though initially he was supplying his products only to the parent company, he now started looking for an alternative, broad-based market. By virtue of his past experience and connections, he could procure orders from other two-wheeler manufacturing companies of repute, viz., Hero Honda, Bajaj Auto, Gujarat Narmada, Escorts, LML Vespa, etc., as also from some firms dealing in spare parts. With his technical competence, he had developed some dies in his unit. His products were of good quality and were picking up well in the market.

The unit had obtained firm orders from the companies of repute to the tune of Rs. 20 lakh, which were of a repeat nature. Messrs Bajaj Auto tested the samples of the unit and initially gave an order for Rs. 1 lakh, which was expected to go up to Rs. 20 lakh annually.

But the unit was not in position to execute these orders due to lack of funds. Sri Ram Kumar, therefore, approached the bank for release of further funds with a view to rehabilitating the unit.

Keeping in view the technical competence and marketing ability of Sri Ram Kumar, good quality of the products and substantial firm orders in hand and, above all, the sincerity of purpose on the part of Sri Ram Kumar, the bank, based on the detailed viability study of the unit, its past performance and future prospects, decided to rehabilitate the unit by granting the following concessions and enhancement in the working capital limit in September 1990:

(i) An interest-free Funded Interest Term Loan (FITL) of Rs. 5.40 lakh (comprising total amount of interest, right from the beginning till September 1990) was granted, repayable in 24 monthly instalments of Rs. 22,500 each, commencing from 31-10-1990.

(ii) A Working Capital Term Loan of Rs. 8.40 lakh (comprising total irregularity on the account, excluding the interest component) was also granted at a concessional rate of interest of 10% p.a., repayable in 30 monthly instalments of Rs. 28,000 each, commencing from 31-10-1992, i.e., after the

FITL was fully repaid.

(iii) A fresh working capital limit of Rs. 12.70 lakh, against stocks and bills, was sanctioned, after duly assessing the total working capital requirement of the unit.

The entrepreneurs also pumped in additional funds to the tune of Rs. 1 lakh; Rs. 80,000 by way of equity (raising the paid-up capital to Rs. 5 lakh i.e., up to the level of the authorised capital), and Rs. 20,000 by way of unsecured loans from friends and relatives, not to be withdrawn during the currency of the advance without the specific written permission from the bank.

Besides, a consortium meeting was held on 9-6-1990 between the bank and the State Financial Corporation, wherein the SFC also agreed to suitably rephase the repayment programme on the term loan and to sanction a margin money assistance of Rs. 1 lakh.

Further, the rehabilitation programme was being regularly monitored by the bank, both at the branch and the controlling office levels, at monthly intervals, in close coordination with the entrepreneurs. Besides, the working capital loan was being disbursed by the bank strictly on cash budget basis, ensuring end-use of funds. The unit was now working satisfactorily and all its accounts with the bank were running regular.

Comments

The unit, being an anciallary one, fell sick mainly due to the failure of its parent company. It could, however, be rehabilitated successfully, largely due to the following favourable features:

Sri Ram Kumar, the Managing Director, did not give up hopes and, instead, continued to work with confidence and commitment, patience and perseverance. He continued the production activity, though on a lower scale. He maintained the quality of his products which enjoyed a good reputation in the market. Besides having the requisite technical competence, he possessed the marketing ability whereby he could obtain firm and repeat orders from reputed companies. He brought in further funds of Rs. 1 lakh which showed his sincerity and determination to revive the unit.

The bank, on its part, conducted an in-depth study to assess the technical feasibility and economic viability of the unit. It brought out a detailed rehabilitation package in close coordination with the term lending institution (SFC). Additional funds were released in a phased manner, ensuring end-use of funds. The unit's performance was being effectively monitored by the bank at regular monthly intervals, both at the branch and the controlling office levels, in close coordination with the entrepreneurs. The entrepreneurs also adhered to the financial discipline of the bank and worked on sound lines.

20. BIG BITE BISCUITS

Big Bite Biscuits (Private) Limited was established in December 1980, with Mr Bhaskar as the Managing Director and Ms Bhanupriya (wife) as the Director, for manufacturing biscuits. Mr Bhaskar was a food-technologist of national repute. He had served, for several years, as a consultant to various well established companies manufacturing biscuits and such other food products.

The company was sanctioned a term loan of Rs. 7.67 lakh by the State Financial Corporation for the purchase of land, building and machinery, and a working capital limit of Rs. 4.35 lakh by the bank in February 1981.

The company had hired a portion of a building, in a posh market place in the city, to establish a full-fledged office. The office was set up on a divisionalised basis. There was a Production Department headed by a Production Manager and aided by a Production Assistant and a Lab Assistant. Similarly, there were other departments viz., Marketing

Department, Finance Department, etc.. The products were being marketed all over India including far flung areas like Guwahati, Bombay, Calcutta, Madurai, Surat, etc.. The company commenced its production in April 1982. But its sales could not pick up in the market due to stiff competition from 35 biscuit manufacturing units in the State, out of which 25 units were located in the same city. Besides, there were several bakeries in the city in the unorganised sector operating on a much smaller scale. The unit had not conducted a market survey/census and had projected a higher level of profitability based on over-ambitious sales and conservative cost estimates.

With poor realisation of bills, the company's sundry debtors kept on rising. Its bills for over Rs. 2 lakh were long outstanding, payment whereof was considered doubtful. Some of its bills were returned unpaid. The distributors and sales-representatives of the company were luke warm in regard to the sales promotion and recovery of the dues, due to lack of sufficient incentives.

The unit was operating at the level of 30 TPM, i.e., at 23% of its installed capacity, and well below the break-even point computed at 46 TPM. It was, therefore, incurring losses right from the inception. In 1982 its losses amounted to Rs. 4.18 lakh which increased to Rs. 15.18 lakh by September 1987.

The unit was brought under the rehabilitation programme by the bank in September 1987. As per the rehabilitation package, the total irregularity of Rs. 2.93 lakh on the company's account was converted into a working capital term loan, repayable in instalments. A further sum of Rs. 1 lakh was advanced to the unit to finance the rigorous advertisement strategy, to boost its sales. The strategy included advertisement on autobacks, banners and sunshades, cineslides, free sampling, "taste-and-buy" scheme, stalls in exhibitions, advertisement in magazines, etc.

But the strategy did not pay. The sales did not pick up. By October 1989, the company's turnover came down to 25%

of the projected level of 50 TPM. The company, therefore, could not pay a single instalment on its working capital term loan. By January 1990, the unit had stopped functioning and was contemplating to sell all its assets, including fixed assets, to repay its loan to the State Financial Corporation and the bank.

The State Financial Corporation, on their part, had sealed the factory in August 1990 and initiated the recovery proceedings against the company. They had also given an advertisement in the local papers dated the 25th September 1990 for the sale of the fixed assets (land, building and machinery) financed by them.

The rehabilitation programme thus failed and the bank filed a civil suit against the company to recover its dues.

Comments

The instant case goes to indicate that merely having technical competence is not enough for the success of a unit. The economic viability of the project and the managerial skills on the part of the entrepreneurs are of essence.

The unit had faltered on various counts right from its inception. A market survey or market census was not done to ascertain the extent of competition from the large, small and tiny sectors. Being in a brand-conscious market, the unit failed to compete with other well-established and popular brands of biscuits. The local mini-bakeries also had an edge over it due to their cheaper and fresh products, different from the usual packed brands. The projections of the unit's production and sales proved to be overambitious as it always operated at well below the break-even point.

The establishment of a full-fledged office on a divisionalised basis in a posh market area had led to the avoidably high overheads by way of high salary and rent. The useful purpose behind the appointment of a Production Manager, when Mr Bhaskar himself was technically qualified, was not clear to us. The widely spread market, in far-flung areas, had made the effective monitoring of the sales promotion and recovery of the dues rather difficult and costly due to long travels and high transportation costs involved. The long distances, in different directions, had adversely affected Mr Bhaskar's effective personal supervision and control over the company's distributors and the sales-representatives.

The long overdues, bad debts, return of bills and steadily increasing sundry debtors speak adversely of the company's credit policy and the system of realisation of its bills. The bank and the State Financial Corporation did not undertake an in-depth viability study of the unit at the project appraisal stage. Further, the bank did not thoroughly weigh the various factors that had led to the sickness of the unit to stipulate the right remedial measures to revive the unit. Instead of formulating a comprehensive rehabilitation programme, the bank suggested the advertisement strategy which alone could not remedy the problems of poor sales, sub-optimal production, accumulated losses, etc.. The prospects of revival of the unit, by operating above the break-even point and by achieving the desired level of sales, were not assessed by the bank on a realistic basis. The performance of the unit was not being effectively monitored by the bank. The unit had fallen sick in 1982 but it was brought under the bank's rehabilitation programme in September 1987.

21. RANGOLI PRINTS

Sri Raghu established a proprietary concern named *Rangoli Prints* in November 1984 for printing and dyeing of saries. He had the requisite technical competence and past experience in the line of the business. He had purchased land, building and machinery from his own resources. The unit was sanctioned a working capital limit of Rs. 2.30 lakh by the bank in March in 1985. It started working well with a turnover of Rs. 18.75 lakh in 1985. But gradually its turnover came down to Rs. 8.97 lakh in 1986 and Rs. 4.04 lakh in

1987.

Sri Raghu had diverted a sum of Rs. 60,000 from the working capital funds for acquiring fixed assets like screens, designs, etc.. Further, a sum of Rs. 1.20 lakh was embezzled by his selling agents. The level of sundry debtors was steadily rising. The sale proceeds were not being deposited by the firm in the bank account. The cash credit account with the bank had become irregular by Rs. 2.88 lakh with outstanding at Rs. 3.08 lakh as on 31-3-1988 as against the drawing power of Rs. 20,000. Its production activity had stopped since 1988. Under the circumstances, the unit was declared by the bank as sick in April 1988.

The unit was first brought under the rehabilitation programme by the bank in June 1988, whereby the irregularity of Rs. 2.88 lakh on the firm's account was converted into a working capital term loan, repayable in instalments. But, during the first six months, the firm could achieve a sales turnover of Rs. 9.53 lakh i.e., 70% of the projected level of Rs. 13.5 lakh. Besides, it did not adhere to the bank's financial discipline and kept on issuing cheques indiscriminately whereby the irregularity on its account rose to Rs. 2.50 lakh, over and above the previous irregularity of Rs. 2.88 lakh. Further, the unit did not pay a single instalment on its working capital term loan account and also stopped routing the sale proceeds through its bank account. Moreover, Sri Raghu diverted a portion of the short term sources for some construction work. Sri Raghu was making vague promises to the bank and was not keeping any of them.

Despite the aforesaid unsatisfactory features connected with the conduct of the advance and the continued non-adherence to the bank's financial discipline by the unit, the bank had been liberal enough to give as many as three chances to the unit, by way of three rehabilitation packages, one after the other. But the unit did not show any sign of improvement. By September 1991, however, the bank was inclined to call up the loan and proceed legally against the unit, if Sri Raghu did not come forward with some reasonable proposals, by December 1991, for the revival of the unit. Finally, the bank initiated the recovery proceedings against the unit in 1992.

Comments

The main cause of the sickness of the unit was the diversion of funds by Sri Raghu and embezzlement of Rs. 1.20 lakh by his selling agents. These facts indicate some lack of managerial skills and financial knowledge on the part of Sri Raghu.

The rehabilitation programmes had failed because the bank did not undertake an in-depth viability study of the unit at any stage. The various factors that had led to the sickness of the unit were not thoroughly weighed by the bank to stipulate suitable strategies to guard against them. Instead of formulating a comprehensive rehabilitation package, the bank resorted to *ad-hoc* arrangements, one after the other, which could not succeed. Further, the bank could not enforce the financial discipline on the unit and, instead, allowed frequent over-drawings on the account. Moreover, the performance of the unit was not being effectively monitored by the bank at regular monthly intervals, with a view to taking suitable remedial measures, including counselling the entrepreneur, well in time.

22. RAKESH ENTERPRISES

Rakesh Enterprises, a proprietary concern, was established by Sri Rakesh in 1971 for manufacturing electro-magnetic clutches and electrical control panels. The unit was sanctioned a working capital limit of Rs. 45,000 and a term loan of Rs. 1.42 lakh by the bank the same year, under the bank's entrepreneur scheme.

The unit could, however, commence the production of electrical control panels in May 1972 due to the late receipt of the main items of machinery. But, in the mean time, the unit was undertaking some job work so as to meet a portion of the fixed costs and overheads. Its products were well received and soon gained good reputation in the market.

But, during the year 1975-76, Sri Rakesh faced some financial difficulties as he had diverted a portion of the working capital loan for repayment of the instalments on the term loan. Ultimately, the unit's bank account had become irregular by Rs. 47,000 by May 1977.

The unit was studied in detail by the bank's consultancy cell in 1978 and was found to be viable with all the items of machinery in good condition. The bank, therefore, decided to rehabilitate the unit. The production activity of the unit, however, continued to be at a low level and the irregularity on the bank account went up to Rs. 1.58 lakh by November 1980.

But, by the year 1982, the unit could turn the corner by procuring orders of a substantial amount from some companies of repute. The irregularity on its cash credit account came down to Rs. 8,500. The unit had also been able to repay the instalments on its term loan account.

In February 1984, the working capital limit of the unit was enhanced to Rs. 4.44 lakh, commensurate with the increased scale of operations. The unit was also sanctioned a medium term loan of Rs. 2.45 lakh, which it utilised only to the extent of Rs. 83,000 for liquidation of the term loan of the Small Scale Industrial Development Corporation (SSIDC).

The unit was, by now, well established and was working on sound lines. But, in September 1987, Sri Rakesh, unfortunately suffered from a serious stroke of paralysis. He had to be immediately hospitalised where he had to stay for long. Even after he came back home, he was advised complete rest till May 1990. Thus, the factory remained closed for around three years in the absence of Sri Rakesh. Consequently, the irregularity on the account kept on rising, and by May 1990 it stood at Rs. 7.06 lakh, including Rs. 2.60 lakh by way of interest for the period September 1987 to May 1990.

But since Sri Rakesh had resumed his work, he was trying hard to, at least, contain the level of irregularity on the account. Thus, by February 1991, the irregularity on the account stood at Rs. 7.31 lakh, showing a small rise of Rs. 25,000 during the period of nine months.

In October 1990, Sri Rakesh brought in a further sum of Rs. 80,000 in the business by way of an unsecured loan from his wife. He also inducted his son in the business so as to serve as a second line of management.

But the level of its sundry debtors was showing a rising trend. By February 1990, it stood at Rs. 3.47 lakh, out of which the bills aggregating Rs. 2.95 lakh were outstanding with one single large scale unit. The company had, however, promised to make the payment within 3/4 months, after the unit restarted functioning on a fuller scale.

The unit, therefore, decided to undertake only job work from large industries of repute, so as to keep the level of its investments at a lower level, till it came out of the financial difficulties. Further, as the job work (machining) was labour intensive, the unit expected a surplus of Rs. 1.25 lakh out of the orders worth Rs. 2.50 lakh in hand. It was expecting yet another order worth Rs. 2 lakh shortly and further orders in the near future.

But the existing items of machinery were not found suitable for executing the current type of job work. The unit, therefore, proposed to the bank that it would dispose of the old items of machinery and deposit the sale proceeds in the bank account towards reduction of the irregularity. It also requested the bank to sanction a term loan of Rs. 4.90 lakh — Rs. 4.50 lakh for the purchase of the required items of machinery and Rs. 0.40 lakh for the purchase of a generator.

Keeping in view the honesty and sincerity of Sri Rakesh, his pragmatic and cautious approach, his ability to procure and execute orders to the full satisfaction of the clientele, his technical competence and economic viability of the project the bank finally decided to rehabilitate the unit. The detailed rehabilitation package, however, was being worked out by the bank, in consultation with the entrepreneur.

Comments

The main cause of the sickness of the unit was the long illness of the entrepreneur and the absence of the second line of management. Diversion of funds had caused the financial constraint on the unit at the initial stage, which was, however, overcome by the unit with the timely assistance from the bank. The long overdues with large scale industries had also increased the financial hardship of the unit.

The sincerity and earnestness of Sri Rakesh to revive the unit and the technical feasibility and economic viability of the unit had facilitated the bank's decision to rehabilitate the unit.

III

HEALTHY UNITS

22. CUREWELL PHARMACEUTICALS

Sri Yogesh Chandra and Sri Ravi Shankar had established a partnership firm named *Curewell Pharmaceuticals* in June 1981 for manufacturing pharmaceutical items like saline water, dextrose tablets, injections, syrups, etc. Sri Yogesh Chandra, the Managing Partner, was an honours graduate in Pharmacy and had sufficient experience in the pharmaceutical line.

The entrepreneurs were sincere, honest and hard-working persons fully committed to the venture. They had conducted a market survey and found that their products had a good market potential in the government hospitals and departments as also in the open market, provided the quality of their products was of the required standard. They also found that the necessary infrastructure, like building, power, transport, etc., the skilled labour and the required raw materials were available locally.

The partners started the venture with an initial capital base of Rs. 1.83 lakh and obtained a working capital limit of Rs. 4 lakh from the bank in July 1981.

The unit started the commercial production in July 1982. By virtue of good quality and competitive rates of its products, it established itself well in the market.

Moreover, the unit entered into a rate contract with the State Governments of Andhra Pradesh and Karnataka for the bulk supply of drugs to the government hospitals and government departments. Sri Yogesh Chandra had established a good rapport with the government officials, by virtue of which the quantum of government orders was steadily rising and accounted for about 75% of the total sales. The unit's sales in the open market were also showing a rising trend.

Keeping in view the steady progress and profitability of the unit and the increased scale of its operation, the bank enhanced the working capital limit to Rs. 25 lakh in March 1984.

The unit had appointed its representatives in the State of Andhra Pradesh to procure orders and to closely follow-up the payment of bills. The unit had also appointed distributors in Andhra Pradesh, and sales agents outside the State, on a commission basis.

Besides, the entrepreneurs continued to maintain good rapport with the government officials, distributors and the dealers, coupled with strict quality control. They also maintained good industrial relations with their workers so as to ensure their productivity at higher levels at all times.

The unit achieved the total sales of Rs. 85 lakh and Rs. 132 lakh during the years ended 31-3-1989 and 31-3-1990 respectively. During the period April to November 1990 its sales stood at Rs. 130 lakh and by the year ended 31-3-1991 it crossed the Rs. 200 lakh mark.

A substantial portion of its sales (Rs. 55.46 lakh), however, got locked up in sundry debtors, mostly with the government departments and hospitals, causing liquidity problem to the unit. But, instead of requesting the bank for allowing temporary overdrawings on the account, the partners geared up their collection machinery and gradually recovered the over-due bills within a reasonable time.

The unit was adhering to the financial discipline stipulated by the bank by routing its entire sale proceeds through the bank account and by maintaining sufficient stocks to cover the outstandings on the account, as is revealed by the position of its account given hereunder :

(Rs. in lakh)

Stock Cash Credit Limit	Market Value	Advance Value	Drawing Power	Outstandings
25	60	45	25	24

The bank, on its part, had also adopted a positive and helpful attitude towards the unit. At the same time, it was exercising effective supervision and control over the conduct of the advance and was meaningfully monitoring the activities of the unit, at regular monthly intervals, in an atmosphere of mutual trust and confidence. Any shortage in, or over-valuation of, the stocks was detected in time and the position was got regularised, with the cooperation of the borrowers. Various problems confronting the unit were sorted out through free and frank discussions at the initial stage itself ensuring uninterrupted activity of the unit on sound lines.

The unit was earning profit from the very first year and had registered a net profit of Rs. 12 lakh during the year ended 31-3-1989. It had also adopted the policy of ploughing back a substantial portion of the profit in the business so as to expand and diversify its activity in due course. Thus, the equity base of the unit had gone up from Rs. 1.83 lakh to Rs. 25.36 lakh as on 31-3-1989.

The unit started selling saline water (its main product) in plastic sachets, instead of glass bottles, which proved to be much cheaper and safer in handling. This innovative step resulted in high turnover, reduction in overheads like cost of transport and breakage, and substantial increase in the profitability of the unit.

In 1989, the unit expand its activity and commenced production of some new tablets and syrups which were received well in the market. Recently the unit had introduced some tonic and syrup, specifically meant for infants, which had received a good response from the market. Besides, the unit had obtained license for manufacturing several other pharmaceutical preparations for supply to the government hospitals and departments. All these augured well for its steady growth and prosperity.

Comments

The entrepreneurs, while preparing the project report, had considered the various factors connected with the technical feasibility and economic viability of the project. They had ensured that the required infrastructure, skilled labour, raw materials, etc., were available. Sri Yogesh Chandra, the Managing Partner, was endowed with sufficient technical competence and marketing ability. Before starting the venture, the entrepreneurs had conducted a market survey. They had also estimated the levels of costs, sales and profitability on a realistic basis. They had entered into a rate contract with the State Governments of Andhra Pradesh and Karnataka for bulk supply to the government hospitals and departments.Further, instead of over-dependence on bulk supply the State Governments, they had also taken due care and pains to establish their products in the open market. They had exercised effective quality control whereby the products of the unit enjoyed a good reputation in the market. They were also maintaining good rapport with the government officials and the dealers whereby the level of their sales was steadily rising and the profitability therewith.

The entrepreneurs had started the venture with sufficient capital base and on a scale that they could well manage initially. They had obtained a working capital loan from the bank as per their requirement, knowing well that the limit would be suitably enhanced with the growth of the business.

They were adhering to the financial discipline stipulated by the bank and were getting the problems sorted out at the initial stage itself by maintaining good relations, of mutual trust and confidence, with the bank. They did not resort to diversion of funds and, instead, adopted a policy of ploughing back a substantial portion of the profit in the business. Thus, the capital base of the firm became stronger, year after year.

The unit had first consolidated its position in the market and thereafter had gone into diversification of products, one after the other, at a slow and steady pace.

22. TIRUMALA TRANSFORMERS

Sri Alok Rao, M.Tech., along with his younger brother Sri Prakash Rao, B.Tech., established a partnership firm named *Tirumala Transformers Company* in 1974 for manufacturing transformers for supply to the various State Electricity Boards. As the business of the firm grew gradually, it was converted into a Private Limited Company in May 1981 and subsequently into a Public Limited Company in June 1989.

The unit has been dealing with the bank since its inception. It was initially sanctioned a working capital limit of Rs. 50,000 in 1974 under the bank's entrepreneur scheme for technocrats. The limit was gradually enhanced, commensurate with the increase in the level of its activity. The aggregate working capital limit of the unit now stands at Rs. 33.60 crore since February 1990, comprising fund based limit of Rs. 15.00 crore (against stocks of inventory Rs. 9.75 crore and against outward bills Rs. 5.25 crore) and non-fund based limit of Rs. 18.60 crore (for issuance of Letters of Credit

Rs. 12.60 crore and Bank Guarantees Rs. 6.00 crore).

The share capital of the company has also been gradually augmented. It now stands at Rs. 110 lakh since 30-6-1988, enhanced from Rs. 22 lakh as on 30-6-1987.

The company is manufacturing different types of transformers, viz.,

(i) Three-phase distribution transformers;
(ii) Single-phase oil filled transformers; and
(iii) Single-phase cast resin transformers, for supply to the various State Electricity Boards.

Sri Alok and Sri Prakash, besides being qualified engineers, have, by now, gained 19 years and 14 years experience respectively in the line of the business. Further, they have employed qualified and trained engineers to look after the production and after-sales service. The products, being of good quality, have been received well by the various State Electricity Boards, who keep giving repeat orders to the company. The net sales of the company at Rs. 2277.10 lakh for the year ended 30-6-1988 registered an increase of 111% over the previous year (Rs. 1076.17 lakh) mainly due to the thrust given to the power distribution by the various State Electricity Boards. After having achieved 67% utilisation of the installed capacity in 1988, the net sales of the company at Rs. 2435.35 lakh in the year ended 30-6-1989 registered an increase of only 7% over the previous year.

The company's profit before tax (PBT) for the year 1988 (Rs. 192.51 lakh) rose by around 142% over the previous year (Rs. 79.30 lakh). In the year ended 30-6-1989, the profit before tax (Rs. 304.87 lakh) increased by around 58% over the previous year, though the increase in the net sales for the corresponding period was only 7%.

The company's profit after tax (PAT) was steadily rising from Rs. 51.43 lakh in 1987 to Rs. 126.51 lakh in 1988 and Rs. 251.87 lakh in 1989. As the company was retaining a substantial portion of the profit in the business, the tangible net worth (TNW) of the company also increased from Rs. 139.26 lakh in 1987 to Rs. 294.43 lakh in 1988 and Rs. 546.30 lakh in 1989. Consequently, the company's Total Outside Liabilities/Tangible Net Worth also gradually improved from 4.27 times in 1987 to 3.78 times in 1988 and 2.45 times in 1989.

While most of the required raw materials are available indigenously, the imported components of the raw materials are procured by the company under the import licences without difficulty. All the infrastructural facilities are also available to the unit. Further, the unit has installed two generators, of 100 KVA and 20 KVA respectively, which are sufficient for ensuring continued production even in the event of power cuts.

The company adheres to the financial discipline stipulated by the bank. It submits the stock statements, QIS forms and such other financial statements to the bank regularly. The operative working capital limits of the company are fixed by the bank for each quarter on the basis of the QIS forms.

Of late, the company was experiencing some financial difficulties as the payment of its bills aggregating Rs. 12.00 crore was held up with the Bihar State Electricity Board (Rs. 7.90 crore) and the U.P. State Electricity Board (Rs. 4.10 crore) since December 1990. Keeping in view the satisfactory conduct of the account of the unit, the bank discounted the bills amounting to Rs. 3.80 crore, pending with the U.P. State Electricity Board, under the IDBI Bills Discounting Scheme. Further, the company vigorously followed up the matter with the Bihar State Electricity Board and could obtain payment from them to the tune of Rs. 6.60 crore. As regards the balance amount of the overdue bills aggregating Rs. 1.60 crore, the bank has allowed temporary overdrawings on the account to that extent. The company has now approached the bank for sanction of a working capital term loan for Rs. 1.50 crore repayable in three years in six-half-yearly instalments. The proposal was being examined by the bank favourably.

Comments

Sri Alok and Sri Prakash, besides being technically qualified, had started the venture on a limited scale with an initial capital base of Rs. 20,000 and working capital loan of Rs. 50,000. Their products were of the standard quality as they were exercising effective quality control all through. This way they could procure repeat orders from the various State Electricity Boards. They were adhering to the financial discipline of the bank. They did not resort to diversion of funds at any stage. Instead, they were ploughing back a substantial portion of their profit in the business whereby they could expand their business gradually and could achieve the present level of their activity.

The entrepreneurs are hard working and fully committed to the venture. As their personal stake is sufficiently high, they have sustained interest in their business. This has also helped them in tiding over their financial difficulties caused by unduly delayed payment of their bills by the State Electricity Boards. They are men of patience and perseverance whereby they could obtain the payment of a substantial portion of their overdue bills from the Bihar State Electricity Board. Further, as the conduct of their bank accounts was satisfactory, the bank came forward to meet their genuine financial requirements from time to time. They have courage and determination to face problems and come out of the wood. They have developed a good rapport with the officials of the bank and the various State Electricity Boards. Their industrial relations are cordial. They have recently obtained firm export orders to the tune of Rs. 10 crore from Dubai, Ghana, Cyprus, and Brazil.

All considered, the unit is working on sound lines and its prospects seem to be bright.

25. TIRUPATI ENTERPRISES

Sri Alok, M.Tech., established a proprietary concern named

Tirupati Enterprises in February 1987 for manufacturing distribution transformer components like transformer core laminations, and paper—covered aluminium wires and strips. Initially, the firm was undertaking only job work for its sister concern, Messrs Tirumala Transformers Limited, where Sri Alok himself is the Managing Director.

The unit was sanctioned a term loan of Rs. 18.17 lakh by the bank on 21-2-1987. It did not avail of any working capital loan from the bank at this stage, as it was undertaking only job work. The firm was regularly paying the instalments on the loan which now stands fully repaid.

The unit commenced production in February 1987 and achieved a net sales of Rs. 131 lakh in the very first year of its operation. In 1989, it acquired some additional machinery and commenced manufacturing complete distribution transformers for several State Electricity Boards, in addition to the job work for its sister concern. At this stage, Sri Alok approached the bank for a working capital loan. On 20-4-1989, the bank sanctioned an aggregate working capital limit of Rs. 245 lakh, comprising fund based limit of Rs. 100 lakh (against stocks of inventory Rs. 70 lakh and against outward bills Rs. 30 lakh) and non-fund based limit of Rs. 145 lakh (for Letters of Credit Rs. 100 lakh and for Bank Guarantees Rs. 45 lakh). Further, with the increase in the scale of operations of the unit, its aggregate working capital limit was enhanced on 16-11-1990 to Rs. 870 lakh, comprising fund based limit of Rs. 400 lakh and non-fund based limit of Rs. 470 lakh.

Sri Alok, having 19 years of experience in manufacturing distribution transformers, exercises personal overall supervision on the affairs of the firm. The day-to-day management, however, is being looked after by the General Manager, Sri Hari Prasad, having 15 years of experience in the line to his credit. The unit has employed qualified and trained engineers and other officers to ensure smooth production, sales and after-sales service, and strict quality control.

The firm's net sales increased from Rs. 131 lakh in 1988 to Rs. 483 lakh in 1990, and the profit after tax rose from Rs. 56 lakh in 1988 to Rs. 105 lakh in 1990. The unit is ploughing back a substantial portion of its profit in the business whereby its capital base has got strengthened from Rs. 22 lakh in 1988 to Rs. 128 lakh in 1990. The Total Outside Liability/Tangible Net Worth ratio of the firm, which was by itself satisfactory at 2.19 in 1988, improved further to 1.59 in 1990. The current ratio for the year 1990 at 1.41 is also considered satisfactory.

The unit has an assured market because its sister concern, Messrs Tirumala Transformers Limited, already enjoys a good reputation with the various State Electricity Boards. Besides, the products of the unit are of the required standard as it exercises effective quality control on a continuous basis. Further, the demand of its products is ever increasing due to the thrust given to the rural electrification. The unit is on the approved list of suppliers of several State Electricity Boards. It has already supplied its transformers worth over Rs. 3.00 crore during the nine months period ended 31-3-1990 and has firm orders in hand to the tune of over Rs. 6.00 crore.

The unit started the production of the single-phase electrical monoblock pump sets on a trial basis in 1990 for sale in the open market. It had undertaken the diversification as the Andhra Pradesh State Electricity Board had recommended such pump sets as the most suitable ones for power connections provided from the single-phase transformers. The new product has been well received in the market as its sales have crossed the Rs. 1 crore mark during the year ended 30-6-1992. A substantial portion of the sales (Rs. 75 lakh) is, however, blocked in sundry debtors. Sri Alok is vigorously following up the matter and expects to realise the dues shortly.

While most of the required raw materials are available indigenously, the imported components of the raw materials are procured by the unit against import licences issued from time to time. All other necessary infrastructural facilities are also available to the unit. As the requirement of the unit is minimal, the power cuts are not expected to adversely affect its production activity.

The unit adheres to the financial discipline stipulated by the bank. It is regular in the submission of the stock statements, QIS forms and other financial statements required by the bank. It does not resort to diversion of funds or overdrawings on the account, as may be observed from the position of its bank account as on 27-6-1992 given hereunder:

(Rs. in lakh)

Limit	Market Value of security	Drawing Power	Outstandings	Irregularity
400	506	379	379	Nil

Sri Alok is maintaining good inter-personal relations with the officials of the various State Eectricity Boards and its valued customers in the open market. The industrial relations are cordial so much so that there has been no strike or lock-out in the factory so far.

Comments

Sri Alok had established this firm after substantially consolidating the position of his first company, Messrs Tirumala Transformers Limited. Further, he had initially undertaken only the job work for his sister concern. He started manufacturing the transformers when the demand therefor had gone up significantly. He continued to undertake the job work also side by side. He lately realised the risk of over-dependence on State Electricity Boards and entered the open market also with his new product. He started the mass production of his new product only after it was received well in the market. He was maintaining good relations with his buyers and bankers as also with his own workers and officers.

Sri Alok is hard working and fully involved in the business. He is ambitious but not over-ambitious. He has the courage and patience to face the problems, as and when they come. He is ploughing back a substantial portion of the profit in the business which augurs well for the future growth of his unit.

He has been adhering to the bank's financial discipline. He had repaid his term loan on time and is regular in submission of the stock statements, QIS forms and other financial statements to the bank. As the conduct of all the bank accounts of the unit is satisfactory, the officers of the bank are always willing to extend the financial help and cooperation to the unit.

The officers of the bank had thoroughly examined the techno-economic viability of the unit before meeting its genuine credit requirements. The working capital requirement of the unit was properly assessed by the bank which was subsequently enhanced, commensurate with the increase in the scale of operations of the unit. The bank has been enforcing the financial discipline on the unit and periodically monitoring its performance with a view to ensuring that it worked on sound lines on a continuing basis.

26. BREEZY FANS

Sri Mukesh, along with his brother Sri Rakesh, established *Breezy Fans (Private) Limited* in 1987 for manufacturing ceiling fans and washing machines. The performance of the unit during the first four months of its operation was encouraging in that the sale of its ceiling fans had crossed the projected level of 2,000 numbers per month. As the washing machines manufactured by the unit on trial basis could not pick up well in the market, the entrepreneurs started concentrating exclusively on the production of the ceiling fans. The sale of its ceiling fans was steadily rising from Rs. 258.03 lakh during the 15 months period ended

31-12-1989 to Rs. 646.38 lakh during the 15 months period ended 31-3-1991, registering a net increase of 150 per cent. After consolidating the position, the entrepreneurs had, of late, gone into backward integration to manufacture castings and bearings for their fans as also for sale to the other manufacturers.

The unit was initially sanctioned a working capital limit of Rs. 15 lakh by the bank in 1987. The limit was, however, gradually increased, commensurate with the increase in the scale of its operations. As on 1-4-1992, the unit was enjoying a fund based working capital limit of Rs. 475 lakh and a non-fund based limit of Rs. 610 lakh (for Letters of Credit Rs. 520 lakh and for Bank Guarantees Rs. 90 lakh).

The unit was adhering to the bank's financial discipline and was regular in submission of the stock statements, QIS forms and other financial statements to the bank. It had not resorted to diversion of funds at any stage and its bank accounts were being conducted satisfactorily.

The company has graduated from a small scale industry to large scale industry, and from a Private Limited Company to a Public Limited Company since October 1990. Its public issue was oversubscribed by nearly four times. Its capital base has thus gone up from Rs. 27.73 lakh as on 31-12-1989 to Rs. 120.99 lakh as on 31-3-1991. Its profit after tax (PAT) has gone up from Rs. 15.25 lakh to Rs. 33.41 lakh during the corresponding period. As the company has been ploughing back a substantial portion of its profit in the business, its tangible net worth (TNW) also improved from Rs. 44.87 lakh as on 31-12-1989 to Rs. 158.36 lakh as on 31-3-1991. Accordingly, its Total Outside Liability/Tangible Net Worth improved from 5.18 to 3.78 during the corresponding period.

Comments

The entrepreneurs are sincere, hard working and fully devoted to their business. They are assisted by professionally qualified managers in the areas of production, marketing and finance. Their industrial relations are cordial. They have developed a good marketing network through a trading firm. They are exercising effective quality control and are able to push up their sales at a competitive price. They undertook the expansion and backward integration only after sufficiently consolidating their financial position and standing in the market. They have been adhering to the bank's financial discipline by virtue of which all their financial requirements were promptly and adequately met by the bank. By increasing their capital base and ploughing back a substantial portion of the profit in the business, they seem to be determined to grow on sound lines.

27. AIR PURIFICATION SYSTEMS

Sri Krishna Kumar, along with his brother Sri Ram Kmar, established *Air Purification Systems (Private) Limited* in December 1979 for the designing, manufacturing, erecting, testing and commissioning of pollution control equipments and systems like humidification and ventilation plants, dust collection systems, fume extraction systems, industrial fans, air curtains, etc.

The unit commenced its production in August 1980 and has installed several large-size equipments and systems in many reputed companies like BHEL, HMT, ECIL, BDL, HAL, VST Industries, Bakelite Hylam, etc.

The company is manufacturing industrial fans of 1000 H.P. capacity, an import substitute item, costing Rs. 17.50 lakh each, for cement industries like Deccan Cements Limited, etc. The unit has developed large-size axial flow fans for ventilation purposes in textile industries. It has supplied the product to two major textile units in the cooperative sector under the World Bank Scheme. It is, at present, executing orders for humidification and ventilation systems for the spinning mills financed by the World Bank and the National Cooperative Development Corporation.

Sri Krishna Kumar, Managing Director, is a graduate in

Mechanical Engineering. He has varied experience in designing and installing various pollution control systems referred to above. He has worked with a Swedish company as a Design Engineer and has visited several European countries to study different types of pollution control systems. He has worked for three years with Electron Devices (Private) Limited, Palghat, who were associated with the execution of a Rs. 1.00 crore project for manufacturing semi-conductors. He has also worked with an international firm of consultancy services for two years, looking after the finance and administration. As he is a qualified technocrat, with varied and long experience in the line, he is personally ensuring effective quality control of the products. The company's products are enjoying a good reputation in the market and it is getting repeat orders from all its valued customers. Accordingly, its net sales have steadily risen from Rs. 71.23 lakh in 1988 to Rs. 75.47 lakh in 1989 and Rs. 82.36 lakh in 1990. In view of the growing demand for the products, the company does not envisage any marketing problem.

The unit experienced some financial difficulties in the past due to the delayed payment of its bills by the government departments and public sector undertakings. It has now geared up its collection machinery and is able to realise its dues within a reasonable time. Further, the unit had earlier entered into a long term contract for supply of its products at fixed price, without taking into account the factors like the increase in the cost of raw materials, etc. Thus, its net profit (PAT) had declined from Rs. 1.61 lakh in 1988 to Rs. 1.12 lakh in 1989 which had marginally improved to Rs. 1.19 lakh in 1990. The unit has, however, since changed its strategy and is expected to do better in the future. Further, as the unit is ploughing back the entire profit in the business, its tangible net worth (TNW) has gradually increased from Rs. 5.25 lakh in 1988 to Rs. 6.37 lakh in 1989 and Rs. 7.56 lakh in 1990, with the share capital base maintained uniformly at Rs. 2.50 lakh.

The unit is dealing with the bank since its inception. It

has been adhering to the bank's financial discipline and submitting the stock statements, QIS forms and the other financial statements to the bank on a regular basis. Keeping in view the satisfactory conduct of its bank accounts, the bank has been gradually enhancing its working capital limit, commensurate with the increase in the scale of its operations. The unit is now enjoying an aggregate working capital limit of Rs. 31 lakh comprising fund based limit of Rs. 13 lakh and non-fund based limit (for issuance of Bank Guarantees) of Rs. 18 lakh. All its bank accounts were running regular as may be observed from the position of the accounts as on 27-11-1991 given hereunder:

(Rs. in lakhs)

Facility	Limit	Drawing Power	Outstandings	Irregularity
Stock Cash Credit (Hypothecation)	13.00	13.00	12.63	Nil
Bank Guarantee	18.00	—	16.49	Nil

The unit has been regular in the payment of the periodical instalments on its term loan accounts aggregating Rs. 5.31 lakh, out of which a sum of Rs. 3.95 lakh has already been repaid as on 27-11-1991.

Comments

Sri Krishna Kumar, a technically qualified person with varied experience, had started the venture after properly assessing the demand for the products and his company's share in the market on a realistic basis. He was exercising effective quality control whereby the products enjoyed a good reputation in the market. He was maintaining good personal relations with the officers of the reputed companies buying the products and was rendering prompt and efficient after sales service to them. This way, he was able to procure repeat orders from them and realise the payment of the bills within a reasonable time. He has learnt from his mistakes and taken suitable corrective measures in time so that his unit runs on healthy line on a continuing basis. Both the entrepreneurs are sincere, hard working and fully committed to their venture. Their industrial relations are also cordial.

The unit is adhering to the bank's financial discipline and is regular in submitting the required statements to the bank. Keeping in view the satisfactory conduct of its bank accounts and the growing demand for its products, the bank has been gradually enhancing its credit limits promptly to meet its genuine financial requirements, though its Current Ratio, during the years 1988 through 1990, at 1.1 was not considered satisfactory. The bank has, however, advised the company to improve its Current Ratio gradually. The company's Total Outside Liability/Tangible Net Worth (TOL/TNW) has marginally improved from 4.98 in 1989 to 4.92 in 1990. With the pursuance of the present policy of ploughing back the entire profit, or a substantial portion thereof, in the business, the position is expected to improve further in due course. As the bank officers are periodically monitoring the performance of the unit with the active cooperation of the entrepreneurs, the unit is expected to do even better in the future.

28. RETREADING RUBBERS

Sri Ravi Shankar, along with his brother Sri Kavi Shankar and son Sri Shiv Shankar, established a partnership firm named *Retreading Rubbers,* in September 1971 for manufacturing precured tread rubber, cushion compound, vulcanising solution, tyre flaps, etc. Sri Ravi Shankar, the Managing Partner, is a technically qualified person, having 21 years of experience in the line of the business. He is assisted by Sri Kavi Shankar and Sri Shiv Shankar in the day-to-day working of the unit.

The peoducts of the unit, being of the standard quality, have good demand in the market. The new product introduced by the unit, viz., precured tread rubber, has been received well in the market. While a major portion of its products are being supplied to the State Road Transport Corporations of Andhra Pradesh, Tamil Nadu and Gujarat, the remaining products are sold to the local tyre retreading companies and the owners of fleets of trucks and taxies.

The net sales of the unit have been steadily rising from Rs. 20.56 lakh in 1977 to Rs. 222.36 lakh in 1985 and Rs. 429.24 lakh in 1992. As there has been a continuous flow of orders, the sales are expected to grow still further.

Share capital of the firm has increased from Rs. 12.37 lakh in 1985 to Rs. 16.77 lakh in 1986. As the firm has been ploughing back a substantial portion of its profit in the business, the Tangible Net Worth (TNW) of the firm has increased from Rs. 17.14 lakh in 1986 to Rs. 24.18 lakh in 1992.

The unit has been dealing with the bank since its inception and was initially financed under the bank's entrepreneur scheme for technocrats. With the increase in the scale of operations of the unit, its working capital limit was gradually enhanced to meet its genuine credit requirements. The unit is now enjoying a working capital limit of Rs. 49 lakh, and all its accounts are being conducted satisfactorily. The unit has been adhering to the bank's financial discipline and is regular in the submission of the stock statements, QIS forms and other financial statements to the bank.

Sri Ravi Shankar is maintaining good rapport with the officers of the various State Road Transport Corporations and the other local buyers which facilitates timely payment of the bills. Further, the unit has its sales offices at Vijayawada, Madras and Ahmedabad for procuring orders from the respective State Road Transport Corporations and other local buyers as also to expedite the payment of the bills. The industrial relations of the firm are cordial. However, the

Current Ratio of the firm at 1.12 is considered to be rather unsatisfactory. The unit has, therefore, been advised by the bank to bring in some more capital in the business so as to improve its financial position, and its prospects therewith.

Comments

Sri Ravi Shankar, the Managing Partner, is technically competent and has long experience and standing in the business. All the three entrepreneurs are fully committed to their venture and are working hard together for the success of the unit. They started the venture on a modest scale and, after consolidating their position, expanded their business gradually. Besides supplying their products to some bulk buyers, they were simultaneously selling their products in the open market. They have opened their offices in some important centres to procure orders and to vigorously follow-up the payment of their bills. Their new product has also been received well in the market. They have been consistently maintaining the high quality of their products by exercising effective quality control. This way they are getting repeat orders from the bulk buyers and also fresh orders from their broad based customers. They, therefore, do not envisage any marketing problem.

The unit is adhering to the bank's financial discipline and is submitting the required financial statements to the bank regularly. As the conduct of all the bank accounts of the unit have been satisfactory, its genuine credit requirements have been met by the bank promptly and fully. As the entrepreneurs are ploughing back a substantial portion of the profit in the business, and are managing the affairs of the unit on sound lines, they seem to be determined to grow from strength to strength.

29. OFFICE EQUIPMENTS

Sri Om Prakash, along with his wife Srimati Lakshmi Devi,

established *Office Equipments (Private) Limited* in May 1988 for manufacturing pallets, bins, lockers, table trays, etc. The unit subsequently developed a new product, the mobile racks, for supply to the industrial concerns and the government departments. The new product was first manufactured on a trial basis and was subsequently improved upon, as per the market feed-back, before commencing the mass production. The unit later added the fabrication of industrial structure/ furniture as also the heavy duty storage systems to the list of its products.

Sri Om Prakash, having 10 years of experience in the family business of similar products, personally oversees the production, sales, marketing and financial management of the unit. Srimati Lakshmi Devi helps in the general administration. The entrepreneurs have employed a Design Engineer, an Erection Engineer and other professional managers to look after the day-to-day working of the unit. The quality of management of the company is, therefore, considered satisfactory. Besides, the company has been maintaining cordial industrial relations all through.

The products of the unit enjoy a good reputation in the market as these are of the standard quality and are produced under strict quality control.This is evident from the fact that the net sales of the company have progressively increased from Rs. 35 lakh in 1990 to Rs. 50 lakh in 1991 and Rs. 97 lakh in 1992. The valued customers of the unit include ITC, VST, BHEL, BDL, Ordnance Factories, etc. It has firm orders worth Rs. 45 lakh in hand. Further, it has been receiving enquiries from several companies of repute like L & T, Mec-Neil, Crompton and Greaves, etc., for the supply of its new product, viz., the mobiles storage system. It has supplied pallets of different types worth Rs. 19 lakh to ITC and has secured a repeat order from them for the same amount.

Under the circumstances, the company's projected sales for the year 1993 at Rs. 120 lakh may be considered achievable. Sri Om Prakash has been maintaining good rapport with the customers which facilitates continuous flow of orders and timely payment of the bills.

The unit has been dealing with the bank since its inception. It was sanctioned a term loan of Rs. 2 lakh by the bank on 24-6-1988 for the purchase of machinery and a working capital loan of Rs. 4.5 lakh on 3-7-1988. It was sanctioned another term loan of Rs. 1.75 lakh by the bank for the purchase of a generator with a view to ensuring continued production even in the event of frequent power cuts. The unit has been regular in the payment of the instalments and both its term loans now stand fully repaid. With the increase in the scale of its operations, its working capital limit was gradually enhanced to Rs. 13 lakh on 7-2-1990 and Rs. 18 lakh on 1-4-1992.

The entrepreneurs have been adhering to the bank's financial discipline and submitting the stock statements, QIS forms and other financial statements to the bank regularly. They are routing the entire sale proceeds through bank account as is evident from the credit summations of Rs. 118.40 lakh for the period 1-4-1991 to 28-3-1992. They are conducting the bank account in a satisfactory manner as may be seen from the position of the account as on 27-6-1992 given hereunder:

(Rs. in lakh)

Facility	Limit	Drawing Power	Outstandings	Irregularity
Working Capital	18	17.85	16.37	nil

The unit earned a net profit of Rs. 2.11 lakh in 1990. But in 1991, it incurred a loss of Rs. 1.40 lakh because it had entered into a long term supply contract at fixed price, without providing for the increase in the cost of raw materials, etc. The entrepreneurs, however, realised their mistake and changed their strategy appropriately. They also brought in further funds in the business whereby their share capital increased from Rs. 3.30 lakh in 1990 to Rs. 4.80 lakh in 1991. Subsequently, the company registered a net profit of Rs. 7.32 lakh in 1992. Further, as the company has been ploughing back a substantial portion of its profit in the business, its Tangible Net Worth (TNW) improved from Rs. 3.33 lakh in 1991 to Rs. 10.33 lakh in 1992. The company's Current Ratio has also improved from 1.00 in 1990 and 1991 to 1.25 in 1992. Further, the Total Outside Liability/Tangible Net Worth (TOL/TNW) at 3.05 is also considered satisfactory.

Comments

Sri Om Prakash is an experienced businessman and has the required managerial skills to run the venture on sound lines. His wife gives him the necessary help in the general administration. They had started the venture on a modest scale and expanded their business gradually. They were cautious to introduce their product in the market on trial basis before going in for mass production. They are maintaining the quality of their products whereby they are now well established in the market.

Besides, the entrepreneurs are able to collect the payment of their bills within a reasonable time. As the conduct of their bank accounts is satisfactory, their genuine credit requirements have been met by the bank fully and promptly. They have learnt from their mistakes and changed their strategy appropriately. As they have recently augmented their capital base and are ploughing back a substantial portion of their profit in the business, they are expected to perform even better in the future.

30. SUNSHINE BATTERIES

Dr. Prabhakar, Ph.D. in Engineering, along with his son Sri Diwakar, B.E., established *Sunshine Batteries (Private) Limited* in March 1986 for designing, assembling, erecting and commissioning solar photo-voltaic systems. They had carefully selected this project as it involved a modest capital investment, high technical input and value added, and better prospects for profitability and growth. They had initially invested a share capital of Rs. 50,000 and obtained a working capital loan of Rs. 2.50 lakh and a term loan of Rs. 1.82 lakh under the bank's entrepreneur scheme for technocrats.

The unit commenced its commercial production in 1987. Its net sales have been progressively increasing from Rs. 6 lakh in 1987 to Rs. 18 lakh in 1988, Rs. 110 lakh in 1990 and Rs. 210 lakh in 1992. The unit has firm orders in hand to the tune of Rs. 20 crore, mainly from the BDL, its bulk buyers, to be executed over a period of five years. The unit also supplies its products to the DRDL and other defence departments.

Dr. Prabhakar, Chairman, personally looks after the technical aspects of the products, quality control and development of new products. The unit has a strong Research and Development (R & D) set-up. After consolidating its position in the aforesaid product, it has diversified into the production of thermal batteries since July 1992. These are special types of batteries exclusively used in the missiles by the defence department, and the unit is said to be the only supplier thereof in the private sector. By 1993, the unit expects to perfect and produce yet another product, viz., lithium sulpha-dioxide batteries. In recognition of its R & D activities, the unit received the national award in 1991 from the Department of Science and Technology, Government of India. It was also awarded by the Federation of Andhra Pradesh Chambers of Commerce and Industries for the best technological innovations.

Sri Diwakar, the Managing Director, looks after the day-to-day operations of the unit with the assistance of a team of professional managers in the respective functional areas of finance, production, marketing and personnel. He maintains good personal relations with the officers of the government departments and the companies purchasing the products of the unit, which facilitates the continuous flow of fresh and repeat orders from them. He is able to negotiate long term contracts at favourable rates, and takes special care to make provisions for the corresponding increase in the price of the products with every rise in the cost of the raw materials and such other variable costs.

The entrepreneurs take pride in their people and treat them with respect. The employees are paid well and are imparted the necessary training to enable them to prosper in their career path. They have thus developed a sense of belonging to the organisation and feel that they are also growing with it. Under the circumstances, the 140 employees of the unit have not so far considered it necessary to form a formal union. The personnel management and industrial relations of the unit may, therefore, be considered as excellent.

The unit is adhering to the bank's financial discipline and is complying with the various terms and conditions of the advances stipulated by the bank. It is regular in the submission of the stock statements, QIS forms and other financial statements required by the bank. It adheres to the inventory norms and conducts its bank accounts in a satisfactory manner.

The company has augmented its paid-up capital from Rs. 0.50 lakh in 1986 to Rs. 9.38 lakh in 1991 and Rs. 11.30 lakh in 1992. With the increase in the net sales of the company, as aforesaid, its net profit has increased from Rs. 0.42 lakh in 1988 to Rs. 5.05 lakh in 1990, Rs. 5.96 lakh in 1991 and Rs. 17.66 lakh in 1992. As the company has been ploughing back a substantial portion of its profit in the business, its Tangible Net Worth (TNW) has steadily increased from Rs. 6.01 lakh in 1990 to Rs. 20.85 lakh in 1991 and Rs. 40.43 lakh in 1992. The Current Ratio of the company has also been gradually improving from 1.16 in 1990 to 1.19 in 1991 and 1.22 in 1992. The position is expected to improve further to 1.42 by 1993, after the disbursement of term loans and quasi equity by the State Financial Corporation and the Canbank Venture Capital Fund for the implementation of the company's expansion programmes, as aforesaid. In view of the foregoing, the past performance and the financial position of the company may be considered satisfactory.

Keeping in view the increase in the scale of operations of the unit, the gradual growth in its sales, profitability and order book, and the other satisfactory features connected with the advance, as aforesaid, the working capital limit of the unit has been enhanced by the bank from time to time. The unit is at present enjoying a fund based working limit of Rs. 65 lakh and non-fund based working capital limit of Rs. 130 lakh (for issuance of Letters of Credit Rs. 30 lakh and Bank Guarantees Rs. 100 lakh).

By virtue of close follow-up, the unit has been usually obtaining the payment of its bills from the government departments and the public sector undertakings within a reasonable time. But, of late, its bills aggregating Rs.112 lakh have become overdue for payment, mainly by the BDL. This has caused some financial difficulties to the unit. Keeping in view the past performance and satisfactory conduct of the accounts, the bank has extended the timely financial help to the unit and allowed temporary overdrawings on the account. The stock cash credit account of the unit has, thus been running irregular since 19-3-1992, as may be seen from the position of the account given hereunder:

(Rs. in lakh)

Limit	Market Value of Security	Advance Value of Security	Drawing Power	Outstandings	Irregularity
65	115.96	86.59	65.00	72.69	7.69

It may, however, be observed that though the outstandings have exceeded the limit and the drawing power, these are still well within the market value and advance value of the security. As the payment of the bills was not forthcoming, mainly from the BDL, the irregularity on the account gradually rose to Rs. 20.50 lakh as on 30-4-1992 and Rs. 34.41 lakh as on 27-6-1992. The bank has, however, sanctioned an ad-hoc working capital limit of Rs. 37 lakh to the unit on 16-6-1992, raising the total fund based limit to Rs. 102 lakh. The unit is vigorously pursuing the matter with the BDL and the government departments and expects to obtain the payment of its long outstanding bills from them at an early date. The position of its bank account may thus be regularised in the near future. Further, with a view to avoiding the recurrence of such financial difficulties caused by high sundry debtors, the unit is now endeavouring to simultaneously sell its solar photo-voltaic systems to a broad-based clientele in the open market.

Comments

The entrepreneurs are technically qualified and have gradually acquired the required managerial skills in various functional areas like production, marketing, finance and personnel. They selected the project after due deliberations and started the venture on a limited scale which they could ably manage. They developed high-tech products which had a higher margin of profit and was in great demand by the government departments and public sector undertakings. They have maintained the quality of their products through effective quality control. They have thus been able to procure substantial firm orders, including repeat orders, and have not faced any marketing problems so far. They first consolidated their position in one of their products and thereafter diversified into other products in a gradual and planned manner.

The unit has been adhering to the financial discipline stipulated by the bank and conducting its bank accounts in a satisfactory manner. The bank, therefore, gradually enhanced the working capital limit of the unit, commensurate with the increase in the scale of its operations. Further, when the unit started experiencing some genuine financial difficulty, due to blockage of substantial funds in high sundry debtors, the bank adopted a helpful attitude and allowed temporary overdrawings on the account. Later, the bank even sanctioned an ad-hoc working capital limit of Rs. 37 lakh, until the overdue bills were finally paid. The entrepreneurs have also, by now, realised the imminent risk of over-dependence on a few bulk buyers. They have, therefore, decided to sell their solar photo-voltaic systems, a popular product of common use, in the open market, too.

The entrepreneurs are hard working, sincere and fully committed to the venture. They also have the courage to face problems with patience. They have adopted the sound policy of ploughing back a substantial portion of their profit in the business so that they may expand further with the sound equity base. Their inter-personal competence is of a high order. They maintain good personal relations with their bankers and customers, as also with their employees and officers.

At this rate, the unit is expected to do even better in the future.

5

ANALYSIS AND INTERPRETATION OF DATA

ANALYSIS OF THE CAUSES OF SICKNESS FOUND IN CASES 1 TO 22

The case-wise distribution of the various causes of sickness found in the foregoing 22 cases of sick small scale industrial (SSI) units are presented in Tables 5.1. to 5.9.

The causes of sickness have been presented under two broad classifications, viz.

A. *Internal causes* (i.e., due to the factors within the control of the entrepreneurs).

B. *External causes* (i.e. due to the factors beyond the control of the entrepreneurs).

The internal and external causes have been further classified under the following heads with the number of the relevant Table noted against each head:

A. Internal Causes of Sickness Pertaining to

(i)	Marketing Management Area	Table : 5.1
(ii)	Financial Management Area	Table : 5.2
(iii)	Production Management Area	Table : 5.3
(iv)	Corporate Management Area	Table : 5.4

B. External Causes of Sickness Relating to

(i)	Commercial Banks	Table : 5.5
(ii)	State Financial Corporations	Table : 5.6
(iii)	Central and State Governments	Table : 5.7
(iv)	Large Scale Industries	Table : 5.8
(v)	Miscellaneous Factors	Table : 5.9

The serial numbers of the cases have been given against the relevant causes, listed in the Tables, due to which the respective units had fallen sick. Such numbers of the cases have been presented in separate columns for the four different categories of the cases, viz. *category 1, category 2.1, category 2.2, and category 2.3, as classified in Table 1.6.*

A. Internal Causes of Sickness

TABLE 5.1: Internal Causes of Sickness Pertaining to Marketing Management Area

Causes of Sickness	Category 1	Category 2.1	Category 2.2	Category 2.3	Total
	Case No.	Case No.	Case No.	Case No.	
1	2	3	4	5	6
1. Lack of Sales	1 to 12	13 to 16, 18, 19	20, 21	–	20
Further break-up of the causes of lack of sales:					
(i) Poor quality of product	1, 4 to 7, 9, 10	16	–	–	8
(ii) Highly competitive market	1, 6	13, 14, 18	20	–	6

(Contd.)

TABLE 5.1 *(Contd.)*

1	2	3	4	5	6
(iii) Over-dependence on one or a few bulk buyers Further break-up of bulk buyers:	3, 4, 7, 9, 10	14,15, 19	–	–	8
(a) Govt. departments	3, 4, 10	14, 15	–	–	5
(b) Large scale industries	7, 9	–	–	–	2
(c) Parent unit of ancillary SSI unit	–	19	–	–	1
(iv) Inaccurate demand forecasting	2, 5, 6	–	20, 21	–	5
(v) Highly brand-loyal market	–	–	20	–	1
2. Exorbitant Expenses on advertisements, etc.	12	–	–	–	1
3. Wrong selection of distributors/selling agents	–	18	20, 21	–	3
4. Far-flung market	–	–	20	–	1
5. Others (Marketability suffered due to lack of second line of management)	8	–	–	–	1

TABLE 5.2 : Internal Causes of Sickness Pertaining to Financial Management Area

Causes of Sickness	Category 1	Category 2.1	Category 2.2	Category 2.3	Total
	Case No.	Case No.	Case No.	Case No.	
1	2	3	4	5	6
1. Weak equity base as compared to high outside borrowings	1 to 12	–	20, 21	–	14
2. Poor utilisation of assets i.e. operating at sub-optimal level or below breakeven point	1 to 12	19	20, 21	22	16
3. Poor Working Capital Management:					

(Contd.)

TABLE 5.2 *(Contd.)*

1	2	3	4	5	6
(a) Poor inventory management control :					
(i) Depletion of stocks	1 to 12	19	20, 21	–	15
(ii) Slow/non-moving items in stocks	3, 4, 10, 11	16	–	–	5
(iii) Stocks of returned goods	1, 10	15, 16	–	–	4
(b) Poor Sundry debtors management :					
(i) Poor collection and follow-up system	2, 8, 12	16, 18	20, 21	22	8
(ii) Disputed bills due to poor quality of goods supplied	1, 9	16	–	–	3
(iii) Return of substandard goods	1, 7, 10	–	–	–	3
(iv) Long outstanding bills with					
(a) Government departments	3, 4	15	–	–	3
(b) Large scale industries	9	19	–	22	3
4. Frequent overdrawing on bank account	1 to 12	13,14,18,19	21	–	17
5. Diversion of Funds:					
(i) For acquiring fixed assets	1, 2, 8	–	21	–	4
(ii) For payments of instalments and interest on term loans	1	–	20	22	3
(iii) For unplanned expansion/ diversification	1, 4, 5, 7	–	–	–	4
6. Selling at a lower price to get established in the market	–	18	–	–	1
7. Inability to raise price with the rise in the cost of raw material	1	13	–	–	2
8. Long-term contract in an inflationary market	–	13	–	–	1
9. Non-adherence to the bank's financial discipline	1 to 12	13, 14	20, 21	22	17

TABLE 5.3: Internal Causes of Sickness Pertaining to Production Management Area

Causes of Sickness	Category 1	Category 2.1	Category 2.2	Category 2.3	Total
	Case No.	Case No.	Case No.	Case No.	
1	2	3	4	5	6
1. Poor quality control	1, 4 to 7, 9, 10	16	–	–	8
2. Lack of raw materials	1, 11	–	–	–	2
3. Lack of skilled labour	2	–	–	–	1
4. Lack of power	–	–	–	22	1
5. Sub-standard items of machine/moulds	–	15	–	–	1
6. Wrong selection of site (away from source of raw material and market)	1	–	–	–	1
7. Poor maintenance management causing frequent break-downs	2	–	–	–	1

TABLE 5.4: Internal Causes of Sickness Pertaining to Corporate Management Area

Causes of Sickness	Category 1	Category 2.1	Category 2.2	Category 2.3	Total
	Case No.	Case No.	Case No.	Case No.	
1	2	3	4	5	6
1, Lack of managerial competence	1, 2, 5 to 8 10, 11	13, 16	20	–	11
2. Lack of technical competence	1, 2, 5, 6 7, 9, 10	16	–	–	8
3. Lack of marketing ability	2, 5, 6, 7, 10, 11	–	–	–	6
4. Lack of second line of management	8	–	–	22	2

(Contd.)

TABLE 5.4 *(Contd.)*

1	2	3	4	5	6
5. Dispute among top management	1, 5	16	–	–	3
6. Lack of self-restraint on expenses (e.g. personal drawings, travelling, office lay-out, etc.)	1	–	20	–	2
7. Lack of integrity in top management	3, 5, 10	–	–	–	3

B. External Causes of Sickness

TABLE 5.5: External Causes of Sickness Relating to the Commercial Banks

Causes of Sickness	Category 1	Category 2.1	Category 2.2	Category 2.3	Total
	Case No.	Case No.	Case No.	Case No.	
1	2	3	4	5	6
1. Faulty project appraisal	1 to 7	–	20	–	8
2. Lack of effective supervision and follow-up of advances					
(i) Security level	1 to 12	–	–	–	12
(ii) Activity level	1 to 12	–	20	–	13
3. Indiscrete/unrestricted permission of overdrawings on accounts	1 to 12	13	–	–	13
4. Failure to detect early signals of sickness	1 to 12	–	20	–	13
5. Unit declared sick and no-viable after some delay	1 to 12	–	–	–	12

TABLE 5.6: External Causes of Sickness Relating to the State Financial Corporations

Causes of Sickness	Category 1	Category 2.1	Category 2.2	Category 2.3	Total
	Case No.	Case No.	Case No.	Case No.	
1	2	3	4	5	6
1. Faulty Project appraisal	1, 2, 6	–	20	–	4
2. Lack of post-sanction performance monitoring of the units	1, 2, 6	–	20	–	4
3. Lack of coordination with the bank	1, 2, 6	–	20	–	4
4. Failure to detect early signals of sickness	1, 2, 6	–	20	–	4

TABLE 5.7: External Causes of Sickness Relating to the Central and State Governments

Causes of Sickness	Category 1	Category 2.1	Category 2.2	Category 2.3	Total
	Case No.	Case No.	Case No.	Case No.	
1	2	3	4	5	6
1. Change in government policy regarding :					
(i) Development programmes	3, 4	15	–	–	3
(ii) Taxation policy	–	13	–	–	1
(iii) Imposition of restrictions	11	–	–	–	1
2. Delayed payment of bills by government departments	3, 4	15	–	–	3

TABLE 5.8: External Causes of Sickness Relating to the Large Scale Industries

Causes of Sickness	Category 1	Category 2.1	Category 2.2	Category 2.3	Total
	Case No.	Case No.	Case No.	Case No.	
1	2	3	4	5	6
1. Delayed payment of bills	9	19	–	22	3
2. Selling at lower price to drive the SSI units out of the market	–	13	–	–	1

TABLE 5.9 : External Causes of Sickness Relating to Miscellaneous Factors

Causes of Sickness	Category 1	Category 2.1	Category 2.2	Category 2.3	Total
	Case No.	Case No.	Case No.	Case No.	
1	2	3	4	5	6
1. Destruction of plant and machinery and stocks due to accident (fire, etc.)	–	17	–	–	1
2. Sickness of the entrepreneur or his/her family members	3	–	–	22	2

ANALYSIS AND INTERPRETATION OF DATA

Before suggesting the remedial measures for preventing sickness in SSI units and the necessary steps to be taken for rehabilitating the sick units, it would be pertinent to analyse and interpret the facts contained in the foregoing 22 cases of sick units, and the data presented in the Tables 5.1 to 5.9 on the following parameters :

1. The factors due to which the units were considered

non-viable for rehabilitation by the bank *(units under category 1, cases 1 to 12).*

2. The factors due to which the units were found viable for rehabilitation by the bank *(units under categories 2.1 and 2.3, cases 13 to 19, and 22 respectively).*
3. The factors which had facilitated the success of the bank's rehabilitation programmes *(units under category 2.1, cases 13 to 19).*
4. The factors which had led to the failure of the bank's rehabilitation programmes *(units under category 2.2, cases 20 and 21).*

The factors due to which the units were considered non-viable for rehabilitation by the bank (units under category 1, cases 1 to 12)

The study has revealed that lack of marketability of the products had been the main cause of sickness in all the 12 units (100%) which were found non-viable for rehabilitation by the bank. In 7 units (58%) the sales could not pick up due to poor quality of the products, not accepted in the market. This also speaks of the lack of technical competence on the part of the entrepreneurs.

Five units (42%) were largely depending on one or a few bulk purchasers, like the government departments (3 units or 25%), and the large scale industries (2 units or 17%), instead of having a broad-based clientele in the market, too. Changes in the government policy had caused serious set-back to 3 units (25%). Further, 2 units (17%) were operating in a highly competitive market. They had obviously not conducted a market survey, or a quick market scanning, to ascertain the extent of competition. They had, instead, over-estimated their own share in the market. One unit (8.33%) had indulged in exorbitant expenditure on advertisement, incommensurate with its scale of operation. Due to poor marketability of the products, all the 12 units (100%) were operating at sub-optimal level, well below the break-even point, resulting in rising accumulated losses.

Seven units (58%) suffered from lack of quality control of their products. While 2 units (17%) were facing scarcity of raw materials, one unit (8.33%) was facing lack of skilled labour. While one unit (8.33%) had selected a wrong site, the other unit had frequent break-downs, indicative of poor maintenance management.

All the 12 units (100%) did not adhere to the financial discipline stipulated by the bank. In all the 12 units (100%) the level of stocks of raw materials and finished goods, charged to the bank, had got depleted over a period of time. Further, while 4 units (33.3%) were carrying stocks of slow-moving/non-moving items, the other 2 units (17%) were carrying stocks of finished goods of sub-standard quality, returned by the bulk buyers.

A substantial portion of funds of 9 units (75%) was locked up in high sundry debtors for various reasons, viz.

(i) poor collection and follow-up system, (3 units or 25%)

(ii) disputed bills due to

- (a) supply of sub-standard goods (2 units or 17%), or
- (b) return of sub-standard goods (3 units or 25%),

(iii) long overdues with the government departments (2 units or 17%) and large scale industries (1 unit or 8.33%).

In the remaining 3 units (25%) the level of sundry debtors was low because their goods had not picked up in the market. Due to the aforesaid financial constraints, all the 12 units (100%) had resorted to frequent and excess over-drawings on their bank accounts, well above their sanctioned limits, and against 'nil' or nominal drawing power. The level of outside borrowings of all the 12 units (100%) had steadily increased and had ultimately reached a high level, disproportionate to their equity base. The bank had consequently taken a firm stand not to grant further credit facilities unless the entrepreneurs brought in further funds in the business, which they were unable to comply. Six units (50%) had resorted to diversion of funds (short-term sources for long-term uses) for acquiring fixed assets, for unplanned expansion/diversification, and/or for payment of instalments on term loans.

Three units (25%) had suffered due to changes in the government policy and two units (17%) due to undue delay in the release of payments of bills by the government departments. In one case (8.33%) the government department had cancelled the orders due to the dubious design of the entrepreneur and in the other case (8.33%) due to poor quality of the products.

In two cases (17%) the large scale industries had cancelled the orders due to poor quality of the products. Undue delay in the payment of the bills by a large scale industry (the bulk purchaser) had caused financial constraint to one unit (8.33). While in 8 cases (67%) the entrepreneurs lacked the managerial competence, in 7 cases (58%) they lacked in technical competence, too. Besides the poor quality of the products, 6 units (50%) lacked in marketing ability also. While in two cases (17%) the units fell sick due to the dispute among the partners, in other two cases (17%) the units suffered due to lack of the second line of management. In one unit (8.33%) the entrepreneurs were resorting to unrestricted personal drawings and excessive travelling, though the unit was incurring losses right from the beginning.

The gradual depletion of stocks, excess over-drawings on the accounts, high sundry debtors etc., are also indicative of lack of supervision and control on the part of the bank officers, both at the security and activity levels. They had allowed frequent overdrawings on the accounts and had failed to pick up early signal of sickness so as to take the timely remedial measures, to check the sickness at the incipient stage itself. They had somehow faltered at the project appraisal stage, too. Besides, there had been some delay on their part in declaring the units as sick and non-viable for rehabilitation.

The factors due to which the units were found viable for rehabilitation by the bank (units under categories 2.1 and 2.3 cases 13 to 19, and 22 respectively)

The study has revealed that in all the cases of sick units found viable for rehabilitation by the bank, the undernoted positive factors were present:

(i) The entrepreneurs, instead of stopping the production continued the activity, though on a limited scale.

(ii) Though the entrepreneurs initially faced the problem of marketing their products, they gradually stabilised themselves in the market and/or obtained sufficient firm orders.

(iii) The integrity of the entrepreneurs of such units were above board, though some of them had initially resorted to violation of the bank's financial discipline viz. routing of sale proceeds through other banks, depletion of stocks, frequent overdrawings on their accounts, etc., to tide over their financial difficulties. It may, however, be pertinent to mention here that none of these units had diverted short term funds for long term uses, except one (case 22) and that, too, for payment of instalments on the term loan.

(iv) All the entrepreneurs were serious and sincere about the revival of their units and they extended their whole-hearted cooperation to the bank in this regard.

(v) The entrepreneurs had learnt from their mistakes and had, in due course of time, gained sufficient experience and expertise in the line of their business, which held them in good stead in the later years.

The Factors which had facilitated the success of the bank's rehabilitation programmes (units under category 2.1, cases 13 to 19)

The study has further revealed that the bank's rehabilitation programmes had succeeded due to the following factors:

(i) The bank had thoroughly considered various causes of sickness and had undertaken an in-depth study of the economic viability and technical feasibility of the units, *de novo*, keeping in view the changed circumstances.

(ii) The bank had chalked out a comprehensive rehabilitation package after duly assessing the total fresh financial requirements and prospects of revival of the unit as also the financial stability, managerial capability, honesty and sincerity of the entrepreneurs.

(iii) Other financial institutions, if any, were also involved in the formulation and implementation of the rehabilitation programme (case 19).

(iv) Further finance was released by the bank in a phased manner with a view to ensuring the end-use of funds.

(v) The performance of all such units was being closely and carefully monitored by the bank, both at the branch and controlling office levels, in close coordination with the entrepreneurs, at regular monthly intervals.

(vi) During the course of the rehabilitation programme, timely corrective actions were being taken by the bank to remedy the malady at the early stage, so as to ensure the working of the unit on satisfactory lines, on an on-going basis.

The Factors which had led to the failure of the bank's rehabilitation programmes (units under category 2.2, cases 20 and 21).

The rehabilitation programmes in some of the cases had failed mainly due to the following factors :

(i) The bank did not thoroughly weigh the various factors that had led to the sickness of such units.

(ii) An in-depth viability study of the units was not undertaken by the bank.

(iii) Instead of working out a comprehensive rehabilitation package, some *ad-hoc* enhancement of limits or release of further funds was resorted to.

(iv) A realistic SWOT analysis of the units, with a view to assessing the chances of their revival, was not undertaken. The capacity and capability of the entrepreneurs, their sincerity and commitment to the projects, were not properly assessed.

(v) While releasing further funds, proper care was not taken to ensure end-use of funds whereby further diversion of funds had taken place (case 21). This also meant that the entrepreneur concerned did not mend his ways and that he even lacked commitment and sincerity of purpose to revive the unit.

(vi) The performance of such units was not being closely and carefully monitored by the branch and the controlling office at regular monthly intervals.

(vii) Instead of enforcing financial discipline on the units and taking suitable corrective measures promptly, the bank had allowed frequent over-drawings on the accounts (case 21). The entrepreneur concerned did not appreciate the ramifications of such overdrawings, either.

PROFILES OF SUCCESSFUL AND UNSUCCESSFUL ENTREPRENEURS – A COMPARISON

The comparative study of the cases of sick and healthy units, the analysis of the factors that had rendered the sick units as viable or non-viable for rehabilitation by the bank, and the study of the facilitating and hindering factors responsible for the success or sickness of the units, have established that the entrepreneurs play a pivotal role in the management of the affairs of their ventures. The study has further revealed that the success of the units largely depends on the character and capability, determination and dynamism, patience and perseverance of the entrepreneurs concerned.

On the basis of the study, the comparative profiles of successful and unsuccessful entrepreneurs have been broadly summarised in Table 5.10. This may serve as a general guideline to the entrepreneurs, both present and prospective, to start and run their units on sound lines as also to guard against the possible pitfalls, on an on-going basis.

Attributes of Successful and Unsuccessful Entrepreneurs

General Comments

It would, however, be pertinent to mention here that these are the general attributes, mostly found in successful or unsuccessful entrepreneurs, as the case be. This does not mean that all the traits of a successful entrepreneur, listed in Table 5.10, should necessarily be present in a person to be treated as such. It is not expected, either, that a successful entrepreneur would be free from all the aforesaid characteristics of an unsuccessful entrepreneur. Similarly, it should not be inferred that an unsuccessful entrepreneur

TABLE 5.10: Comparative Profiles of Successful and Unsuccessful Entrepreneurs

Sucessful Entrepreneurs	Unsucessful Entrepreneurs
1	2
A.Conception (Pre-Project) Stage	
1. While conceiving a project, he is clear about the objectives and the strategies. He is aware of his strengths and does a quick SWOT analysis of the various factors and environments having a bearing on his venture	He conceives a project mostly based on the success of other units in the line, without analysing the factors responsible for their success, and without examining whether the favourable conditions still prevail or the market for the product has already reached a saturation point.
2. Before entering into a venture, he does a quick market survey or market scanning/census to ascertain the extent of existing competition in the market, the demand and supply gap and his own share in the market, on a realistic and conservative basis.	Instead of taking such reasonable care, he tends to be over-optimistic, thinking that he would also be able to sell well, as the others in the line are doing, and ultimately lands himself in trouble when his products do not pick up well in the market.
3. He has a cautious approach and prefers to learn from the experiences of others who are already in the same or similar line of activity.	He tends to be over-confident of himself and ignores to take guidance and advice from the units, operating in the line.
4. He is flexible in his approache, examines the suggestions and is even prepared to change the line of his activity, if considered necessary.	He is rather rigid in his approach and does not seem to be open to reasoned and valuable suggestions to suitably modify or scale down his project, or even to switch over to some other line of activity, if necessary.
B. Project Stage	
1. While preparing the project report he proceeds in a systematic way, taking into account the various factors connected with his venture viz.	He is over-enthusiastic and impatient to launch his project at the earliest. He does not take due care to examine the various factors, listed alongside in items (a), (b) and (c). His main purpose in preparing the project report seems

(Contd.)

TABLE 5.10 *(Contd.)*

1	2
(a) availability of the necessary infrastructure like building, road, power, fuel, etc. (b) availability of the required raw materials, locally or from elsewhere, and whether these would be available in the near future, too. (c) availability of the necessary items of machinery, the names of the manufacturers, their reputation and competitiveness as also whether he should go in for power-operated or hand-operated machines, new of old machines in good condition, depending upon the resources at his command, to begin with, etc.	to be to take the maximum finance from the bank and the term lending institution. He prefers to do some window-dressing in his project report, depicting a rosy picture about his venture. He is prepared to pay the fees to the professional management consultants, to prepare the project report on the lines suggested by him, so as to meet the aforesaid objective, little realising that it may be even suicidal for the project.
2. He assesses the cost of the project on a realistic basis, providing for sufficient margin for cost overruns.	He assesses the cost of his project on a conservative basis and approaches the bank and the term lending institution for further finance, in case of cost overruns, which is usually the case.
3. He estimates the sales and profitability on a conservative basis, so as to be able to withstand the initial difficulties and set-backs.	He projects his sales and profitability on an over-ambitious scale, which he fails to achieve and starts incurring cash losses, usually from the first year onwards, and tends to fall sick.
4. He does the break-even analysis, based on actual and conservative basis, as in items (2) and (3) above.	He usually avoids doing the break-even analysis, or else he does so on an unrealistic basis so as to arrive at a favourable break-even point, for getting the required finance from the bank and other financial institutions.
5. He may also enlist the services of some management consultant for preparation of the project report, with an open mind.	While engaging a management consultant, he asks him to prepare an impressive and favourable project report justifying maximum loans possible.

(Contd.)

TABLE 5.10 *(Contd.)*

1	2
C. Implementation Stage	
1. He prefers to start the venture on a reasonable scale, which he could manage properly, keeping in view the limitations of his means and resources, experience and expertise, etc.	He is over-enthusiastic to start the venture on a larger scale than he can ably manage, to begin with. His main aim seems to be to avail of the maximum credit from banks and other financial institutions, without realising the avoidable interest burden and other risks connected therewith.
2. He tends to go slow and thinks of expansion and diversification only at a later date, after consolidating his position and gaining sufficient experience and confidence in the line.	He wants to grow fast by resorting to diversion of funds for unplanned and non-viable diversification and expansion, adversely affecting his stability and smooth working.
3. He starts the venture with sufficient stake of his own so as to be able to bear the brunt of the initial shocks as also to have sustained interest and involvement in the venture.	He prefers to bring in the minimal capital of his own and is always eager to get his project financed by banks and other financial institutions to the maximum possible extent. This way, he fails to withstand the initial set-backs in his business and tends to lose interest in his venture soon.
4. He approaches the bank and other financial institutions for working capital loan and term loan and is satisfied when his genuine credit requirements are fully met by them. He does not press them for over-financing, because he realises that it would unnecessarily increase his interest burden. He knows that when he would start working on sound and profitable lines, they would definitely enhance his credit limits, as and when deservedly required.	He is eager to obtain the maximum possible credit from the bank and other financial institutions, well beyond his genuine credit requirements by projecting the estimates of costs and sales at a higher level. This way his interest burden goes up and his profitability is adversely affected. He also resorts to diversion of funds, making the position still worse He finds himself unable to service the debt and pay the instalments, with interest, on his term loan, on time. The irregularity on his cash credit acount also starts steadily rising. The unit is ultimately declared sick and mostly found non-viable for rehabilitation.
5. He adheres to the financial	He fails to adhere to the financial dis-

(Contd.)

TABLE 5.10 *(Contd.)*

1	2
discipline of the bank and other financial institutions, by routing his entire sale proceeds through his cash credit account, maintaining sufficient stocks of inventory charged to the bank, managing his sundry debtors and other financial affairs of his unit well, and regularly paying the instalments on his term loan account, timely and promptly, out of the profit generated, and thereby building a relationship of mutual trust and confidence with them.	cipline and resorts to over-drawings on his cash credit account, and does not endeavour to regularise the position. When the bank adopts a firm attitude, he stops routing the sale proceeds through his account. His stocks of raw materials and finished goods also start depleting gradually. His sundry debtors are not well-managed making his financial position still worse. He is unable to pay the instalments on his term loan. The unit is ultimately declared sick and mostly found nonviable for rehabilitation.
6. After the credit limits are sanctioned, he prefers to withdraw the funds only when required so as to save on interest. He also deposits the sale proceeds in his cash credit account promptly to keep the outstandings thereon, and the interest burden therewith, at the minimal level.	He prefers to withdraw the entire loan amount sanctioned by the bank and term lending institution, unnecessarily fearing that the same may not be released to him at a later date. Thus, he incurs avoidable interest burden, besides resorting to uneconomic diversion of surplus funds, detrimental to the satisfactory and profitable functioning of his unit.
7. He avoids overdrawings on his account, except for meeting some emergent commitments, which he pays back fast, at the earliest opportunity, and thereby enhances his credit-worthiness and trustworthiness, in the eyes of his bankers.	He frequently resorts to over-drawings on his account, on some plea or the other, and neglects to regularise the position. This stiffens the attitude of his bankers towards him, who desist from meeting even his genuine requests in times of need.
8. He does not indulge in extravagant and avoidable expenditure, and keeps his personal drawings to the minimal level of sustenance.	He makes substantial personal drawings even out of the loan funds, and indulges in extravagant expenditure in travelling, entertainment, etc.
9. He prefers to plough back the profit in the business so that it may continue to expand and grow on sound and profitable lines.	By resorting to the aforesaid avoidable expenditure and mismanagement of his unit, he is hardly left with any profit and usually incurs cash losses.
10. His refrains himself from diversion of funds (short term sources for	He indulges in diversion of funds and unplanned expansion and diversifica-

(Contd.)

TABLE 5.10 *(Contd.)*

1	2
long term uses) and unplanned expansion and diversification, because he realises that it would create financial difficulties, adversely affecting the operating cycle and the viability and profitability of the unit.	tion, in his over-anxiety to grow fast, adversely affecting the profitability and viability of his unit.
11. He endeavours to manage the affairs of his unit on sound and profitable lines, and gradually develop professionalism and expertise in various facets of management, like financial management, materials management, production management, marketing management, personnel management, etc.	He lacks the ability, and even inclination, for managing the affairs of his unit on sound and profitable lines which ultimately falls sick, beyond rehabilitation.
12. He closely monitors the performance of his unit, on different parameters, on a regular basis, and takes suitable remedial measures promptly so that the unit may continue to work on sound and healthy lines, on an ongoing basis.	He fails to monitor the performance of of his unit, on a regular basis, and realises his mistakes when it is too late to take the required corrective measures.
13. During the course of his business, he may be confronted with problems and difficulties like scarcity of raw materials, shortage of power, blockage of funds in high sundry debtors, etc. But he does not get discouraged and desperate. Instead, he faces the challenge with firm determination, courage and patience, and ultimately comes out of the wood.	He loses his heart and confidence when confronted with problems. He tries to shift the blame on to the bank and other agencies, without making sincere efforts to overcome the problems. As his personal stake in the business is usually of a lower level, he ceases to take interest in his unit and allows it to get defunct.
14. His inter-personal relations with his banker and other financial institutions, trade creditors, customers and government officials, are cordial and of mutual respect and trust, which facilitate smooth working of his unit.	Because of his unsound and unprofitable working and even dishonest designs and dealings, he ultimately develops strained relationship with his banker and others dealing with him.

(Contd.)

TABLE 5.10 *(Contd.)*

1	2
15. His industrial relations are also cordial and congenial. He is an effective manager and a dynamic leader. He motivates his people to work well, with devotion and commitment, with a sense of belonging to the organisation and as a well-knit team. This way, the productivity of the unit goes up, and the profitability and prospects therewith.	He lacks the will and skill of managing the various facets of his unit on professional lines, adversely affecting the prosperity and profitability of his unit.
16. As regards his personality traits, he is a hard working person, fully committed and devoted to his unit. He works with full involvement for the success and growth of his unit. He is a dynamic personality with passion for excellence. He is an ambitious (not over-ambitious) person and works with zeal to make a mark for himself in the line of his business. He is a man of high integrity and enterprising enough to take fair business risks.	He usually starts the venture with the main idea of making a quick buck, at other's cost. He lacks commitment and involvement, patience and perseverance. He lacks courage and confidence to face problems and come out of the difficulties by making sustained efforts. He is over-ambitious and takes high risks initially which lands him in serious trouble, and he usually finds it difficult to come out of it. The risk of his unit falling sick, sooner or later, is usually high and the possibility of its being found viable for rehabilitation rather low, *inter alia*, due to lack of integrity on his part.

would necessarily possess all the traits of an unsuccessful entrepreneur and would be devoid of all the characteristics of a successful entrepreneur. In reality, each entrepreneur is a unique personality, a distinct combination of some of the traits listed above, both positive and negative, of course, in different proportions. And, in fact, it is this difference in the quantum and quality of the traits that differentiates the two.

Successful entrepreneurs were also found to be possessing some negative attributes. But their positive traits were far too many and much more material such that they could easily overcome the adverse effects and initial difficulties, and ultimately came out successful. Their positive characteristics were too over-powering, and their negative traits comparatively too small and insignificant, to block their path to prosperity. But, in the case of unsuccessful entrepreneurs, the proportion was just the reverse, and so was the result. Besides, the element of luck may also play a significant role in some cases. A person, endowed with most of the traits of a successful entrepreneur, may ultimately fail due to a sudden change in the environment well beyond his control, e.g., power cut, change in the market condition, import policy, etc., adversely affecting his business. And, to the contrary, a person possessing most of the characteristics of an unsuccessful entrepreneur may luckily succeed if such sudden changes prove favourable to his business prospects.

For example, in the event of a sudden and sutained power cut, the productivity and profitability of a unit, largely dependent on power, may be adversely affected. The sales of the units manufacturing fans, room coolers, air conditioners, etc., would also go down substantially. But the unit manufacturing candles may start doing a roaring business due to a sudden spurt in the demand of its products.

All considered, the profiles of successful and unsuccessful entrepreneurs can well serve as a list of do's and don'ts, for the benefit of the entrepreneurs, both present and prospective. These may also prove useful for the banks and other financial institutions for appraising a new project, for exercising effective supervision and follow-up of advances and for suitably counselling the entrepreneurs, well in time, so that their units may work on sound lines, on an on-going basis.

6

CONCLUSIONS AND SUGGESTIONS

SUGGESTIONS FOR PREVENTING SICKNESS

We have discussed 30 cases, including 8 success stories, in the small scale sector, in Chapter Four.

On the basis of the facts and figures contained in the cases of 22 sick SSI units (cases 1 to 22), we have identified the various factors that had led to the sickness of these units, as given in Table 5.1 to 5.9.

Subsequently, we have also examined the factors due to which the units were found non-viable (cases 1 to 12) and viable (cases 13 to 19 and 22) for rehabilitation by the bank.

Further, we have studied the facilitating and hindering factors that had led to the success (cases 13 to 19) and failure (cases 20 and 21) of the bank's rehabilitation programmes.

Besides, on the basis of the positive and negative features reflected in the cases of the successful and sick units, we have prepared the comparative profiles of successful and unsuccessful entrepreneurs, as presented in Table 5.10. These profiles, *inter alia*, focus on the various positive and negative factors that the entrepreneurs, both present and prospective, should bear in mind with a view to ensuring the success of their units and arresting and remedying the sickness, if at all, in their units at the incipient stage itself.

We would now examine the roles that:

(a) The Commercial Banks,

(b) The State Financial Corporations and other Financial Institutions,
(c) The Government, and
(d) The Large Scale Industries

may play in preventing the sickness in the small scale sector and in ensuring that the units work on sound lines on an on-going basis.

(A) By the Commercial Banks

The analysis of the cases in the foregoing pages, the study of the bank's laid down systems and procedures and the prevalent practices obtaining at the bank's branches and controlling offices (as contained in the bank's books and records), and the personal discussions with the bank officers of varied ranks and roles, have revealed that the quality of management of advances by banks mainly depends on the undernoted seven factors:

1. Prompt and realistic appraisal of the projects on receipt of the loan applications along with the project reports.
2. Prompt and realistic assessment of the credit requirements, both short term (working capital) and long term (term loan).
3. Phased disbursement of loans to ensure the end use of funds.
4. Effective supervision and follow-up of the advances and periodical performance monitoring of the units through intelligent scrutiny of their books of accounts, stock statements, financial statements, etc., coupled with personal dialogues with the entrepreneurs.
5. Timely detection of early symptoms of sickness at the incipient stage, and prompt and effective implementation of suitable remedial measures to put

the units back to health.

6. Effective supervision and control of the irregularities in the advances at the branches, by the controlling authority.
7. Prompt decision and action in regard to rehabilitation of viable sick units or calling up of the advances of non-viable sick units.

These seven factors have been discussed seriatim in the following pages.

Project Appraisal

Objectives

Project appraisal is the process of critical examination and analytical evaluation of a loan proposal for a project to see whether funds, if lent, can be repaid out of the profit generated within a reasonable time. It provides an analytical base for the decision making process.

The main objectives of project appraisal are:

(a) To assess whether the entrepreneurs are technically and managerially equipped to execute the project, and whether their antecedents like character, credit worthiness, integrity, etc., are satisfactory.

(b) To examine the technical feasibility of the process of manufacturing the product and the availability of the infrastructural facilities, raw materials, etc.

(c) To realistically determine the market demand for the proposed product and the achievability of the projected sales.

(d) To estimate the quantum of bank finance required.

(e) To assess the profitability of the project on a realistic basis and the adequacy of the cash surplus for repayment of the loan within a reasonable time.

Flaws Observed in the Bank's Project Appraisal

In most of the cases of non-viable sick SSI units, these aspects were not thoroughly examined by the bank officers at the project appraisal stage. This vital exercise was, instead, done by them in a rather perfunctory manner, as has been revealed from the perusal of the respective files of such cases and in the course of personal interviews of the bank officers, of different levels, at the controlling offices and the respective branches. Instead of making independent and realistic estimates of the projected sales and profitability, keeping in view the technical competence of the entrepreneurs and the quantum of demand for the products, extent of competition, etc., the operating staff at the branches were largely guided by the estimates of the entrepreneurs, as incorporated in the project reports. These initial lapses, at the project appraisal stage itself, had led to the sickness in most of the non-viable units covered in the study. Such units had fallen sick, beyond rehabilitation, as these were facing serious marketing problems and could not overcome such problems at any stage. Some viable units under study had also initially faced some marketing problems, but the entrepreneurs concerned could overcome these difficulties and could establish themselves well in the market in due course.

Flaws observed in the Project Appraisal by the Bank Officers as revealed in the Specific Cases under Study

The sales of some units (cases 1, 2, 5, 6, 20) had fallen short of the projected levels, estimated in the project reports, due to stiff competition in the market. The extent of competition and the level of achievable sales were not thoroughly examined by the bank officers independently, on a realistic basis, at the project appraisal stage. Some other units also initially faced some competition in the market (cases 13,14,18) but the entrepreneurs concerned strived hard and ultimately succeeded in establishing themselves in the market, by adopting suitable marketing strategies and/or by improving the quality of their products.

The products of some units could not pick in the market due to their poor quality (cases 1, 4 to 7, 9, 10) ultimately resulting in the sickness of these units. As the entrepreneurs concerned could not improve upon the quality of their products, even at a later stage, their units became non-viable and the loans were called up by the bank. The bank officers had thus failed to properly assess the technical competence of the entrepreneurs at the project appraisal stage In case 16 also, the unit had fallen sick due to poor quality of its products, but it could be rehabilitated as the entrepreneurs could succeed in improving upon the quality of their products which ultimately picked up well in the market.

The bank officers did not forewarn the entrepreneurs at the project appraisal stage, regarding the pitfalls of over-dependence on one or a few bulk buyers, viz. government departments (cases 3, 4, 10) or large scale industries (cases 7, 9). They could have counselled the entrepreneurs to explore an alternative broad-based clientele in the open market, too.

Some units, which were initially depending on government departments or a large scale industry (cases 13, 14, 19) and had fallen sick due to change in the government policy or the failure of the parent unit, could be rehabilitated by the bank as the entrepreneurs could subsequently find some alternative buyers to establish themselves in the open market. One unit (case 23), however, did not fall sick at any stage, as it was selling its products to the government departments as also in the open market, right from the beginning.

Bank's Systems and Procedures for Project Appraisal

All the relevant factors required to be considered by the entrepreneurs while preparing the project report, and to be examined by the bank officers while appraising the project reports, are contained in the three loan application forms prescribed by the bank for different quantum of advances. viz.

(i) over Rs. 50,000 and upto Rs. 2 lakh
(ii) over Rs. 2 lakh and upto Rs. 10 lakh
(iii) over Rs. 10 lakh (where Tandon Committee norms apply)

These forms well serve the purpose of check lists to verify whether all the relevant factors have been duly considered. But, unfortunately, in many cases, due attention was not paid to these crucial factors by the bank officers.

Suggestions

(a) It is, therefore, suggested that the bank officers should pay due attention and importance to the project appraisal, so crucial and critical for the success of an enterprise. They must meticulously appraise the technical feasibility and economic viability of the projects and objectively assess the entrepreneurs' managerial competence. The Branch Managers should seek the help and guidance from the specialists in the bank's consultancy services cell for conducting the detailed techno-economic viability study of new units involving highly technical and complex manufacturing process where the experience of the branch staff may be considered inadequate.

(b) It is a well-known fact that no industrial unit can work on sound and profitable lines unless it is able to market its products in sufficient quantity and at a price higher than its cost of production. The bank officers should, therefore, assess the cost of production and marketability of the products of the units on a realistic basis.

(c) They must do the break-even analysis on the basis of actual (not conservative) costs and reasonable (not over-ambitious) estimates of sales, with a view to ensuring that the unit was breaking even at a reasonably lower level so as to be able to withstand the initial shocks of lower sales and profitability.

(d) They would do well to ensure that the entrepreneurs undertake a market survey or a quick market census/scanning to ascertain the extent of competition already/existing in the market from the multinationals and the large, medium and small scale sectors.

(e) They should suggest to the prospective entrepreneurs to explore and tap some alternative broad-based customers also, to the extent of say 50% of their production, so as to guard against the imminent risk of over-dependence on one or a few bulk buyers.

(f) Further, they should impress upon the entrepreneurs the desirability of maintaining the quality of their products upto an acceptable standard so as to pick up in the market, even in the face of competition. They must make the entrepreneurs realise that a sub-standard product may fail in the market, and that even the supply of such products on credit terms may give rise to disputed bills and rising sundry debtors, resulting in liquidity problems, with other ramifications, ultimately leading to the sickness in the units (cases 1, 9).

(g) They must also advise the entrepreneurs to first get the samples approved by the parent units or the bulk purchasers, before going in for mass production, so as to guard against mass rejection and the adverse ramifications connected therewith (cases 1, 10, 15, 16).

(h) Bank officers should as well guide the entrepreneurs in identifying viable projects and assist them in preparing the project reports on a realistic basis. Banks should develop their own data banks on some selected industries, on an on-going basis, and have a list of other banks and institutions maintaining the data banks on some other industries. This may help the bank officers in guiding the entrepreneurs in the preparation of the project reports, as also while appraising the projects. Bank's consultancy services cell could render the necessary help and guidance, wherever required. Besides, the bank may have a panel of some reputed management consultants, to refer the prospective borrowers to, or even to consult them on some highly technical projects.

(i) Many senior retired officers of the banks and term lending institutions, with sufficient financial and technical background, were found to be keen on establishing their private consultancy services. Banks may help them in doing so by rendering them the necessary guidance and even some financial assistance, if necessary. They may as well design and conduct a short duration course for them for the purpose.

(j) The bank officers should apprise the entrepreneurs of the imminent risks, if any, in the project, which may ultimately result in the sickness of the unit. They should also counsel the entrepreneurs, wherever necessary, to start the project on a scale that they may manage effectively, and to go in for expansion and diversification after acquiring some insight and experience in the line of the business (case 1).

(k) Personal interviews with the prospective entrepreneurs would provide the bank officers with some valuable information regarding the competence and commitment of the entrepreneurs to run their units on sound lines. A visit to the factory site by the branch operating staff and an informal dialogue with other managers/workers of the unit, at the project appraisal stage, would also reveal some valuable and vital facts and facets which usually may not be available in the project report or other statements.

Assessment of Working Capital Requirements

Objectives

Prompt and realistic assessment of working capital requirements by banks is crucial for the success of a unit inasmuch as while over-financing may lead to diversion of funds and avoidable interest burden, under-financing may cause financial constraints and avoidable hardship to the unit.

Components of Working Capital

Working capital finance is required to meet the cost of production and sales so as to keep the production cycle moving on an on-going basis. It is, therefore, intended to finance the five components of the production cycle, viz.,

1. Raw Materials
2. Stocks-in-process
3. Finished Goods
4. Bills Receivable
5. Cash

Factors Determining the Quantum of Working Capital

The quantum of funds required to finance the aforesaid components of working capital depends on the nature and level of the activity of the unit and the prevailing market conditions, which are discussed hereunder:

1. Raw Materials

The amount of funds required for holding stocks of raw materials and consumable stores and spares depends on the undernoted factors:

(a) Availability of raw materials in the market and proximity to their source.
(b) Seasonal availability of raw materials.
(c) The normal lead time of delivery, i.e., average time taken for raw materials to reach the factory after an order is placed.
(d) The maximum lead time of delivery.
(e) Minimum order quantity stipulated by suppliers.
(f) The quantity that can be transported economically and the discounts on bulk orders, provided the amount saved by the bulk purchase is sufficient to cover the interest on the funds blocked.
(g) Government quotas/controls.
(h) In the case of imported raw materials, the time taken for the issuance of import licence and other relevant factors.
(i) The normal rate of consumption of raw materials, depending on the level of activity.
(j) Fluctuations in the requirements of raw materials.
(k) Seasonal peak requirements, if any.
(l) Safety level of stocks to take care of delay in supply or high consumption of raw materials to meet an urgent order.
(m) Storage facility available.
(n) Economic order quantity based on the cost considerations i.e., cost of holding the inventory versus cost of frequent ordering.

2. Stocks-in-Process

The level of stocks-in-process depends on the following

factors:

(a) Manufacturing process.
(b) Manufacturing time.
(c) Batch quantity (i.e., number of units manufactured in a batch).

3. Finished Goods

The stocking period of finished goods depends on the factors given hereunder:

(a) Delayed inspection by the government officials/customers.
(b) Time involved in the preparation of documents.
(c) Average minimum quantity of despatch.
(d) Transportation facilities.
(e) Market demand (only in the case of goods manufactured against anticipated orders).
(f) Purchasing pattern of buyers.
(g) Storage space/facility available.
(h) Seasonal demand like for firecrackers, çalendars, fans, woollens, etc.
(i) Maximum shelf life of the product, if perishable.
(j) Seasonal availability of raw materials.

4. Bills Receivable

The amount of advance required against bills receivable depends on the undernoted factors:

(a) Percentage of credit sales to total sales.
(b) Period of credit allowed as per the existing business practices.
(c) Normal realisation time as determined by the existing business practices.

Bank's Systems and Procedures for Assessment of Working Capital Requirement

The bank's instructions are clear and detailed, covering all the foregoing points, for consideration by the operating staff, while assessing the total working capital requirements. The bank has also prescribed three separate detailed loan application forms for the purpose, for different levels of such financial requirements, as discussed earlier.

As per these forms, the bank officers are required to consider the various factors for the assessment of the total working capital requirements as given in Table 6.1.

Flaws observed in the Assessment of Working Capital Requirements by the Officers of the Bank

A proper assessment of the working capital requirements by the bank depends on the realistic assessment of two main factors, viz.,

(i) Anticipated monthly sales; and
(ii) Period of stocking/payment of the various components of working capital.

On perusal of the bank's records, it was observed that in most of the cases the level of estimated sales was taken on an over-ambitious basis, as projected in the relative project reports, resulting in over-financing and extra interest burden and even diversion of funds, ultimately resulting in the sickness of the units (cases 1 to 5, 7, 8). The bank officers did not make their own independent estimates of sales, on a realistic basis, at the project appraisal stage itself, keeping in view the installed capacity, the demand for the product, the extent of competition in the market, etc.

It was further observed that the bank officers usually arrived at the total working capital requirements on an *ad hoc* basis, and thereafter computed the period of stocking/

TABLE 6.1 : Factors to be considered by the Bank Officers for the Assessment of the Total Working Capital Requirements

A.	Anticipated monthly sales	Rs. ....
B.	Cost of raw materials per month	Rs. ....
C.	Total expenses per month	Rs. ....
D.	Cost of production per month	Rs. ....

Item	Period of stocking/ payment	Working capital require-ment	Margin %	Value Rs.	Permi-ssible limit
1	2	3 Rs.	4	5 Rs.	6 = (3-5) Rs.
a. Imported raw materials	-month (s)	–	–	–	–
b. Indigenous raw materials	-months (s)	–	–	–	–
c. Stock-in process	-week (s)	–	–	–	–
d. Finished goods	-week (s)	–	–	–	–
e. Receivables	-month(s)	–	–	–	–
f. Expenses	-month (s)	–	100%	–	NIL
Total		–	–	–	–

payment so as to conform to such figures. In some cases even this exercise was not done and only the total working capital requirement was put in the assessment form.

Reasons for Such Flaws in the Assessment of Working Capital Rquirements by the Bank Officers

Personal interviews with the bank officers revealed that the system of realistic assessment of working capital requirements, though meticulously laid down by the bank, was not being followed at the branch level, mainly due to:

(i) lack of job knowledge and skills in these areas on the part of the operating staff at the branches; and
(ii) ever-increasing work-load at the branches, incommensurate with the staff strength.

Suggestions

(a) It is, therefore, suggested that the operating staff lacking in such job knowledge and skills, should be imparted the required institutional training in these areas in the bank's Staff Colleges and Staff Training Centres.
(b) On perusal of the existing curricula and programme designs of such in-house training programmes, it was observed that these were more theory based and academic in character. These should, therefore, be suitably modified so as to provide the required pragmatic orientation to the operating staff, by including more inputs by way of practical exercises, live case studies, group discussions etc., instead of the lecture method. The involved members of the faculty would do well to prepare some relevant exercises, live case studies, and a list of common discrepancies, usually found in the working capital assessment, by visiting some intensive centre branches and controlling offices.
(c) It was also observed that some of the officers, who had attended special programmes for SSI lendings, including those of high-value SSI advances, were subsequently transferred to agricultural branches or were posted in some such assignments where the training could not be put to much use. It is, therefore, suggested that, barring some exigencies

of circumstances, the post-training assignments should be so planned as to enable the trained officers to make full use of the training in their respective areas of specialisation.

The bank has prepared a comprehensive but concise *Hand Book on SIB Lendings*, covering various aspects of the conduct of SSI advances, viz., project appraisal, assessment of credit requirements, supervision and follow-up, rehabilitation of sick units, recovery of bad debts, etc.

During the course of personal interviews with the bank officers, it was found that the *Hand Book* had proved to be very informative and extremely useful for them, both at the branches and the controlling offices. They had found it handy for reference purposes, in cases of doubts. It also served as a good guide to them in their day-to-day working.

It was, however, observed that though the *Hand Book* was still in great demand by the officers concerned, all the 600 copies of its second edition, published in March 1992, were already exhausted.

It is, therefore, suggested that the bank should come out with the third edition of the *Hand Book*, by updating the instructions, wherever necessary, and print sufficient number of copies thereof, so that each and every officer of the bank, dealing with SIB (Small Industries and Small Business) lendings, may have a personal copy for his guidance and reference purposes. A sufficient number of extra copies should also be kept in stock to be promptly supplied to other officers as and when they get inducted into the work connected with SIB lendings. Such measures will provide a good back-up system to the institutional training imparted to the bank officers, and the incidence of sickness, caused by lack of experience and expertise on their part, would be curbed to a large extent.

(e) All units, including those in the small scale sector,

> enjoying working capital limits of over Rs. 10 lakh are subjected to the inventory norms stipulated by the Tandon Committee. At present, the inventory norms for 22 selected industry groups have been laid down. In case of other industry groups also similar criteria and rationale are to be followed.

However, in the cases of units having working capital requirements upto Rs. 10 lakh, the period of stocking/ payment of the various components of working capital are required to be arrived at by the bank officers on a realistic basis, keeping in view the various factors discussed earlier. The past experience of the bank officers in the cases of similar industries, and personal discussions with the borrowers would also be a good guide.

It is further suggested that, based on all such factors, the banks should build up a data bank on some selected industry groups, on an on-going basis, wherein the inventory norms, the position of demand for the product in the market, the extent of competition and such other relevant information and data could be available, for use by the operating staff.

The bank has built up such data bank in respect of a few industry groups viz., Mangalore tiles, granite, ceiling fans, bulk drugs and food processing industries, and the work in respect of some other industry groups like Kalamkari and silk reeling industries is in progress.

The concept of data bank has proved to be of practical utility to the operating staff. It is, therefore, suggested that other banks should also initiate such good work, if not already done. It would also be a good idea for all the banks, specially in the public sector, to coordinate amongst themselves such that each bank may undertake the task of building up data banks in respect of different selected industry groups, most relevant for the particular region, and these information/data should be freely shared and exchanged amongst themselves. The Reserve Bank of India or the Indian Banks' Association (IBA) could undertake the responsibility of coordinating such activity.

(f) As regards the problem of paucity of staff, the bank may consider the desirability of suitably augementing the staff strength, particularly of the field staff, at the branches, specially at the intensive centre branches, based on the merit of each case.

(g) The other strategy could be to reduce the work-load at the branches, wherever possible, specially at the intensive centre branches. One such strategy could be to take a policy decision not to entertain any small loan under the government sponsored schemes like Self-Employment Scheme for Educated Unemployed Youth (SEEUY), Self-Employment Programme for Urban Poor (SEPUP) etc., at intensive centre branches, already burdened with high-value SSI advances. Such schemes could, however, be financed by other neighbouring branches of the bank. This would be on the similar principle on which the bank has recently set up an Industrial Finance branch in Hyderabad exclusively for the borrowers having financial requirements of Rs. 1 crore and above.

Phased Disbursement of Loans

Objective

The objective of phased disbursement of loans is to ensure the end use of funds. The bank officers are, therefore, required to disburse the working capital loans in a phased manner, in accordance with the gradual increase in the scale of operations of the units and the levels of their stocks of inventory and book debts. Due care is to be taken to avoid double financing of goods supplied on credit. Further, term loans are required to be disbursed in instalments commensurate with the progress made in the implementation of the project.

Flaws in the Disbursement of Loans by the Bnak Officers

On perusal of the bank accounts of sick units under study, it was observed that in most cases the bank officers had allowed the entrepreneurs to withdraw the entire amount of the working capital loans soon after these were sanctioned to them, resulting in avoidable extra interest burden on them. Further, most of them had resorted to diversion of funds, i.e., short term sources of funds (working capital loan) for long term uses, e.g. for acquiring fixed assets or for unplanned expansion/diversification (cases 1, 2, 4, 5, 7, 8, 20, 21). This had led to the problem of paucity of working fund, adversely affecting the operating cycle with other ramifications, ultimately resulting in their sickness, beyond rehabilitation. In some cases it was observed that though the entrepreneurs had stated in the application form that the required quantum of own fund (equity) would be invested by them in the venture, they actually did not do so in full measure, or else they later gradually withdrew their own fund from the business. In one case the bank officers had advanced against goods supplied on credit (case 12).

Suggestions

(a) It is, therefore, suggested that the bank officers should allow drawings in the working capital loan accounts in a phased manner, commensurate with the gradual increase in the scale of operations of the units and the levels of their stocks of inventory and book debts. This way, they would be able to ensure the end use of funds and guard against the risk of diversion of funds by the entrepreneurs.

(b) Further, the bank officers should get the required margin money for working capital loans deposited with the bank in the accounts of the units before releasing the loan amount to them. The margin money so deposited by the entrepreneurs should also be reflected in their books of accounts.

(c) Besides, while encashing cheques, specially those drawn in favour of the entrepreneurs and/or in round thousands, the bank officers would do well to satisfy themselves, beyond doubt, that the amount was being withdrawn for genuine business transactions and not for the purpose of siphoning off of the entrepreneurs' own fund from the business.

(d) Due care must be taken by the bank officers to avoid double financing against the goods supplied to the units on credit.

(e) Term loans, of course, should be disbursed in instalments, commensurate with the stages of progress in the implementation of the project. Payments should preferably be made direct to the suppliers of machinery, etc. Proportionate amount of margin for term loans should be got deposited with the bank before disbursement of each instalment.

These suggestions are based on the fact unless the entrepreneurs would start the venture with sufficient capital base of their own, they would not have sustained commitment and initial financial difficulties and operating losses.

Supervision and Follow-up of Advances and Performance Monitoring of the Units

Objectives

The objectives of post-sanction supervision and follow-up of advances are:

(a) To check the end use of funds.

(b) To verify the quantity and quality of assets charged

to the bank and to ensure that the outstandings in the accounts are covered by security of adequate value.

(c) To assess the health of the unit and to take timely preventive or corrective measures where called for.

Types of Supervision and Follow-up

Such supervision and follow-up could broadly be classified under two categories, viz.

1. Quantitative or Security Oriented.
2. Qualitative or Activity Oriented.

1. Quantitative or Security Oriented Supervision and Follow-up

This helps the bank officers to ensure that:

(a) the condition of the factory premises, machinery and equipment financed by the bank is in order,
(b) the machinery is intact and in good working condition,
(c) the stocks of inventory charged to the bank are adequate to cover the outstandings in the account, and
(d) the insurance cover is adequate

The stocks of inventory charged to the bank are to be verified with the latest stock statements.

2. Qualitative or Activity Oriented Supervision and Follow-up

It is heartening to note that the emphasis on the bank's supervision and follow-up of advances has undergone a healthy change, from security-based inspection to activity-based supervision, from mere physical verification of assets to the monitoring.of performance of the units.

The key indicators of performance are the levels of activity (production and sales) and profitability of the units. The bank has, therefore, laid down the following guidelines for the inspecting officers:

(a) Unit's books of accounts like cash book, sales, purchase and stock registers, should be maintained properly and kept up-to-date and correct. Invoices may be checked by the inspecting officers at random, to know the mode of purchase (credit or cash basis), and terms of purchase.
(b) Stocks should be regularly turned over. If there is any accumulation of slow-moving/non-moving items of finished goods, semi-finished goods and raw materials, reasons therefor should be enquired into.
(c) Where the number of items charged to the bank is large, the inspecting officers may check such items on the principle of 'ABC Analysis', whereby all 'A' class (high value) items are to be checked thoroughly during each visit. A certain percentage of 'B' and 'C' class items, however, may be checked during each visit so that all such items may be covered within say six months. Goods should be stocked according to sizes, weight, lots, groups, etc., to facilitate the inspection.
(d) Stocks-in-process should be in proportion to the time for conversion of raw materials into finished goods.
(e) Activity level may be assessed from the order book, daily production register, general tempo of activity in the unit, number of shifts, etc.
(f) Outstandings in loan accounts should be related to the activity level, and actual activity levels should

be compared with the projected levels. Reasons for major adverse variance, if any, should be enquired into. Debit and credit summations on the accounts are also good indicators of the levels of production and sales of the units.

(g) When there is a decline in sales, production and profitability, the reasons therefor should be ascertained.

(h) Idle machinery, rejected items, and additions or disposal of fixed assets, should also be checked.

(i) Unit's accounts should be scrutinised periodically and where the accounts are irregular due to non-payment of instalments or excess drawings, the entrepreneurs should be promptly advised to regularise the position urgently.

(j) Bills outstanding in Cash Credit (Bills)' account beyond a reasonable period (depending on lead time and transit time) need enquiry.

(k) Sales through associate or sister concerns and the bills drawn on them for the purpose should be monitored with extra care.

(l) The reasons for the return of bills or undue delay in their payments should be enquired into.

(m) Bills outstanding in the bank's book should be compared and cross checked with the unit's bills receivable registers.

(n) The position of orders, pending, being executed and anticipated, should be enquired into and matched with the production and sales. This should be followed up in subsequent inspections.

(o) The inspecting officers should discuss with the entrepreneurs the general trend in the market, the unit's problems regarding supply of raw materials, labour and infrastructural facilities, performance of the unit's competitors, future plans etc., and share their own experiences of other similar units. This would give them a clue to the imminent problems, if any, of the unit.

(p) Surplus cash generated and its utilisation and the management of cash and working capital should be monitored.

(q) Where goods are stored in different places, inspection of all the godowns should be conducted simultaneously on the same day.

(r) Market enquiries may also be made about the unit.

(s) Inspection card/register should be filled in after each inspection.

(t) All units should be advised to maintain visit books at the place of business and the inspecting officers should note down the irregularities observed during the inspection. On return to the bank, the entrepreneurs should be advised in writing about the irregularities observed with a request to set right the position immediately. During the next visit, attention should be paid to check the progress made in regard to the rectification of the irregularities observed, during the previous visits.

The above instructions of the bank, regarding periodical supervision and follow-up of advances, are considered sufficiently detailed, clear and effective, with a view to ensuring the safety of the bank's advances and the health of the units, on an on-going basis. The bank has also been reasonable in stipulating that such detailed supervision and follow-up were required to be done by the inspecting officers in cases of advances of over Rs. 2 lakh.

Frequency of Inspection

The frequency of inspections, for different quantum of advances, has been fixed by the bank as under:

Quantum of Advances		Frequency of Inspection
1, Loans upto Rs. 25,000	-	Once in 3 months by Field Officers
2. Loans above Rs. 25,000 and upto Rs. 2 lakh	-	Once in 2 months by Field Officers
3. Lons above Rs. 2 lakh	-	Monthly by Field Officers

Branch Managers (of branches with SIB Division, SIB Brnahces and Special branches), and Managers/Dy. Managers of SIB Division are also required to inspect the units with loans above Rs. 5 lakh once in 9 months and 6 months respectively.

For the first four months of disbursement of the loan, however, the inspection is required to be done by the Field Officers monthly in all the cases, inasmuch as more than ordinary care needs to be exercised to monitor the activities of the new units and to rectify the initial difficulties, if any.

In case of unsatisfactory accounts, the inspection is required to be carried out at shorter intervals, irrespective of the loan amounts, till the units are nursed back to health or the loans are called up and recovered.

The Branch Manager is required to verify the Inspection Register each month to find out the units not inspected during the previous month and to ensure that such units are inspected during the current month. He is also required to submit to the controlling authority, at half-yearly intervals (in March and September), a list of units with outstandings of over Rs. 2 lakh, not inspected during the last two quarters, indicating the date of last inspection, the reasons for the delay, and the plan of action proposed to rectify the position.

Flaws observed in the Supervision and Follow-up Advances by Bank Officers

The systems and procedures laid down by the bank for supervision and follow-up of advances, as discussed in the foregoing pages, are found to be sufficiently exhaustive and clear with a view to detecting early signals of sickness, and arresting and rectifying the malady in time, at the incipient stage itself, so that all the units financed by the bank could perform on healthy lines, on an on-going basis. But there seems to be something significantly wanting in the implementation of these systems and procedures by the bank officers, as has been revealed from the facts of the foregoing cases of sick units given hereunder:

(a) In all the cases of non-viable units, the stocks of inventory, charged to the bank, had got depleted, completely or substantially, over a period of time (cases 1 to 12, 20, 21).

(b) In a majority of the cases the bank officers had allowed frequent overdrawings on the accounts, well above the sanctioned limit and drawing power (cases 1 to 14, 18, 19, 21).

Reasons for lack of Effective Supervision and Follow-up of Advances by the Bank Officers

Personal interviews with the bank officers, both at the branches and controlling offices, revealed that the extant instructions regarding the supervision and follow-up of advances were not being meticulously and effectively followed by the bank officers at the branches for several reasons, viz.

1. Lack of job knowledge and skills on the part of the Field Officers.
2. Paucity of Field Officers to cope with the ever increasing work-load at the branches.
3. Lack of willingness on the part of the Field Officers to inspect the units periodically, as stipulated by the bank.
4. Lack of efforts on the part of the bank officers to

apprise the entrepreneurs of the adverse effects and ramifications of non-adherence to the bank's financial discipline.

Suggestions

1. Suggestions for Improving the Job Knowledge and Skills of the Field Officers

(a) It is suggested that the bank should impart institutional training to the Field Officers, lacking in the job knowledge and skills in the areas of supervision and follow-up of advances. These areas may be covered in the special courses for SSI advances also with a shift in the emphasis from imparting conceptual knowledge through theoretical lectures, as at present, to developing the required skills and pragmatic approach through practical exercises, live cases, and visits to the units.

(b) Besides the institutional training, Branch Managers and Managers (SIB Division) should invest some of their valuable time in imparting practical training to the Field Officers. They should, for the first few months, take the Field Officers along, while going for inspection of some units, for imparting on-the-job training to them. This way the Managers would become '*Gurus*' (teachers) to the members of the staff, and would enjoy 'personal power' in addition to their 'positions power', making them more effective in the discharge of their managerial role and responsibility.

2. Suggestions for Solving the Problems of Paucity of Field Officers at the Branches

The problems of paucity of Field Officers at the branches may better be tackled by the bank from two directions simultaneously:

1. By suitably augmenting the strength of the Field Officers at the branches.
2. By rationally reducing the work-load of the Field Officers.

I. (a) It is, therefore, suggested that the required number of additional Field Officers should be posted at the branches, specially at the intensive centre branches, having sufficient number of units enjoying credit limits of over Rs. 2 lakh, so that each Field Officer may be required to effectively supervise only a limited number of units, as stipulated by the bank.

(b) Personal interviews with the bank officers revealed that at some branches, specially at the urban and metropolitan centres, the staff position was rather comfortable, as compared to most of the branches in the semi-urban and rural areas. It is, therefore, suggested that the bank should rationally deploy the staff amongst its branches.

(c) Now that the post of the Field Officer does not attract any additional allowance, the bank may as well consider the desirability of promoting some suitable junior officers as Field Officers, after duly training and equipping them for the job.

II. With a view to rationally reducing the work-load of the Field Officers, the bank may consider the following suggestions:

(a) Small loans under the government sponsored schemes like SEEUY, SEPUP, etc., may not be encouraged at the intensive centre branches, already burdened with high-value SSI advances. Such advances may, instead, be diverted to other neighbouring branches. Siphoning off of such existing small loans from the intensive centre branches to some neighbouring branches may as well be considered. This would save sufficient time of the Field Officers at the intensive centre branches to effectively supervise other SSI advances of higher value.

(b) Further, while the Field Officers may be required to supervise the advances of say over Rs. 50,000, the supervision and follow-up of the other smaller advances say upto Rs. 50,000 may be delegated to other junior officers.

(c) Moreover, the frequency of inspection of the units by the Field Officers may be modified on the lines suggested in Table 6.2.

TABLE 6.2.: Present and Proposed Frequencies of Inspection of the Units by the Field Officers

Quantum of Loans	Present Frequency of Inspection	Propsed Frequency of Inspection
(i) Loans upto Rs. 25,000	Once in 3 months	Once in say 6 months
(ii) Loans above Rs. 25,000 and upto Rs. 50,000	Once in 2 months	Once in say 4 months
(iii) Loans above Rs.50,000 and upto Rs. 2 lakh	Once in 2 months	Once in say 3 months
(iv) Loans above Rs. 2 lakh and upto Rs. 5 lakh	Once in 1 month	Once in say 2 months
(v) Loans above Rs. 5 lakh	Once in 1 month	No change suggested

(d) In addition, the branches may categorise their advances into –

(i) satisfactory,
(ii) temporarily irregular, and

(iii) sick.

and gradually increase the rigour of their supervision and follow-up accordingly.

3. *Suugestions for Enforcing Discipline among the Field Officers*

(a) Insincere and recalcitrant Field Officers deserve to be dealt with firmly. Where persuasion fails, punitive measures must prevail. Any dereliction of duty needs to be dealt with severely.

(b) Branch Managers should not pass the TA bills of the Field Officers without perusing their Inspection Diary and satisfying themselves that the necessary corrective steps have been initiated by the Field Officers, wherever necessary.

4. *Suggestions for Enforcing the Bank's Financial Discipline on the Entrepreneurs*

(a) It is suggested that the bank officers should apprise the prospective entrepreneurs of the dangers and adverse ramifications of diversion of funds, frequent and excess over-drawings on the account, and such other violations of the bank's financial discipline, and counsel them to guard against them.

(b) It would also be a good idea to arrange a one-day seminar (a banker-borrower meet), branch-wise, in the branch premises or in some hotel. It would serve as a good forum for an interface between the branch staff and the borrowers enabling them, to appreciate the problems of, and expectations from, each other. The presence of the Regional Manager or the Administrative Officer (Advances) in such meet would give the controlling office a first-hand feedback regarding the position of advances at the branch and the practical difficulties being experienced by the borrowers in the small scale sector.

(c) Regional Managers and Deputy General Managers, during the course of their periodical visits to the branches, would do well to visit some high value SSI units and discuss the problems and prospects with the borrowers. This way the borrowers will feel that they are being cared for by the bank, and the Regional Managers and the Deputy General Managers would get to know of the unsatisfactory features, if any, attached with the advances.

5. *Suggestions for Streamlining the Bank's Performance Monitoring of the Units and Management Information System (MIS)*

With a view to streamlining the bank's system of performance monitoring, a follow-up form may be introduced by the bank on the lines of the suggested proforma placed at *Appendix I.* The proforma contains three parts:

Part I: Control Card (The Unit at a Glance)

It contains the particulars about the unit, relevant for the effective control and security of the advance. It may be got printed on a hard paper and placed in the relative files of the units,for perusal and review of the position of their accounts by the bank's inspecting officers at regular quarterly intervals.

Part II: Performance Monitoring of the Unit

This part includes the main indicators of the unit's performance, viz., levels of activity (production, sales, etc), profitability, cash management, liquidity position, etc., and is required to be compiled by the bank's inspecting officers.

Part III: Quarterly Information System (QIS Form)

This part also contains all the particulars provided in Part II, except item No. 5 (v), and is required to be submitted by the borrowers to the Branch Manager at regular quarterly intervals. This would give a meaningful feedback to the entrepreneurs also as to in which area(s) they were faltering.

Further, keeping in view the quantum of work at the branches, it is suggested that such statements may be submitted only by the units enjoying aggregate credit limits of over Rs. 2 lakh and that, too, at regular quarterly intervals. These statements should be thoroughly and meaningfully examined at the branch level and need not be sent to the controlling office. Any adverse features observed therein should be looked into and necessary remedial measures initiated in consultation with the borrowers concerned. Such regular performance monitoring undertaken, both by the bank and the borrower, and timely corrective actions taken, in mutual cooperation of each other, may go a long way in arresting the incidence of sickness in the small scale sector.

Timely Detection of Early Symptoms of Sickness

Objective

The objective of timely detection of early symptoms of sickness by the bank officers is to enable them to take timely corrective actions in close coordination with the borrowers, so as to remedy the malady at the incipient stage itself.

Reserve Bank of India, in their circular letter dated January 3, 1987, have therefore, advised all the banks that "a culture of identifying the sickness symptoms of assisted units and rendering possible assistance with speed has to be enforced to prevent increasing sickness due to delays and consequent burden to the borrowers and losses to the bank".

Symptoms of Sickness

Symptoms of sickness can be detected in the following areas :

1. Conduct of the Bank Accounts of the Units

(i) Non-routing of the sale proceeds through the account i.e., credit summations in the account are not commensurate with the total sales.
(ii) Frequent requests for excess drawings.
(iii) Non-payment of term loan instalments.
(iv) Non-payment of interest applied periodically.
(v) Irregular or non-submission or delayed submission of stock statements or financial statements.
(vi) Frequent removal of bills from the cover.
(vii) Frequent dishonour of bills or cheques.
viii) Raising of accommodations bills or cheques.
(ix) Progressive reduction in the number and amount of bills lodged with the bank.
(x) Repetition of the same items in the stock statements or in the list of sundry debtors, indicating non-movement of stocks and poor recovery of sundry debtors.

2. Levels of Activities of the Units

A. Production

(i) Low capacity utilisation (of both men and machines).
(ii) Frequent closure of the units.
(iii) Fluctuations in the capacity utilisation in non-seasonal activities.
(iv) High internal rate of rejection of products.
(v) Inadequate maintenance of machinery, resulting in

frequent break-downs.

B. Sales

(i) Decrease in sales turnover.
(ii) Inability to meet delivery schedule.
(iii) Frequent customer complaints.
(iv) High external rate of rejection of products.
(v) Non-moving/non-usable stocks.

3. Financial Indicators

(i) Negative liquid surplus (i.e., current ratio less than one).
(ii) Increase in sundry creditors/sundry debtors.
(iii) Increase in debt/equity ratio.
(iv) Decrease in net profit to sales ratio.
(v) External borrowings at exorbitant rates of interest.
(vi) Excessive drawings by the Promoters or Directors.
(vii) Changing pattern of cash to credit sales.
(viii) Non-payment of statutory dues.
(ix) Sale of fixed assets.

Reasons or Non-detection of Early Symptoms of Sickness by the Bank Officers

Personal interviews with the bank officers revealed that the branch field staff avoided to record and refer such unsatisfactory features to the higher authorities as it involved more work for them by way of closer performance monitoring of such units failing which they could be held personally responsible by the bank.

Personal interviews with the entrepreneurs revealed that instead of discussing their genuine problems and financial difficulties with the bank officers freely and frankly, they preferred to conceal them, at the initial stages, apprehending that the bank may adopt a strict and unhelpful attitude towards them.

In the process, the small malady, not tackled and remedied at the incipient stage, kept on accumulating and ultimately the units became non-viable, beyond rehabilitation, to the mutual detriment of the bank and the borrowers.

Suggestions

(a) It is, therefore, suggested that the bank officers should work in close coordination with the entrepreneurs, in an atmosphere of mutual trust and confidence, and with the positive attitude of timely and sustained help and cooperation towards each other, based on the genuineness of the problem and sincerity of purpose. The bank officers may, however, bear in mind that the symptoms of sickness, discussed earlier, are sometimes found even in healthy units. They may, therefore, take suitable action, based on the merit of each case.

(b) Further, the cases of dereliction of duty on the part of the operating staff, in regard to detection of early symptoms of sickness and initiation of suitable remedial measures in time, should be severely dealt with by the bank.

Supervision and Control of the Irregularities in the Advances at the Branches by the Controlling Authority

Objectives

The objectives of the system of reporting the irregularities in the advances, by the branches to the controlling authority, at periodical intervals, are :

(a) To provide the controlling authority with the total

picture of the position regarding the irregular accounts at the branches for control and monitoring purposes.

(b) To enable the controlling authority to help and guide the branches in taking some further suitable corrective measures, in addition to the ones already initiated by the branch staff, to regularise the position of the accounts and to keep the interest of the bank, as also that of the borrowers, safeguarded at all times.

Periodical Stagements on Irregular Accounts Required to be Submitted by the Branches to the Controlling Authority

Branches are required to submit to the controlling authority a detailed statement on all irregular accounts, containing all relevant particulars, at regular quarterly intervals as on the last Friday of each quarter.

The under-noted types of irregular accounts are required to be reported:

(a) All accounts which were irregular during the quarter, even though standing regularised as on the date of the statement, must be reported.

(b) In case of loans upto Rs. 25,000, a summary of irregular accounts is required to be enclosed to the main statement.

(c) Accounts which were irregular merely due to application of interest need not be reported.

(d) A separate summary of loans upto Rs. 25,000 which were persistently irregular for more than three quarters, inclusive of accounts which were irregular for more than three quarters due to application of interest, is required to be enclosed to the quarterly statement of June every year.

Rationale behind the Submission of the Statements

(a) The rationale behind the submission of such detailed statements is to enable the controlling ofice to exercise an effective control over the advances at the branches.

(b) All irregularities on the accounts during the quarter are required to be reported, even though such accounts may stand regularised as on the date of the statement, so as to guard against manipulations or unauthorised accommodations, etc., if resorted to at the branches.

(c) Further, based on the principle of "Management by Exception", all advances irregular only due to application of interest are exempt, and only a summary of irregular advances of small amount, i.e., upto Rs. 25,000, is called for.

(d) A separate summary of such small advances irregular for three consecutive quarters is required inasmuch as the persistent irregularity itself could be indicative of the imminent sickness of such units.

Reasons for Non-submission of the Statements

It thus appears that the bank's system of control is well designed and well intentioned. But, as revealed by the bank records, the system was, of late, not working well, inasmuch as most of the branches were not submitting the statements. Personal interviews with the bank officers of various levels revealed the undernoted reasons for non-submission of the statements by the branches.

(a) The number of accounts with credit limits above Rs. 25,000 had substantially increased.

(b) The number and extent of irregularities on such accounts were on the rise.

(c) Reporting of all irregularities, whether material or

marginal, during the quarter, on all accounts above Rs. 25,000, even if subsequently adjusted, involved substantial quantum of work. Besides, the Branch Managers feared that even small and unintended omissions could be termed by the controlling office as a wilful concealment of facts.

Under the circumstances, the non-submission of the statements was considered by the branches to be the easier and safer option.

Suggestions

During the course of discussions with the bank officers, it was gathered that the controlling office, in its over-anxiety to exercise rather absolute control over the advances at the branches, was gradually loosening its grip thereon. It was generally felt that the system of control, prevalent in the sixties and seventies, may not necessarily prove effective in the nineties, too. The circumstances have changed. The delegation of power of the bank officers has recently been suitably revised upward to cope with the ever increasing quantum of advances to the small scale sector. The level of trust reposed in the bank officers also needs to go up accordingly. Consequently, the extent of control over the branches by the controlling office may be reduced suitably, somewhat on the lines suggested hereunder:

(a) Only the undernoted category of irregular accounts may be reported in detail by the branches to the controlling office as on the last Friday of each quarter :

All accounts with credit limits of over Rs. 50,000, standing irregular as on the date of the statement by more than 10% of the amount of the sanctioned limit or in excess of a specified amount, given hereunder, whichever is lower :

(i) Say Rs. 1,00,000 in case of special branches
(ii) Say Rs. 50,000 in case of Category 'A' branches
(iii) Say Rs. 30,000 in case of Category 'B' branches
(iv) Say Rs. 20,000 in case of Category 'C' branches
(v) Say Rs.10,000 in case of Category 'D' branches

(b) Irregularities due to application of interest for the quarter in question may not be reported.

(c) Irregularities allowed during the quarter, within the discretionary powers of the Branch Manager, and subsequently rectified as on the date of the statement, may not be reported.

(d) Irregularities allowed on the accounts beyond the discretionary powers of the Branch Manager, however, may continue to be reported separately in each case, for reporting and ratification purposes.

(e) In the case of loans upto Rs. 50,000, a summary of accounts irregular by more than 10% of the sanctioned limit may be enclosed to the main statement.

(f) All irregular accounts not reported in the statements must be got rectified at the branch level within a reasonable period, under the direct supervision of the Branch Manager and the Manager of the Division.

(g) A separate summary of loans upto Rs. 50,000, which are persistently irregular for more than three quarters, inclusive of accounts which are irregular for more than three quarters due to application of interest, should be enclosed to the quarterly statement of June every year.

(h) In the case of such persistently irregular accounts of over Rs. 50,000, each case must be reported to the controlling office separately, with reasoned recommendations whether to treat the unit as sick or otherwise, and if declared sick whether considered viable for rehabilitation or rated as non-viable, justifying calling up of the loan. The required action must also be initiated promptly.

The suggested changes in the quarterly statements of irregular accounts, excluding smaller accounts and smaller irregularities in other accounts, would considerably reduce the quantum of work involved, facilitating its submission by the branches regularly and thereby ensuring effective control of the advances by the controlling office. Further, the non-submission or inordinately delayed submission of these statements must be taken up with the defaulting branches strongly and dealt with severely.

Rehabilitation of Viable Units by the Bank

Objectives

The objective of the bank's rehabilitation programme is to bring the sick units back to health by restoring their capacity to generate internal surplus.

Eligibility Criteria for Rehabilitation

The units which satisfy the following criteria are to be considered for rehabilitation by the bank:

(a) The entrepreneurs' dealings with the bank in the past should have been satisfactory and above board. There should have been no serious negative features connected with the advance like diversion of funds, or neglect of the business. Besides, the entrepreneurs should be fully committed to the enterprise and sincerely interested in the revival of the unit.

(b) The unit should be potentially viable, i.e.,

(i) It should be able to generate sufficient surplus to repay the loans within a reasonable time, after the initiation of the rehabilitation programme, i.e., within 3 years in the case of tiny, village and cottage industries, and within 5 to 7 years in other cases.

(ii) Period of reliefs and concessions should not exceed 2 years in the case of tiny, village and cottage industries, and 5 years in other cases.

Factors to be Considered for Taking a Rehabilitation Decision

Rehabilitation programme is a medium term plan to overcome the weaknesses of a sick industrial unit and to face the threats by cashing on the strengths and opportunities available to it. Such a plan of action involves due consideration of the following factors:

(a) Identification of the causes of sickness of the unit.

(b) Analysis of the past performance of the unit from its financial statements, its books of accounts and its bank accounts.

(c) Study of the functional aspects like product, market, technology, cost structure, pricing, overheads and organisational set-up. This, together with the analysis of the past performance, will help in the identification of the causes of sickness of the unit as also its strengths, weaknesses, opportunities and threats.

(d) Evaluation of the present position of the unit and the financial implications thereof to the bank. This may be done by preparing a provisional balance sheet and the statement of clean drawings.

(e) Determination of a viable level of operation which will generate sufficient internal surplus to repay the loans. The new break-even point will naturally be higher than the previous break-even point.

(f) Drawing up of a time-bound action plan for regularising the position of the bank accounts.

(g) Identification of the key performance indicators for close monitoring with particular reference to the areas of weakness and threats.

The bank officers concerned should exercise due care, patience and understanding, while taking a rehabilitation decision, so as to avoid any error or *ad-hoc* decisions. Other financial institutions, if any, should also be involved in the formulation and implementation of the rehabilitation programmes.

Performance Monitoring of the Rehabilitation Programmes

The success of the rehabilitation programmes largely depends on the close monitoring of the performance of the units, on all the critical area, as identified in the plans. The general guidelines for the performance monitoring of the units, under the bank's rehabilitation programme, are given hereunder :

(a) Management Information Systems (MIS): A monthly report on the working of the unit is required to be submitted by the entrepreneurs to the Branch Manager who, in turn, forwards the same, along with his comments, to the controlling office, on the proforma placed at Appendix II. The main indicators reported in the proforma include the level of activity (i.e., production, sales, etc.) profitability, cash management, position of various accounts, and the liquidity position of the unit.

(b) The achievement of the various budgeted goals, drawn up by the entrepreneurs, in consultation with the bank, are to be reviewed monthly, with a view to ensuring the end use of funds. Significant adverse variances, if any, are to be enquired into and suitable remedial measures taken.

(c) A meeting between the bank and the entrepreneurs is to be arranged every month with a view to assessing the progress and rectifying the adverse features, if any, in time.

(d) The assistance of the bank's Consultancy Services Cell may as well be sought whenever considered necessary.

Attitudinal Aspects of Rehabiliation

Reserve Bank of India in their letter dated the 3rd January 1987 have advised the banks as under:

> "In regard to sick units, particularly in the small scale sector, it was observed that in a number of cases although units were found to be viable, they were not placed under nursing programme. It need hardly be emphasised that under such circumstances, even a potentially viable unit is likely to become non-viable if timely assistance is not offered.
>
> "Further, it was observed that a very large number of units has been classified as non-viable. This is a matter of anxiety and the classification needs a second look at the appropriate level after taking into account all the relevant factors".

During the course of the study and personal interview with the bank officers, it was observed that some of the viable units, for want of timely and proper assistance, ultimately became non-viable, due to some delay on the part of the bank. It was also gathered that most of the bank officers usually preferred to declare marginal cases as non-viable inasmuch as such decisions were found to be easier and safer in that the matter almost ended by calling up the advances and filing civil suits against the units. As against this, the decision to rehabilitate the sick units involved a higher risk and extra work by way of an indepth viability study of the units, preparation of comprehensive rehabilitation programmes and, above all, a closer and regular monthly performance monitoring of the units. Such negative attitude on the part of the bank officers would be detrimental to the mutual interest of the bank and the borrowers.

(A) The Profile of Bank Officers Facilitating the Rehabilitation of Sick Units

A proper and positive, healthy and helpful, attitude on the part of the bank officers, at all levels, is one of the most important prerequisites for drawing up a comprehensive rehabilitation programme and for its earnest implementation and success.

It is heartening to note that the desired positive attitude and attributes were also found in some bank officers, both at the branches and the controlling offices, as has been gathered from the bank records and correspondence files pertaining to the cases 13 to 19, as also from the personal interviews with the bank officers.

Profile of such bank officer is given hereunder

(a) He listens to the problems and plights of the entrepreneurs of sick units with patience, compassion and empathy.
(b) He identifies and analyses the causes of sickness in the unit, and examines and explores the possibility whether the unit can be rehabilitated, by carrying out a detailed SWOT (Strength, Weakness, Opportunity and Threat) analysis of the unit.
(c) He conducts a thorough study of the technical feasibility and economic viability of the unit, *de novo*, with care and commitment to revive the unit.
(d) He collects all relevant information and data so as to consider the various dimensions of the problem and to explore possible solutions thereto.
(e) He allows sufficient time for the study. He works

with patience and perseverance, and believes in doing a thorough job of preparing a comprehensive rehabilitation programme, which may usually succeed in the long run (cases 13 to 19). He also knows well that such programmes, finalised in a hurry and on an *ad-hoc* basis, may ultimately fail (cases 20 and 21).

(f) He, at the same time, realises that any avoidable delay in such cases may make a viable sick unit as non-viable, if timely help is not provided. He, therefore, does not procrastinate and, instead, takes a quick (though not rash) decisions in such matters.

(g) He appreciates that rehabilitation of a sick unit is not a short term affair and, therefore, he never expects that the irregularity on the account would be rectified soon. He realises that revival of a sick unit is a medium term programme which may usually take 3 to 5 years or even 7 years in some cases, before the unit may be completely rehabilitated back to health.

(h) He accepts that a rehabilitation programme, instead of reducing the outstandings on the account, may even mean larger investments by the bank in most cases. He also knows that the programme may not always run as per the expectations and the budgeted levels. There may, instead, be some set- back in the unit and consequent deterioration in the account. He, therefore, restraints himself from imposing some sudden restrictions on the drawings on the account, etc. He, instead, acts patiently and takes a proper, pragmatic and courageous course of action, most suited for steering the unit out of the current difficulties.

(i) He is objective, rational and unbiased in his approach. If there had been some irregular and unsatisfactory features in the conduct of the account in the past, like discounting of bills or deposit of sale proceeds through other banks, he does not get permanently prejudiced against the entrepreneurs. He, instead, examines the reasons therefor with an unbiased and free mind, and if these are found genuine, he prefers to recommend rehabilitation of viable units, instead of calling up such advances on the grounds of the aforesaid lapses on the part of the entrepreneurs.

(j) He is consistent in the implementation of the programmes once these have been evolved and accepted by the bank. He takes these as the bank's programmes and, therefore, implements the programmes prepared by his predecessors also with equal zeal, care and commitment.

(k) He is clear in his mind that the rehabilitation of a sick unit is not a zero-risk proposition. He is dynamic and courageous enough to take fair banking risk. He takes personal pride and experiences tremendous satisfaction in the revival of the units back to health (cases 13 to 19), and thereby boosts the confidence and morale of other entrepreneurs, both present and prospective.

(l) He is also confident of the positive and reasonable approach of his controlling authority and is convinced that he would not be unnecessarily held personally responsible in the event of the failure of rehabilitation programme, provided suitable actions and precautions were taken in the case, as far as possible, keeping in view the genuine difficulties, constraints and limitations, and above all, the unforeseen circumstances, beyond the control of the bank and the borrower.

Suggestions

(a) It is well known that the prompt action by the bank officers is crucial for the rehabilitation of a sick unit.

When the necessary remedial measures taken at the incipient stage of sickness fail to produce the desired results, the unit should be declared as sick within a reasonable time. A detailed viability study, including the economic viability and technical feasibility, should be undertaken by the bank officers expeditiously.If the unit is found viable for rehabilitation, a comprehensive (not *ad-hoc*) rehabilitation package should be promptly formulated by the bank, in close coordination with the borrower, which must be implemented expeditiously, coupled with more regorous performance monitoring, at regular monthly intervals, till the unit regains its normal health. In case, however, the unit is found non-viable for rehabilitation, the loan should be called up by the bank and legal action initiated without avoidable delay.

(b) The study has revealed that the officers of the commercial banks, though expected to discharge the functions as development bankers, are still functioning as the traditional lenders of money. They mostly restrict their role to the routine assessment of the credit requirements of the units, and disbursal of the loan amount. The operational working of the units is still considered to be the exclusive responsibility of the units. The banks are, at best, interested in the security and repayment of the loans, after the unit gets sick and defunct. This traditional and routine approach must change. The officers of the commercial banks should, therefore, assume an innovative role of true development bankers by treating the SSI units, financed by them, as the joint ventures of both the bank and the borrowers. With such positive approach and attitude, they should closely monitor the performance of the unit at regular intervals, on an on-going basis. They would thus develop the sensitivity and techniques of detecting early signals of sickness at the incipient stage itself, and would initiate the required remedial measures, with willing cooperation and close coordination with the borrowers, in a healthy atmosphere of mutual trust and confidence. Further, if the unit ultimately fell sick, they would be positively and favourably disposed towards undertaking the rehabilitation of the unit and would strive hard to put it back on healthy lines, and would experience a sense of pride and achievement in the process.

(c) The present system of performance appraisal of the bank officers is based on the number of new accounts brought to the books and the quantum of such new loans sanctioned and disbursed. Thus, the quantitative aspect of lending gets over-emphasised and the qualitative aspect tends to take a back seat. It is, therefore, suggested that a suitably ammended performance appraisal system of reward and punishment, should be evolved by the bank.

Under the revised system, an officer should be given commendable remarks and higher ratings in his annual confidential report (ACR) if the incidence of sickness in the units financed by him are negligible or of a reasonably lower order, say five per cent. Similarly, in case the extent of sickness happens to be of an unreasonably higher order, suitable adverse remarks must be given in the ACR of the officer concerned, affecting his future promotions and prospects in the organisation.

A reasonable margin for honest and genuine mistakes has been suggested, keeping in view the fact that even if due care and precautions are taken, some units may fall sick, all the same, for some reason or the other, beyond the control of the bank officers and the borrowers.

This way the officers of the bank would exercise greater care and attention at the various stages of advance viz. project appraisal, assessment of credit needs, disbursement of loan, supervision and follow-up of the advance and conduct of the account, periodical performance monitoring of the unit, etc. They would also get alerted at the appearance of the early signals of sickness, and would take the necessary remedial measures, in time, so as to bring the unit back to health.

The new performance appraisal system should also have suitable parameters of reward and punishment to assess the performance of the officers in terms of the positive attitude and sincere efforts made in regard to rehabilitation of sick units. This way the extent and pace of rehabilitation of viable sick units would show a marked improvement.

(d) The cases of corruption among the bank officials must be severely dealt with by the bank. As of now, the disciplinary authorities refrain from initiating departmental proceedings against corrupt officials for want of documentary evidences, even though there may be sufficient circumstantial evidences to substantiate the charge. Thus, the corrupt officials mostly go unpunished and other honest officers also feel tempted to indulge in such malpractices.The trend needs to be reversed.It is, therefore, suggested that even in the absence of documentary evidences (which would mostly be the case), the suspected corrupt official may be suspended, pending departmental enquiry, provided, of course, a *prima-facie* case gets established on the basis of the available circumstantial evidences. Technically speaking, suspension may not be said to be a punishment but only a preventive measure. But the suspended officer would feel humiliated and experience the agony, all the same. It would also serve as a deterrent to the other officials and the extent of corruption may be curbed. The suspended officer may thereafter be proceeded against departmentally wherein the charges all or some, may be proved on the basis of the circumstantial evidences. And even if the charges are not proved, justifying any punishment, and the official is reinstated, the ends of justice would be suitably met and the magnitude of the malady of corruption would be minimised. Meticulous care, however, will have to be taken to see that innocent officials are not unnecessarily harassed by vindicative officers, by misusing such provisions.

(e) There is a felt need for continued and close coordination between the banks and other financial institutions, and a joint concerted action on their part in regard to credit appraisal, sanction and disbursal of loans, effective supervision and follow-up of advances, and rehabilitation of sick SSI units. It is, therefore, suggested that the officers of the banks and term lending institutions should periodically meet, both at the State and district levels, wherein the relevant information and problems, pertaining to the SSI units financed by them, should be fully and frankly discussed, and suitable remedial measures jointly evolved and acted upon.

State Level Inter-Institutional Committees, represented by the State Governments concerned, Reserve Bank of India, commercial banks and other financial institutions, provide adequate forum for an interface amongst them, for exchange of relevant information and opinions, and meaningful discussion problems faced by the small scale sector. The working of such committees needs to be made more meaningful and effective.

(B) Suggestions for Preventing Sickness – By the State Financial Corporations and Other Financial Institutions

During the course of our study, it has been observed that the officers of the State Financial Corporation did not properly assess the technical feasibility and economic viability of the units, on a realistic basis, at the project appraisal stage (cases 1, 2, 6, 20). They also faltered in conducting post-sanction performance monitoring of the units, in detecting early signals of sickness, and in taking suitable remedial measures, in time, in close coordination with the bank officers concerned.

(a) It is, therefore, suggested that the officers of the State Financial Corporations and other financial institutions should undertake a detailed and realistic appraisal of the technical feasibility and economic viability of the projects, and objectively assess the entrepreneurs' managerial competence in the areas of finance, production, marketing and personnel, before sanction and disbursement of loans. The suggestions, given in the foregoing pages, meant for the bank officers, should be borne in mind by these officers, too.

(b) The officers should assess the quantum of term loans on a realistic basis and avoid over-financing and under-financing so as to guard against the risks of diversion of funds and financial hardships to the units, respectively. Further, they should pay due attention to the prospects of repayment of loans, instead of over-stressing the need for achieving the target set for sanction and disbursement of new loans (case 1).

(c) The loans should be disbursed in suitable instalments, in accordance with the progress of the project, and preferably by way of direct payments to the suppliers of plant and machinery, etc., as far as possible, so as to ensure the end use of funds.

(d) The officers of the term lending institutions should undertake effective and meaningful post-sanction performance monitoring of the units, say at regular quarterly intervals, in close coordination with the officers of the banks financing the working capital requirements of the units.

(e) As we all know, the term loans can be repaid out of the internal surplus generated, which largely depends on efficient management of working capital. It is, therefore,desirable for the officers of the term lending institutions to maintain regular contacts with the bank officers concerned. This way they would be able to know whether the units were working on sound lines. They would also be able to detect early signals of sickness and jointly take timely remedial measures, at the incipient stage itself.

(f) In case some units ultimately fall sick, the officers of the term lending institutions should independently conduct detailed viability study of such units, and expeditiously formulate and implement the mutually agreed comprehensive rehabilitation programmes, in close coordination with the bank officers concerned. If some units are found non-viable for rehabilitation, they should initiate recovery proceedings against such units, without avoidable delay, in consultation with the bank officers concerned.

(C) Suggestions for Preventing Sickness – By the Government

(a) Our study has revealed that the government departments and the public sector undertakings withhold the payments of the bills of SSI units for an unduly long time (cases 3, 4, 15, 19). This causes liquidity problems to the SSI units, adversely affecting their production cycle, which may culminate in their sickness.

Central and State Governments have issued directives to their departments and public sector undertakings to make payments of the bills of SSI units within three months. But this has not been of much avail. The governments should, therefore, take some firm measures to ensure that these directives are meticulously adhered to by the government departments and the public sector undertakings.

(b) Further, the government may defer the recovery of statutory dues like excise duty, sales tax, etc., from the sick units, which may be paid by them after their rehabilitation, in suitable instalments, without interest or penalty.

(c) Frequent changes in the taxation laws and government policies also adversely affect the units in the small scale sector. (cases 3, 4, 11, 13, 15). The government should, therefore, exercise due care in such matters to safeguard the interest of the small scale sector.

(d) The small scale sector usually face the problem of scarcity of raw materials. The government may, therefore, arrange for the supply of scarce raw materials through some government agencies, on quota basis, commensurate with the scale of operation of the units. Preference should be given to the smaller of the SSI units.

(e) While resorting to load-shedding, the government may adopt a liberal attitude towards the small scale sector so that their production may not get adversely affected.

(f) Small scale industrial units are required to deal with many inspectors and officers from various government departments and agencies like excise and customs, Bureau of Indian Standard, Factory Inspectors, Labour Inspectors, fire brigade, municipal sanitary department, etc. They are also required to submit several proforma to different government authorities, and to meet the provisions of various laws and rules passed from time to time.

It is, therefore, suggested that one comprehensive proforma should be designed, incorporating all the relevant information required to be submitted by the SSI units, copies whereof may be sent to all the authorities concerned, for information and control purposes. The number of such authorities should as well be kept at the minimal level.

Further, all the laws and rules, relevant to the small scale sector, should be codified in one volume, which the small entrepreneurs may easily comprehend and follow.

These measures would substantially reduce the extent of their confusion and harassment and they would be able to utilise their time and energy, so saved, for more productive purposes, for the profitability and progress of their units.

(g) "The total number of items reserved exclusively for production in the small scale sector stood at 836 as at the end of March 1990".[1] Besides, the medium and large scale units which were already producing any such items prior to the notifications, were not allowed to increase their capacity.

But the benefit of the scheme was not reaching the small scale sector in full measure. Medium and large scale industries, even without increasing their capacity, compete rigorously with the small scale sector, even by substantially reducing the price, at least temporarily, which the SSI units find difficult to withstand (case 13). Further, the medium and large scale units also establish some units in the small scale sector to circumvent the restrictions and to avail of the concessions.

Such loopholes in the scheme need to be plugged and the enforcement of the scheme made more rigorous and effective, so that the desired benefits may reach the SSI sector in full measure. It is further suggested that a suitable legislation may be passed to take care of the genuine grievances of the small scale sector.

(h) A random sample survey of the units in the small scale sector, conducted by the Development Commissioner (SSI), New Delhi, in 1982-83, revealed that 69.20 per cent of the units had investment in plant and machinery of less than Rs. 50,000, 89.06 per cent had investment of less than Rs. 2 lakh, and 95.76 per cent of less than Rs. 5 lakh.

Thus, only 4.24 per cent of the SSI units had investment in plant and machinery of Rs. 5 lakh and above. Further, the units in the sector, with investment in plant and machinery of Rs. 15 lakh and above accounted for only 0.80% of the total units.[2]

The Government of India, in the Industrial Policy announced on May 31, 1990, has enhanced the investment ceiling in plant and machinery for the small industries from Rs. 35 lakh to Rs. 60 lakh (from Rs. 45 lakh to Rs. 75 lakh for ancillary units)[3]. Such liberalisation would benefit less than one per cent of the units in the small scale sector, at the detriment of the remaining over 99% units, which is against the principle of "Bahujan Hityae Bahujan Sukhaye". There is, therefore, a felt need to suitably reduce the ceiling on investment in plant and machinery for the small scale sector, so that the benefits of the various concessions may be available to a majority of the smaller units in the sector, who deserve these most.

It is, therefore, suggested that the Government of India may reconsider its Industrial Policy in this regard, and constitute a Committee for the purpose, to examine the issue in detail and come forward with reasoned recommen-dations within a given time frame.

(i) The aforesaid survey further revealed that about 60

> per cent of the SSI units have an annual turnover of less than Rs. 2 lakh and about 90 per cent of them below Rs. 15 lakh. Besides, while about 90 per cent of these units account for 20 per cent of the value of production, the remaining 10 per cent of them account for the balance 80 per cent. Further, 1.2 per cent of the units contribute 41.5 per cent of the total production value.

There is, therefore, a felt need to formulate a new scheme of concessions, and criteria therefor, for the small scale sector, so that the smaller of the SSI units may receive more concessions and care than the bigger units in the sector, inasmuch as the smaller child deserves as a greater motherly care than the bigger ones.

It is, therefore, suggested that the units in the small scale sector may be further classified into three categories, as in Table 6.3.

TABLE 6.3: Suggested Further Classification of the Small Scale Sector

Category	Criteria i.e. investment in plant and machinery
A. Small SSI(or tiny sector)	Say upto Rs. 5 lakh
B. Medium SSI	Say over Rs. 5 lakh and upto Rs. 20 lakh
C. Large SSI	Say over Rs. 20 lakh

Separate nature and extent of subsidies and concessions may be stipulated for these three categories of units, depending upon their genuine requirements.

It is further suggested that the subsidies and concessions, though considered necessary for some time in beginning, should be gradually withdrawn over a period, inasmuch as prolonged support makes one complacent and retards further growth.

(j) A suitable incentive scheme may also be formulated to motivate the SSI units to graduate to the next higher category. Further, if large SSI units grow and enter into the medium scale sector, the package of concessions available to them may be withdrawn only gradually with suitable incentive schemes to motivate them to do so. This way the present tendency on their part, not to cross the *'Laxman Rekha'* of investment in plant and machinery stipulated for the small scale sector, would be curbed and they may prefer to grow vertically, instead of horizontally. The aforesaid Committee may examine these aspects also.

(D) Suggestions for Preventing Sickness – By the Large Scale Industries

(a) *Prompt payment of bills*

As has been revealed by our study, the large scale industries, both in the public and private sectors, unduly delay the payment of bills of the small scale industrial (SSI) units (cases 9, 19, 22). This causes paucity of funds to the SSI units which adversely affects the smooth functioning of their production cycle and may even lead to their sickness.

The large scale industries should, therefore, bear this aspect in mind and endeavour to make timely payment of the bills of the SSI units, specially those of the smaller units of the small scale sector.

(b) *Prompt payment of bills through the intervention of some external authorities*

(i) It has further been found that some of the large scale industries were sometimes unable to make the payment of the bills of SSI units within a reasonable time as the payment of their own bills were not forthcoming from the government departments and the public sector enterprises.

The government should, therefore, issue the necessary directives to the various government departments and public sector enterprises with a view to ensuring that they make timely payment of the bills of the large scale industries, too.

(ii) The Reserve Bank of India has issued the guidelines to all banks to ensure that the large scale industries financed by them do not withhold the payment of the bills of small scale industries for an unduly long time. At the time of sanction, renewal and enhancement of the credit limits of large scale industries, the banks are required to incorporate a confirmation to this effect in their loan proposals. It has, however, been found that unsually they do so on the basis of such written confirmations obtained from the borrowers concerned which, in most cases, may not be true.

It is, therefore, suggested that the Reserve Bank of India should issue directives to all commercial banks, requiring the bank officers to personally ascertain the correct position, by perusal of the books of accounts of their borrowers in the large scale sector at regular quarterly intervals, and to charge a penal rate of interest of say 1%, over and above the usual rate, on the entire outstandings on their accounts, if the payment of the bills of the small scale sector remained unpaid with them beyond 60 days.

(iii) The government may also pass an appropriate legislaion so that the large scale industries may avoid withholding the payment of the bills of the units in the small scale sector beyond 60 days.

(iv) Further, the facility of factoring, now being offered by some selected banks, should be made available to the units in the small scale sector also, based on the merit of each case.

(c) Approval of Samples

(i) Large scale industries, making bulk purchases from the small scale sector, should impress upon the small entrepreneurs to first get the samples approved by them before going in for mass production so as to avoid mass rejection and adverse ramifications connected therewith (case 1).

(ii) Further, the large scale industries should make some technical guidance, including modern technology, available to the small entrepreneurs, enabling the latter to improve upon the quality of their existing products as also to venture into the production of some new products.

(d) Avoiding Unhealthy Competition

Large scale industries would do well to resist the temptation of entering into unhealthy competition with the small scale industries, e.g.

(i) Selling the goods at a sufficiently lower price to drive the SSI units out of the market (case 13);

(ii) producing goods specified in the reserved list by circumventing the existing provisions of law; and

(iii) expanding horizontally, instead of vertically, to avail of the concessions and facilities meant for the small scale sector.

CONCLUSIONS

In conclusion, we may say that for arresting the growing

incidence of sickness in the small scale sector, and for dealing with the problems of rehabilitation of sick units, the commercial banks and other financial institutions should work hand in hand, in close coordination with the entrepreneurs, in an atmosphere of mutual trust, and should adopt the following strategies effectively, with a view to bringing about the desired results:

1. At the project appraisal stage itself, the various relevant factors, including the technical feasibility and economic viability of the projects, should be examined thoroughly by the officers of the banks and other financial institutions, so as to ensure that only viable units are financed.
2. The quantum of term loans and working capital requirements of the units must be properly assessed by them so as to avoid both over-financing and under-financing of the units. The loans should be sanctioned expeditiously and disbursed by them in a phased manner, so as to ensure the end use of funds.
3. The various factors that tend to cause sickness in a unit should always be borne in mind by them so as to guard against them on an on-going basis.
4. They should be alert and sensitive to pick up the early signals of sickness, whenever they appear, through an effective monitoring system, so as to take suitable and timely remedial measures, at the incipient stage of the sickness itself, and thereby to prevent the units from falling sick.
5. If the aforesaid preventive measures would be earnestly taken by them, the risk of the units falling sick would be substantially reduced, though not eliminated completely, because sickness may be caused by several factors, well beyond their control. In such an eventuality, the units should be declared sick by the banks and the other financial institutions, without avoidable delay, under advice

to the entrepreneurs.

6. The borrowers tend to hide their real problems from their bankers, fearing that the latter may adopt a strict and unhelpful attitude towards them. The bank officers, on their part, also delay reporting the matter to their controlling authority, for fear of its being viewed with disfavour. Such delays only aggravate the problems. All concerned should therefore, develop a positive attitude towards each other, in *bona fide* cases. The bank officers should take timely and expeditious action for the rehabilitation of the viable sick units, as it substantially enhances the chances of their revival.
7. While examining the prospects for rehabilitation of sick units, the technical feasibility and economic viability of such units must be studied by the bank officers, with greater care and rigour, in close coordination with the other financial institutions. The various factors, leading to the sickness of the units, should also be examined by them in detail and suitable remedial measures suggested and implemented.
8. The sincerity and honesty of the entrepreneurs should be carefully assessed. Further, if a unit is found viable, a comprehensive (not *ad-hoc*) rehabilitation programme should be worked out by the banks, in close coordination with the borrowers and the other financial institutions.
9. The performance of the units, under the rehabilitation programme, should be monitored by the banks, as also by the other financial institutions, with more than ordinary care at regular monthly intervals, with a view to ascertaining whether the units are working on satisfactory lines by achieving the budgeted levels of their various activities, as stipulated in the respective rehabilitation programmes. The specialized officers, at the

controlling offices of the banks, should oversee the performance of the units, in adition to the Branch Managers, till the units are fully revived and start working on sound lines.

10. The Bhide Committee (1976) emphasised the need for effective coordination between the commercial banks and the State Financial Corporations, and made recommendations pertaining to the sharing of the securities against the advances, exchange of information regarding credit reports, project appraisal, sanction of loans, conduct of the advances, detection of early symptons of sickness and prompt initiation of corrective measures, stipulating of non-conflicting terms and conditions of the advances, frequent meetings to settle the differences, if any, etc. The committee also recommended concerted and coordinated action by them in regard to the rehabilitation of the viable sick units by identifying the causes of sickness, evolving a comprehensive rehabilitation programme and periodical monitoring of the performance of the units jointly. The Bhucher Committee (1979) also stressed the need for close and effective coordination between the banks and the term lending institutions for the success of the units as also for the rehabilitation of the viable sick units.

    But, unfortunately, the lack of the desired cooperation and coordination between the banks, and the State Financial Corporations and other term lending institutions still continues to be the Achilles' heel in the efforts to arrest the growing incidence of sickness. Sincere efforts, therefore, need to be made by all concerned such that the various credit institutions work in close coordination with each other, on a continuous basis. This may go a long way in ensuring the continued health of the units and in facilitating the rehabilitation of the viable sick units.

11. In the cases where the units are found non-viable for rehabilitation, the loans must be called up without losing any valuable time, as otherwise it would be detrimental to the mutual interest of the banks, the borrowers and the other financial institutions.
12. The government departments and large scale industries, both in the public and private sectors, should avoid unduly delaying the payment of the bills of SSI units. They should adopt positive attitudes towards them which may be conducive for the healthy growth and prosperity of the small scale sector.

If the various steps and strategies, as suggested on the basis of the findings of the study, would be effectively implemented by the banks, and others, in close coordination with the other financial institutions and the entrepreneurs, the incidence of sickness in the small scale sector, and the extent of the problem of rehabilitation of sick units, would be substantially reduced, to the mutual advantage of all concerned, and would augur well for the steady growth of the small scale sector and the national economy.

REFERENCES

1. Reserve Bank of India, Bombay, Report on Currency and Finance, Vol. I: *Economic Review*, 1989-90, p. 69.
2. Hand Book of Statistics 1989: Small Scale Industries in India, Development Commissioner (SSI), New Delhi, p. 49.
3. Reserve Bank of India, Bombay, Report on Currency and Finace, Vol. I: *Economic Review*, 1989-90, p. 70.

APPENDICES

APPENDIX I

FOLLOW-UP FORM FOR USE BY THE BANK'S INSPECTING OFFICERS

Part I: Control Card (The Unit at a Glance)

1. Name of the unit
2. Constitution
3. Address (i) office
   (ii) factory
4. Telephone Number
   (i) office
   (ii) factory
5. (i) Name(s) of the Proprietor/Partners/ Directors
   (ii) Name(s) of key person(s)
6. Products manufactured
7. Installed Capacity
   (i) Quantity per annum
   (ii) Value per annum Rs.
8. Credit facilities

Facility	Limit	Margin
(a)		
(b)		
(c)		
(d)		

9. Date of Sanction/ last renewal
10. Collateral security

11. Due dates

   (a) For renewal of documents
   (b) For renewal of insurance policies
   (c) For renewal of working capital limits
   (d) Of medium term loan instalments

Amount	Date

12. Inspection due in the month of — Inspection conducted on (date)

Inspection due in the month of	Inspection conducted on (date)
....	....
....	....
....	....
....	....

PART II : PERFORMANCE MONITORING OF THE UNIT

(For use by the Bank's Inspecting Officers for Units Enjoying Working Capital Limits of over Rs. 2 lakh)

Name of the Unit : Messrs..
For the quarter ended : ....

1. Production

Budgeted	Actual	Variance	Reasons for variance
Quantity/ Value	Quantity/ Value	Quantity/ Value	

2. Sales

Budgeted	Actual	Variance	Reasons for variance
Quantity/ Value	Quantity/ Value	Quantity/ Value	

3. Purchases

Budgeted	Actual	Variance	Reasons for variance
Quantity/ Value	Quantity/ Value	Quantity/ Value	

4. Performance of Working Capital Loan Account

(a) (i) Drawing power Rs.

(ii) Debit balance Rs.

(iii) Amount of irregularity, if any, Rs.

(iv) Reasons for the irregularity

(v) Remedial measures taken for regularising the position

(b) (i) Debit summations for the period under review Rs.

(ii) Credit summations for the period under review Rs.

(iii) If credit summations are not commensurate with the actual sales for the period, the reasons therefor

5. Review of Bills Receivable

	No.	Value
(i) Bills withdrawn from the cover during the period under review		
(ii) Reasons for the delay in payment		
(iii) Bills returned unpaid during the period under review		
(iv) Reasons for such return		
(v) Do frequent withdrawals/return of bills, specially those drawn on one or a few drawee(s), suggest 'kite flying' business, and/or such unsatisfactory features? If so, what corrective steps have been taken?		

6. Performance of Term Loan Account

(i) Are the instalments, with interest, paid up-to-date? Yes / No

	No. of instal-ments	Amount of Prin-cipal Rs.	Amount of Inte-rest Rs.
(ii) If reply to 6 (i) is 'NO', the position of overdue instalments			

(iii) Reasons for non-payment of instalments

(iv) Steps taken to regularise the position

7. General Remarks

PART III : QUARTERLY INFORMATION SYSTEM (QIS FORM)

(To be submitted to the Branch Manager by the Units enjoying Working Capital Limits of over Rs. 2 lakh)

Name of the Unit : Messrs..

for the quarter ended : ....

1. Production

Budgeted	Actual	Variance	Reasons for variance
Quantity/ Value	Quantity/ Value	Quantity/ Value	

2. Sales

Budgeted	Actual	Variance	Reasons for variance
Quantity/ Value	Quantity/ Value	Quantity/ Value	

3. Purchases

Budgeted	Actual	Variance	Reasons for variance
Quantity/ Value	Quantity/ Value	Quantity/ Value	

4. Performance of Working Capital Loan Account

(a) (i) Drawing power Rs.

(ii) Debit balance Rs.

(iii) Amount of irregularity, if any, Rs.

(iv) Reasons for irregularity

(v) Remedial measures taken for regularising the position

(b) (i) Debit summations for the

period under review Rs.

(ii) Credit summation for the period under review Rs.

(iii) If credit summations are not commensurate with the actual sales for the period, the reasons therefor

5. Review of Bills Receivable

	No	Value
(i) Bills withdrawn from the cover during the period under review		
(ii) Reasons for the delay in payment		
(iii) Bills returned unpaid during the period under review		
(iv) Reasons for such return		

6. Performance of Term Loan Account

(i) Are the instalments, with interest paid up-to-date? Yes / No

	No. of instal-ments Rs.	Amount of Prin-cipal Rs.	Amount of Inte-rest Rs.
(ii) If reply to 6 (i) is 'NO', the position of overdue instalments			

(iii) Reasons for non-payment of instalments

(iv) Steps taken to regularise the position

7. General Remarks

Note : Simpler forms, on the suggested lines, may be designed and used by the banks, for small advances upto Rs. 2 lakh.

APPENDIX II

MONTHLY PERFORMANCE REPORT

For the month of 1999

PART I : INFORMATION FROM THE UNIT

(To be submitted to the Branch Manager by the Unit under the Bank's Rehabilitation Programme)

Name of the Unit: Messrs..
Name of the Branch :..

Date of Implementation of
the Rehabilitation Programme ....

1. Production and Sales

(Rs. in lakh)

Item	Actuals from April '98 (Progressive figures)	Performance during the month under review			Budgeted level for the next month
		B	A	V*	
1	2	3	4	5	6
1. Production					
(a) Quantity					
(b) Value					

* B = Budgeted; A = Actual; V = Variance

1	2	3	4	5	6
2. Sales					
3. Receipts/ Realisation					
4. Payments					
5. Sundry debtors					
6. Sundry creditors					

Comments on Adverse Variances, if any:

2. Cumulative Position

(i) Projected Annual Sales –
(ii) Sales upto the last month –
(iii) Sales in the current month –

3. Break-even Level

(i) Projected (a) per annum
(b) per month
(ii) Actual average per month

4.1 Break-up of outstanding bills (Sundry Debtors)

Age	No. of bills	Amount	Probable date of realisation
(i) Over 90 days			
(ii) 61 to 90 days			
(iii) 31 to 60 days			
(iv) upto 30 days			

4.2 Position of bills Returned unpaid

	No. of Bills	Amount
(i) Total bills submitted from		

1.4.98 to the current month Rs.

(ii) Total bills returned unpaid Rs.

(iii) Percentage

(iv) Reasons for return of such bills

(a)

(b)

(c)

5. Break-up of stocks

(i) Total Value of Stocks

(ii) High-value stocks

(iii) Slow-moving/Nonmoving Stocks i.e. Value of stocks stored for more than 3 months

(a) Raw Materials

(b) Finished Goods

6.1 Current Financial Position of the Unit

Current Liabilities (C.L.)			Current Assets (C.A.)		
Previous month	Items	Current month	Previous month	Items	Current month
	Bank borrowings			Stocks of inventory	
	Sundry creditors			Sundry debtors	
	Statutory dues			Advances	
	Others			Others	
	Total			Total	

6.2

(i) **Liquid Surplus (CA - CL)**	(a) Estimated
	(b) Actual
(ii) **Current Ratio (CA / CL)**	(a) Estimated
	(b) Actual

7. Order Book Position

7.1. Pending Orders

Name of the buyers	Amount	Expected date of completion

7.2. Expected Orders

Name of the prospective buyers	Amount	Date by when expected

8. Performance Statement for the Month of.................. 1998 with Projections for the Next Month

	Current Month		Next Month
	Projections	Actuals	Projections
(i) **Raw Materials:**			
Opening Stock			

Purchases
Consumption
Closing Stock

(ii) Stocks-in-Process

Opening Stock
Additions
Conversions
Closing Stock

(iii) Finished Goods

Opening Stock
Production
Sales
Closing Stock

(iv) Sundry Creditors

Opening Balance
Purchases
Payments
Closing Balance

(v) Sundry Debtors

Opening Balance
Sales/Bills
Receipts
Closing Balance

9. Cash Flow Statement for the Month of .... 1998 with Projections for the Next Month

	Current Month		Next Month
	Projections	Actuals	Projections
	1	2	3
Cash In-Flow			
Cash Receipts			
Bill Realisations			

	1	2	3
Miscellaneous			
Others (e.g. Fresh Capital)	....	....	....
Total: (A)	....	....	....
Cash Out-Flow			
Cash Purchases			
Creditors			
Consumable Stores			
Fuel			
Wages & Salary			
Admn. Expenses			
Power			
Maintenance, etc.			
Miscellaneous			
Bank Interest	....	....	....
Total: (B)	....	....	....
Surplus/Deficit (A — B)			
Outstandings in the Bank account at the end of the month			

Date: ....

Signature of the unit's representative

PART II: INFORMATION FROM THE BRANCH

(To be submitted to the Controlling Office by the Branch Manager alongwith PART I)

10. Position of Accounts as on .... 1998.

Facility and Limit	Market value of stocks	Advance value of stocks	Drawing power	Outst-andings	Irregu-larity	Clean
TOTAL						

11. Date of Stock Statements : ....
12. Summations

Period	Debit Summations	Credit Summations
(i) From April 1998 upto the last month		
(ii) During the current month		
TOTAL		

13. Date of Inspection of the Unit

    (i) By the Field Officer
    (ii) By the Manager (SIB)
    (iii) By the Branch Manager

14. Comments/Reasons for Irregularities, if any, under each Facility

15. General Comments on the conduct of

the Account and the Implementation
of the Rehabilitation Programme.

Date .... Signature of the Branch Manager

Note : Simpler forms, on the suggested lines, may be designed and used by the banks for small advances upto Rs. 2 lakh.

APPENDIX III

SEMI-STRUCTURED QUESTIONNAIRE USED FOR ELICITING OPINION REGARDING CAUSES AND CURES OF SICKNESS IN THE SMALL SCALE SECTOR FROM THE BANK OFFICERS

(a) At the Controlling Ofices
(b) At the Branches
(c) At the Banks' Colleges and Training Centres

1. Name of the Officer
2. Designation
3. Address (official)
4. Experience in advances to SSI units
5. Your opinion, in general, regarding the causes of sickness in SSI units

A. Internal

(i) Faulty Project Selection
(ii) Lack of managerial competence in the areas of

(a) Marketing
(b) Finance
(c) Production
(d) Personnel
(e) Corporate
(f) Others (please specify)

(iii) Any other (please specify)

B. External

(a) Banks faltering in the areas of

(i) Prompt and realistic project appraisal
(ii) Prompt and realistic assessment of credit requirements
(iii) Phased disbursement of loans
(iv) Effective supervision and follow-up of advances
(v) Prompt detection of early symptoms of sickness and timely corrective actions, at the incipient stage of sickness
(vi) Effective overseeing and control of advances by the controlling office
(vii) Prompt decision and action in regard to
  (a) rehabilitation of viable units
  (b) calling up of loans of non-viable units
  (c) any other (please specify)

(b) Government

(i) Change in government policy
(ii) Delayed payment of bills by the government departments
(iii) Any other (please specify)

(c) Large Scale Industries

(i) Delayed payment of bills
(ii) Selling at lower price to drive out SSI units from the market
(iii) Any other (please specify)

(d) Other Financial Institutions

(i) Lack of realistic project appraisal
(ii) Lack of post-sanction performance monitoring

(iii) Lack of coordination between banks and other financial institutions

(iv) Any other (please specify)

(e) Other Agencies/Institutions, etc.
(please specify)

(f) Miscellaneous

(i) Fire, flood, etc.

(ii) Sickness of entrepreneurs or their family members

(iii) Any other (please specify)

6. What are your suggestions for arresting/averting sickness in the small scale sector that could be adopted by the

(i) Entrepreneurs

(ii) Banks

(iii) Governments

(iv) Large Scale Industries

(v) Other Financial Institutions

(vi) Other Agencies/Institutions

7. In case of successful SSI units, what are the main factors conducive to their success:

(i) Internal

(ii) External

8. Any other suggestions
9. General comments

Note : The questionnaire was supplemented by extensive personal interviews with the bank officers.

APPENDIX IV

SEMI-STRUCTURED QUESTIONNAIRE USED FOR ELICITING OPINION REGARDING CAUSES AND CURES OF SICKNESS IN THE SMALL SCALE SECTOR FROM THE OFFICERS OF THE STATE FINANCIAL CORPORATIONS AND OTHER FINANCIAL INSTITUTIONS

1. Name of the Officer
2. Designation
3. Address (official)
4. Experience in advances to SSI units
5. Your opinion, in general, regarding the causes of sickness in SSI units

A. Internal

(i) Faulty Project Selection
(ii) Lack of managerial competence in the areas of

(a) Marketing
(b) Finance
(c) Production
(d) Personnel
(e) Corporate
(f) Others (please specify)

(iii) Any other (Please specify)

B. External

(a) Banks faltering in the areas of

(i) Prompt and realistic project appraisal
(ii) Prompt and realistic assessment of credit requirements
(iii) Phased disbursement of loans
(iv) Effective supervision and follow-up of advances
(v) Prompt detection of early symptoms of sickness and timely corrective actions, at the incipient stage of sickness
(vi) Effective overseeing and control of advances by the controlling office
(vii) Prompt decision and action in regard to
  (a) rehabilitation of viable units
  (b) calling up of loans of non-viable units
  (c) any other (please specify)

(b). Government

(i) Change in government policy
(ii) Delayed payment of bills by the government departments
(iii) Any other (please specify)

(c). Large Scale Industries

(i) Delayed payment of bills
(ii) Selling at lower price to drive out SSI units from the market
(iii) Any other (please specify)

(d) State Financial Corporations and other Financial Institutions

(i) Lack of realistic project appraisal
(ii) Lack of realistic assessment of quantum of loan
(iii) Over-enthusiasm for achieving the target set for disbursement of new loans, adversely affecting the

quality of lending

(iv) Faulty disbursement of loans *i.e.,* disbursement of the entire loan amount to the entrepreneurs, instead of disbursements in instalments, at the various stages of the implementation of the project, and that too, to the suppliers of machinery etc. direct, as far as possible.

(v) If the response to item (iv) above is, by and large, positive, does it lead to:

(a) Diversion of funds

(b) Erosion of equity

(c) Any other (please specify)

(vi) Lack of post-sanction performance monitoring

(a) at the various stages of the implementation of the project

(b) after commencement of commercial production by the units

(vii) Lack of effective supervision and follow-up with a view to detecting early signals of sickness in the units and to take timely remedial measures to arrest the sickness at the incipient stage itself.

(viii) Avoidable delay in identifying sick units and conducting detailed viability study of such units.

(ix) Avoidable delay in formulating comprehensive (not *ad-hoc*) rehabilitation programmes or calling up the loans of non-viable units.

(x) Lack of coordination with the banks, *inter alia,* pertaining to items vi(b), vii, viii and ix above.

(xi) Any other (please specify).

(e) Other Agencies/Institutions, etc.
(please specify)

(f) Miscellaneous

(i) Fire, flood, etc.

(ii) Sickness of entrepreneurs or their family members.
(iii) Any other (please specify).

6. What are your suggestions for arresting/averting sickness in the small scale sector that could be adopted by the

(i) Entrepreneurs,
(ii) Banks,
(iii) Governments,
(iv) Large Scale Industries,
(v) Other Financial Institutions,
(vi) Other Agencies/Institutions.

7. In the cases of successful SSI units, what are the main factors conducive to their success.

(i) Internal,
(ii) External,

8. Any other suggestions

9. General Comments

Note : The questionnaire was supplemented by extensive personal interviews with the officers of the State Financial Corporations and other financial institutions.

APPENDIX V

SMI-STRUCTURED QUESTIONNAIRE USED FOR ELICTING OPINION REGARDING CAUSES AND CURES OF SICKNESS IN THE SMALL SCALE SECTOR FROM THE ENTREPRENEURS OF SICK SSI UNITS

(a) Found non-viable for rehabilitation

(b) Found viable and where rehabilitation programme was successful

(c) Found viable but where rehabilitation programme was unsuccessful

1. Name of the unit
2. Address : (i) Factory
   (ii) Office
3. Date of establishment
4. Constitution : Proprietary/Partnership
   Private Ltd. Company/Public Ltd. Company
5. Name(s) of the Proprietor/Partners/Directors:
6. Products manufactured
7. Date of commencement of commercial production
8. Capital (equity) base
9. Date when the unit came to the books of the bank
10. Credit Facilities granted by the bank

Name of the Bank	Faciltiy	Limit

11. Credit facilities granted by other financial institutions

Name of the Financial Institution	Facility	Limit

12. In your opinion, what are the main causes of sickness of your unit

A. Internal

(i) Faulty project selection,
(ii) Faulty project report,
(iii) Lack of managerial competence in the areas of:

(a) Marketing
(b) Finance
(c) Production
(d) Personnel
(e) Corporate
(f) Others (please specify).

(iv) Any other (please specify).

B. External

(a) Banks

(i) Faulty project appraisal
(ii) Unrealistic assessment of credit requirements

(a) Underfinancing,
(b) Overfinancing.

(iii) Delay in disbursement of loans,
(iv) Failure to detect early symptoms of sickness,
(v) Unhelpful/non-cooperative attitude of the bank officers,

(vi) Delay in decision and action to rehabilitate the unit,
(vii) Any other (please specify).

(b) Government

(i) Change in government policies,
(ii) Delayed payment of bills by the government departments,
(iii) Any other (please specify).

(c) Other Financial Industries

(i) Delayed payment of bills,
(ii) Selling at lower price to drive out SSI units from the market,
(iii) Any other (please specify).

(d) Other Financial Institutions

(i) Lack of realistic project appraisal,
(ii) Lack of post-sanction performance monitoring,
(iii) Lack of coordination between banks and other financial institutions,
(iv) Any other (please specify).

(e) Other Agencies/Institutions, etc. (please specify)

(f) Miscellaneous

(i) Fire, flood, etc.,
(ii) Sickness of entrepreneurs or their family members,
(iii) Any other (please specify).

13. Has your unit been found non-viable for rehabilitation by the bank? If so, the main

reasons therefor

14. Has your unit been found viable and the rehabilitation programme has been successful? If so, the main facilitating factors therefor:
15. Has the rehabilitation programme of your unit failed? If so, the main hindering factors therefor:
16. Is the rehabilitation package of your unit still under consideration of the bank? If so, what are the prospects of its favourable finalisation?
17. In the case of successful SSI units, what are the main factors conducive to their success?

    (i) Internal,
    (ii) External.

18. What are your suggestions for arresting/averting sickness in the small scale sector that could be adopted by the

    (i) Entrepreneurs,
    (ii) Banks,
    (iii) Governments
    (iv) Large Scale Industries,
    (v) Other Financial Institutions,
    (vi) Other Agencies/Institutions.

19. Any other suggestions

20. General Comments

Note : The questionnaire was supplemented by extensive personal interviews with the entrepreneurs of sick SSI units.

APPENDIX VI

SEMI-STRUCTURED QUESTIONNAIRE USED FOR ELICITING OPINION REGARDING THE FACILITATING FACTORS CONDUCIVE TO THE SUCCESS OF THE UNITS IN THE SMALL SCALE SECTOR FROM THE ENTREPRENEURS OF SUCH SUCCESSFUL UNITS

1. Name of the unit
2. Address : (i) Factory
   (ii) Office
3. Date of establishment
4. Constitution: Proprietary/Partnership
   Private Ltd. Company/Public Ltd. Company.
5. Name(s) of Proprietor/Partners/Directors
6. Products manufactured
7. Date of commencement of commercial production
8. Capital (equity) base
9. Date when the unit came to the books of the bank
10. Credit facilities granted by the bank

Name of the Bank	Facility	Limit

11. Credit facilities granted by other financial institutions:

Name of the Financial Institution	Facility	Limit

12. How did you conceive the project?
13. How did you prepare the project report?

(i) By yourself?
(ii) By some management consultant?
(iii) With the help of the bank and/or other financial institutions?

14. What was the initial quantum of investment?

(i) Equity base
(ii) Working capital loan from the bank
(iii) Term loan from the bank and/or other financial institutions

15. How did you go about implementing the project?
16. What initial problems did you face in the implementation of the project?

(i) Internal
(ii) External

17. How did you tackle these problems?

(i) Internal
(ii) External

18. How would you rate your managerial competence in the areas of

(i) Marketing,
(ii) Finance,
(iii) Production
(iv) Personnel,
(v) Corporate,
(vi) Others (please specify).

19. How did you plan your expansion/diversification?
20. What were the facilitating factors for the success of your unit?

    (i) *Internal*
    - (a) Personal Traits
    - (b) Management Strategies
    - (c) Any other (please specify)

    (ii) *External*
    - (a) Banks,
    - (b) Governments,
    - (c) Large Scale Industries,
    - (d) Other Financial Institutions,
    - (e) Any other (please specify).

21. What, in you opinion, are the main causes of sickness in the SSI units?

    (i) Internal,
    (ii) External.

22. What suggestions would you like to give to the entrepreneurs (present and prospective) to be successful in their ventures?

23. General Comments.

Note: The questionnaire was supplemented by extensive personal interviews with the entrepreneurs of successful SSI units.

APPENDIX VII

TEXT OF THE POLICY MEASURES FOR PROMOTING AND STRENGTHENING SMALL, TINY AND VILLAGE ENTERPRISES*

A. Small and Tiny Enterprises

1.0 *Introduction*

1.1 The small Scale Industrial Sector has emerged as a dynamic and vibrant sector of the economy during the eighties. At the end of the Seventh Plan period, it accounted for nearly 35 per cent of the gross value of output in the manufacturing sector and over 40 per cent of the total exports from the country. It also provided employment opportunities to around 12 million people.

1.2 The primary objective of Small Scale Industrial Policy during the nineties would be to impart more vitality and growth-impetus to the sector to enable it to contribute its mite fully to the economy, particularly in terms of growth of output, employment and exports. The sector has been substantially delicensed. Further efforts would be made to deregulate and debureaucratise the sector with a view to remove all fetters on its growth potential, reposing greater faith in small and young entrepreneurs.

1.3 All statutes, regulations and procedures would be

* The Text of the "Policy for Small, Tiny and Village Industries" announced by Mr. K. Thungon, the Minister of State for Industry, in the Parliament on 6 August 1991.

reviewed and modified, wherever necessary, to ensure that their operations do not militate against the interests of the small and village enterprises.

2.0 *Tiny Enterprises*

2.1 Government have already announced increase in the investment limits in plant and machinery of small scale industries, ancillary units and export-oriented units to Rs. 60 lakhs, 75 lakhs, and 75 lakhs respectively. Such limits in respect of *Tiny Enterprises* would now be increased from the present Rs. 2 lakhs to Rs. 5 lakhs, irrespective of location of the unit.

2.2 Service sub-sector is a fast growing area and there is need to provide support to it in view of its recognised potential for generating employment. Hence all industry-related service and business enterprises, irrespective of their location, would be recognised as small scale industries and their investment ceilings would correspond to those of Tiny enterprises.

2.3 A separate package for the promotion of Tiny Enterprises is now being introduced. This constitutes the main thrust of Government's new policy.

2.4. While the small scale sector (other than 'Tiny Enterprises') would be mainly entitled to one-time benefits (like preference in land allocation/power connection, access to facilities for skill/technology upgradation), the 'Tiny' enterprises would also be eligible for additional support on a countinuing basis, including easier access to institutional finance, priority in the Government Purchase Programme and relaxation from certain provisions of labour laws.

2.5 It has also been decided to widen the scope of the National Equity Fund Scheme to cover projects upto Rs. 10 lakhs for equity support (upto 15 per cent) Single Window Loan Scheme has also been enlarged to cover projects upto Rs. 20 lakhs with working capital margin upto Rs. 10 lakhs. Composite loans under Single Window Scheme, now available only through State Financial Corporations (SFCs) and twin function State Small Industries Development Corporation (SSIDCs), would also be channelised through commercial banks. This would facilitate access to a larger number of entrepreneurs.

3.0 *Financial Support Measures*

3.1 Inadequate access to credit – both short-term and long-term – remains a perennial problems facing the small scale sector. Emphasis would henceforth shift from subsidised/cheap credit, except for specified target groups, and efforts would be made to ensure both adequate flow of credit on a normative basis, and the quality of its delivery, for viable operations of this sector. A special monitoring agency would be set up to oversee that the genuine credit needs of the small scale sector are fully met.

3.2 To provide access to the capital market and to encourage modernisation and technological upgradation, it has been decided to allow equity participation by other industrial undertakings in the SSI, not exceeding 24 per cent of the total shareholding. This would also provide a powerful boost to ancillarisation and sub-contracting, leading to expansion of employment opportunities.

3.3 Regulatory provisions relating to the management of private limited companies are being liberalized. A Limited Partnership Act will be introduced to enhance the supply of risk capital to the small scale sector. Such an Act would limit the financial liability of the new and non-active partners/entrepreneurs to the capital invested.

3.4 A beginning has been made towards solving the problem of delayed payments to small industries by setting up of 'factoring' services through Small Industries Development Bank of India (SIDBI). Network of such services would be set up throughout the country and operated through commercial banks. A suitable legislation will be introduced to ensure prompt payment of Small Industries Bills.

4.0 *Infrastructural Facilities*

4.1 To facilitate location of industries in rural/ backward areas and to promote stronger linkages between agriculture and industry, a new Scheme of Integrated Infrastructural Development (including Technological Back-up Services) for Small Scale Industries would be implemented with the active participation of State Governments and financial institutions. A beginning in this direction will be made this year itself.

4.2 A Technology Development Cell (TDC) would be set up in the Small Industries Development Organisation (SIDO) which would provide technology inputs to improve productivity and competitiveness of the products of the small scale sector. The TDC would coordinate the activities of the Tool Rooms, Process-cum-Product Development Centres (PPDCs), existing as well as to be established under SIDO, and would also interact with the other industrial research and development organisations to achieve its objectives.

4.3. Adequacy and equitable distribution of indigenous and imported raw materials would be ensured to the small scale sector, particularly the tiny sub-sector. Policies would be so designed that they do not militate against entry of new units. Based on the capacity needs, Tiny/Small Scale units would be given priority in allocation of indigenous raw materials.

4.4 A proper and adequate arrangement for delivery of total package of incentives and services at the District level will be evolved and implemented.

5.0 *Marketing and Exports*

5.1 In spite of the vast domestic market, marketing remains a problem area for small and tiny enterprises. Mass consumption labour intensive products are predominantly being marketed by the organised sector. The tiny/small scale sector will be enabled to have a significant share of such markets. In addition to the existing support mechanism, market promotion would be undetaken through cooperative/public sector institutions, other specialised/professional marketing agencies and consortia approach, backed up by such incentives, as considered necessary.

5.2 National Small Industries Corporation (NSIC) would concentrate on marketing of mass consumption items under common brand name and organic links between NSIC and SSIDCs would be established.

5.3 Government recognises the need to widen and deepen complementarity in production programmes of large/ medium and small industrial sectors. Parts, components, sub-assemblies, etc. required by large public/ private sector undertakings would be encouraged for production in a techno-economically viable manner through small scale ancillary units. Industry associations would be encouraged to establish sub-contracting exchanges, in addition to strengthening the existing ones under the SIDO. Emphasis would also be laid in promotion of a viable and competitive 'component' market.

5.4 Though the Small Scale Sector is making significant contribution to total exports, both direct and indirect, a large potential remains untapped. The SIDO has been recognised as the nodal agency to support the small scale industries in export promotion. An Export Development Centre would be set up in SIDO to serve the small scale industries through its network of field offices to further augment export activities of this sector.

6.0 *Modernisation Technological and Quality Upgradation*

6.1 A greater degree of awareness to produce goods and services conforming to national and international standards would be created among the small scale sector.

6.2 Industry Associations would be encouraged and supported to establish quality counselling and common testing facilities. Technology Information Centres to provide updated knowledge on technology and markets would be established.

6.3 Where non-conformity with quality and standards involves risk to human life and public health, compulsory quality control would be enforced.

6.4 A reorinted programme for modernisation and technological upgradation aimed at improving productivity, efficiency and cost effectiveness in the small scale sector would be pursued. Specific industries in large concentrations/clusters would be identified for studies in conjunction with SIDBI and other banks. Such studies will establish commercial viability of modernisation prescriptions, and financial support would be provided for modernisation of these industries on a priority basis.

6.5 Indian Institutes of Technology (IITs) and selected Regional/other Engineering Colleges will serve as Technological Information, Design and Develop-ment Centres in their respective command areas.

7.0 *Promotion of Entrepreneurship*

7.1 Government will continue to support first generation entrepreneurs through training and will support their efforts. Large number of EDP trainers and motivators will be trained to significantly expand the Entrepreneurship Development Programme (EDP). Industry Associations would also be encouraged to participate in this venture effectively.

7.2 EDP would be built into the curricula of vocational and other degree level courses.

7.3 Women entrepreneurs will receive support through special training programmes. Definition of "Woman Enterprises" would be simplified. The present stipulation regarding employment of majority of women workers would be dispensed with and units in which women entrepreneurs have a majority shareholding and management control, would be defined as "Woman Enterprises".

7.4 Additional employment opportunities would be generated through training of multi-disciplinary 'barefoot' managers to suit the special requirements of the small scale sector.

8.0 *Simplification of Rules and Procedures*

8.1 The persistent complaint of small scale units of being subjected to a large number of Acts and Laws, being required to maintain a number of registers and submit returns, and face an army of inspectors, would be attended to within a specified time frame of three months.

8.2 Procedures would be simplified, bureaucratic controls effectively reduced, unnecessary interference eliminated and paper work cut down to the minimum to enable the entrepreneurs to concentrate on production and marketing functions.

B. Village Industries

9.0 *Handloom Sector*

9.1 Handloom sector contributes about 30 per cent of the total textile production in the country. It is the policy of Government to promote handlooms to sustain employment in rural areas and to improve the quality of life for handloom weavers.

9.2 Schemes for the handloom sector will be redesigned keeping in mind the local and regional needs. Constraints of coverage will be removed so as to include bulk of the weavers who are outside the corporate/cooperative fold.

9.3 Existing schemes will be re-drawn and suitably revised under three major heads:

(a) *Project Package Scheme:* Under this scheme, area-based projects for product development, upgradation of technology, improvement of marketing facilities will be drawn up.

(b) *Welfare Package Scheme:* Number of welfare schemes and quantum of funds earmarked for them will be substantially augmented.

(c) *Organisation Development Package:* Schemes for participation in the share capital will be re-drawn under organisational development scheme for imparting a better management system in the existing state agencies.

9.4 Janata cloth scheme which sustains weavers often on a minimum level of livelihood will be phased out by the terminal year of the VIII Plan and replaced by the omnibus project package scheme under which substantial funds will be provided for modernisation of looms, training, provision of better designs, provision of better dyes and chemicals and marketing assistance.

9.5 A vastly expanded role for the National Handloom Development Corporation (NHDC) is envisaged. NHDC would be the nodal agency for increasing the supply of hank yarn and of dyes and chemicals. Spinning capacity in the sector will be increased. National Cooperative Development Corporation will provide more assistance for this in the form of Seed Money, both for cotton growers spinning mills and weavers spinning mills.

9.6 For improving marketing of handloom products, a more intensive implementation of schemes for design and product improvement by national level publicity, exhibitions, and design exercise will be undertaken. A special scheme will be drawn up to graduate the handloom production, which is often of low value items, to high value products suitable for export markets. This will be done by better design inputs, upgradation of technology, diversion of weavers from cotton to silk and tassar weaving. Special projects for modernisation of looms for products suitable for export markets will be drawn up.

10.0 *Handicrafts Sector*

10.1 The key areas in handicrafts that could contribute towards a faster pace of rural industrialisation are production and marketing. Schemes for training and design development and for production and marketing assistance will be given encouragement.

10.2 Considering the importance of this sector from the point of view of employment and exports, it is proposed to provide an integrated development thrust to this sector with a view to enlarging the production base, thus enhancing the opportunities for employment and income through crafts as an economic activity and to giving it necessary inputs for quality improvement and effective marketing support both internal and overseas. Efforts will be made not only to preserve the traditional richness of the crafts but to engage the hereditary skills of the crafts persons to suit modern requirements.

10.3 Emphasis will be given to the following:

* Extension of services like supply of raw materials, design and technical guidance, market support, training and procuring of related materials/inputs in an integrated and area-based manner through the setting up of craft development centres in identified clusters of villages.
* Market development support in the form of a package of assistance through expansion of marketing infrastructure, exhibitions, publicity, etc., through Central and State Handicrafts Corporations, voluntary organisations and support to direct marketing activity by craftspersons.
* Expansion of training activities by greater involvement of State Handicraft Development Corporations, Co-operatives and voluntary organisations.
* Measures to sustain increased exports of handicrafts through new marketing channels like trading companies, departmental stores, etc.

11.0 *Other Village Industries*

11.1 Government recognise the need to enhance the spread of rural and cottage industries towards stepping up non-farm employment opportunities.

11.2 The activities of the Khadi and Village Industries Commission and the State Khadi and Village Industries Boards will be expanded and the organisations strengthened to discharge their responsibilities more effectively.

11.3 There will be greater emphasis on improving the quality and marketability of the products *pari passu* with consumer preferences instead of merely depending on rebates and subsidies.

11.4 While the plan allocation for rural industries will be augmented, effective steps will also be taken to ensure better flow of credit from the financial institutions and a more coordinated and optimal utilisation of different development schemes and agencies operating in the rural sector. Bank ability of projects undertaken in this sector would be stressed.

11.5 The programmes of intensive development of KVI through area approach with tie-up with DRDA, TRYSEM and ongoing developmental programmes relating to weaker sections like Scheduled Castes, Scheduled Tribes and Women would be extended throughout the country.

11.6 The traditional village industries would be given greater thrust. Involvement of traditional and reputed voluntary organisations will be encouraged.

11.7 Agro processing and food processing industries in KVI sector using appropriate technologies would be promoted with a view to utilise locally available agricultural produce and promote employment/ resource generation in the countryside.

11.8 Functional industrial estates would be established in areas with concentration of agricultural/horticultural produce.

11.9 R & D in KVI sector would be strengthened through greater linkages with CSIR and other research institutions in the areas of production, finishing/ packaging, processes and development of new tools and implements.

11.10 The training programmes would be upgraded and augmented to cover the expanded list of industries under the purview of the KVIC.

BIBLIOGRAPHY

Books

Ahmad, N. : *Problems and Management of Small Scale and Cottage Industries.* Deep & Deep Publications, New Delhi, 1987.

Allsop, M. : *Survival in Business : The Dynamics of Success and Failure.* London, 1977.

Altman, E.I.: *Corporate Financial Distress : A Complete Guide to Predicting, Avoiding and Dealing with Bankruptcy.* Wiley Interscience, New York, 1983.

Anderson, D. : *Small Industry in Developing Countries : Some Issues.* The World Bank, Washington, D.C., USA, 1982.

Argenti, J. : *Corporate Collapse : The Causes and Symptoms.* McGraw-Hill, London, 1976.

Ballance, R.H., S.W. Sinclair : *Collapse and Survival : Industry Strategies in a Changing World.* George Allen & Unwin, London, 1983.

Bhandari, P.M. : *A Handbook of Small Scale Industries,* Peerless Publishers, Calcutta, 1975.

Bharati, R.K. : *Industrial Estates in Developing Economies.* National Publishing House, New Delhi, 1978.

Bhattacharyya, H. : *Entrepreneur, Banker and Small Scale Industry.* Deep & Deep Publications, New Delhi, 1984.

Bhattacharya, S. N. : *Development of Small Scale and Cottage Industries – The Indian Experience.* Metropolitan Book Company, New Delhi, 1986.

Bibeault, D.B. : *Corporate Turnaround : How Managers Turn Losers into Winners.* McGraw-Hill, New York, 1982.

Bindani, S.N., P.K. Mitra : *Industrial Sickness : Identification and Rehabilitation.* Vision Books, New Delhi, 1982.

Blanchard, K, Johnson Spencer : *The One Minute Manager.* Fontana Paperbacks, U.K., April 1984.

Blanchard, K., R. Lorber : *Putting the One Minute Manager to Work.* Fontana Paperbacks, U.K., 1984.

Bombay Chamber of Commerce and Industry (ed.) : *Role of Organised Industry in the Effective Development of Small Scale Industry.* (Proceedings of the Seminar held on 8-2-1979), Bombay, 1979.

Bosewell, J. : *The Rise and Decline of Small Firms.* George Allen & Unwin, London, 1973.

Chakraborthy, S.K., P.K. Sen : *Industrial Sickness and Revival in India : Essays, Cases and Debates.* Indian Institute of Management, Calcutta, 1980.

Desai, V. : *Organisation and Management of Small Scale Industries.* Himalaya Publishing House, Bombay, 1983.

–,– *Problems and Prospects of Small Scale Industries in India.* Himalaya Publishing House, Bombay, 1983.

–,– *Management of Small Scale Industries.* Himalaya Publishing House, Bombay, 1989.

Deshpande, M.U. : *Entrepreneurship of Small Scale Industries : Concept, Growth, Management.* Deep & Deep Publications, New Delhi, 1982.

Dhar, P.N., H.F. Lydall : *The Role of Small Enterprises in Indian Economic Development.* Delhi Institute of Economic Growth, Delhi, 1961.

Doshi, A., A.M. Sadare : *Small Scale Industries : Essentials of Marketing Management.* Indian Banks' Association, Bombay, 1986.

Finley, L.: *Entrepreneurial Strategies : Text and Cases.* PWS Kent Publishing Company, Boston, 1990.

Ganapati Iyer, E.V. : *Indian Industrial Development and its Problems.* Ganapati Transwest Associates, Bangalore, 1981.

Ganguli, S., S.C. Guha, S.K. Gupta : *A Management Guide*

for Small Enterprises. Kwality Book Company, Calcutta, 1977.

Gangwal, S. : *New Dimensions in Industrial Sickness.* Sublime Publications, Jaipur, 1990.

Gill, J. : *Factors Affecting the Survival and Growth of the Smaller Company.* Gower Publishing Company, England, 1985.

Gopal Swaroop : *Advances to Small Industries and Small Borrowers.* Sultan Chand & Sons, New Delhi, 1981.

Goyal, S.K., K.S. Chalapati Rao, N. Kumar : *Small Scale Sector and Big Business.* Indian Institute of Public Administration, New Delhi, 1984.

Gupta, M. C. : *Entrepreneurship in Small Scale Industries.* Anmol Publications, New Delhi, 1987.

Hamid, S. A. : *Management and Development in Small Scale Industries.* Anmol Publications, New Delhi, 1989.

Hattangadi, A. : *Bankers' Handbook on Small Scale Industries.* IBH Publishing Company,Bombay, 1973.

ICICI : *Financial Ratios as Forewarning Indicators of Corporate Sickness.* ICICI, Bombay, 1979.

Iyer, T. N. K. : *Guidelines for Financing of Small Scale Industries : A Handbook for Bankers.* Vora & Co., Bombay, 1976.

Jain, P. C. : *Economic Problems of India.* Chaitanya Publishing House, Allahabad, 1967.

Jalal, R. S. (ed.) : *Industrial Entrepreneurship and Small Scale Industries.* Anmol Publications, New Delhi, 1991.

Joshi, V. K. : *Management of Industrial Sickness.* Kuber Associates & Publishers, Jaipur, 1987.

Jyoti, Rani T. : *Sickness in Small Scale Industrial Sector.* Sandeep Publishing House, Warangal (A.P.) 1985.

Kaveri, V. S. : *Financial Ratios as Predictors of Borrowers' Health (with reference to Small Scale Industries in India).* Sultan Chand & Sons, New Delhi, 1980.

Kaveri, V.S. : *How to Diagnose, Prevent and Cure Industrial Sickness : (A Practical Approach).* Sultan Chand & Sons, New Delhi, 1983.

Khan, R.R.: *Management of Small Scale Industries.* S. Chand & Company, New Delhi, 1979.

Khandelwal, N. M. : *Working Capital Management in Small Scale Industries.* Ashish Publishing House, New Delhi, 1985.

Khandwalla, P. N. : *Effective Turnaround of Sick Enterprises (Indian Experience) : Text and Cases.* Commonwealth Secretariat, London, 1989.

Kharbanda, O. P., E. A. Stallworthy : *Corporate Failures.* McGraw-Hill, New York, 1985.

Kumar, V. : *Indian Industries : Predicting Success or Failure.* Commonwealth Publishers, New Delhi, 1987.

Lackey, L. A.: *How to Start a Small Business.* Exposition Press, New York, 1971.

Lakshman, T. K. : *Problems and Prospects of Ancillary Industries in a Growing Economy.* Rekha Publications, Bangalore, 1970.

Lal, S. : *How to Prevent Industrial Sickness: Symptoms and Rehabilitation.* Navrang, New Delhi, 1978.

Little, I. M. D., D. Mazumdar, J. M. Page Jr. : *Small Manufacturing Enterprises : A Comparative Study of India and Other Economies.* (A World Bank Research Publications), Oxford University Press, USA, 1987.

Mahajan, Y. S., M. R. Virmani (eds.) : *Overcoming Sickness in Industries.* Centre for Public Sector Studies, New Delhi, 1988.

Management Development Institute : *Small Scale Industries: An Assessment of Institutional Assistance (Case Studies of Select States in India).* Management Development Institute, New Delhi, 1983.

Mathur, S. P. : *Economics of Small Scale Industries.* Sundeep Prakashan, Delhi, 1979.

Misra, B. : *Monitoring of Industrial Sickness.* Deep & Deep Publications, New Delhi, 1990.

Morris, R. L. : *The Economic Theory of Managerial Capitalism.* MacMillan, London, 1964.

Nagaiya, D. : *Industrial Estates Programme : The Indian*

Experience. SIET Publications, Hyderabad, 1971.

–,– (ed.) : *Industrial Sickness : A Health Monitoring Approach*. Discovery Publishing House, New Delhi, 1991.

Narasimha Murthy, B.E.V.V. : *Entrepreneurship in Small Towns*. Mittal Publications, Delhi, 1989.

Neck, P.A. (ed.) : *Small Enterprise Development : Policies and Programmes*. International Labour Office, Geneva, 1977.

Nelson, R., D. Clutterbuck (eds.) : *Turnaround : How Twenty Wellknown Companies Came Back from the Brink*. Mercury Books, Division of W H Allen & Company, London, 1988.

Newalkar, G. B. : *Small Industry : A Perpetual Economic Necessity*. (Perspective One).

–,–, *Generation of Entrepreneurship in a Developing Economy*. (Perspective Two).

–,–, *Development of Small Industries in Underdeveloped Areas*. (Perspective Three).

–,–, *Management Perspectives for Small Industries Corporations*. (Perspective Four).

–,–, *Dynamics of Economic Development*. (Perspective Five).

–,–, *Executive Perspectives for Small Industries Corporations*. (Perspective Six).

(Sr. Nos. 61 to 66 published by Maharashtra Small Scale Industries Development Corporation (MSSIDC), Bombay, 1973).

Padaki, V., V. Shanbhag : *Industrial Sickness : The Challenge in Indian Textiles*. ITIRA, Ahmedabad, 1984.

Pareek, H. S. : *Financing of Small Scale Industries in a Developing Economy*. National Publishing House, New Delhi, 1978.

Parikh, S. M. : *How to Finance Small Business Enterprises*. MacMillan Company, Delhi, 1977.

Pathak, H. N. : *Problems of Small Scale Entrepreneurs (Report on a Study based on Gujarat)*. IDBI, 1975.

Pattanaik, S. M. : *Development Strategy for Small Industries*.

Himalaya Publishing House, Bombay, 1988.

Penrose, E. T. : *The Theory of the Growth of the Firm.* Basil Blackwell, London, 1980.

Peters, T., N. Austin : *A Passion for Excellence.* Fontana Paperbacks, U. K., 1986.

Peters, T. J., R. H. Waterman Jr. : *In Search of Excellence.* Harpers & Row, New York, 1982.

Prabin Baishya : *Small and Cottage Industries : A Study in Assam.* Manas Publications, Delhi, 1989.

Ramakrishna, K.T. : *Finances for Small Scale Industry in India.* Asia Publishing House, Bombay, 1962.

Ramamohan Rao, T.V.S., S. Acharya : *Management Decisions of Small Scale Firms.* Jaico Publishing House, Bombay, 1978.

Rao, R.V. : *Cottage and Small Scale Industries and Planned Economy.* Sterling Publishers, Delhi, 1967.

Rao, U. M. : *Small Scale Industries.* Popular Prakashan, Bombay, 1965.

Rao, V. S. P., D. Nagaiya (eds) : *Small Industry Development in India.* Discovery Publishing House, New Delhi, 1991.

Reddy, K.C. (ed.) : *Sickness in Small Scale Industries.* Ashish Publishing House, New Delhi, 1988.

–,–, (ed.): *Financing of Small Scale Industries in India.* Himalaya Publishing House, Bombay, 1990.

Reddy, R. J. P. : *Problems and Development of Small Scale Industries in India.* Ashish Publishing House, New Delhi, 1991.

Reddy, T. S., L. V. Reddy (eds.) : *Sickness in Small Industry.* Himalaya Publishing House, Delhi, 1988.

Rodgers, F. G. "Buck", R. L. Shook : *The I B M Way.* Harper & Row, New York, 1986.

Ross, J. E., M. J. Kami : *Corporate Management in Crisis : Why the Mighty Fall.* Prentice-Hall, New York, 1973.

Ryan, F. A. : *Efficiency for Small Manufacturers.* Asia Publishing House, Calcutta, 1962.

Sahu, P. K. (ed.) : *Industrial Sickness (Concepts, Cases & Remedies).* Discovery Publishing House, New Delhi,

1990.

Sami Uddin : *Entrepreneurship Development in India.* Mittal Publications, Delhi, 1989.

Sanghvi, R. L. : *Role of Industrial Estates in a Developing Economy.* Multi-tech Publishing Co., Bombay, 1979.

Satyanarayana, T. : *Financing of Small Scale Industries.* Himalaya Publishing House, Bombay, 1989.

Saxena, K. K. : *Regional Input – Output Model for Small Scale Industries (A Case Study of Rajasthan)* – Himanshu Publications, Udaipur, 1987.

Sharma, R. A. : *Entrepreneurial Change in Indian Industry.* Sterling Publishers, New Delhi, 1980.

–,–, *Entrepreneurial Performance in Indian Industry.* Inter-India Publications, New Delhi, 1985.

Shashi Bala : *Management of Small Scale Industries.* Deep & Deep Publications, New Delhi, 1984.

Simha, S.L.N.: *Sickness of Industrial Units – Some Observations.* Institute for Financial Management and Research, Madras, 1977.

Singh, I., N.S. Gupta : *Financing of Small Industry.* S. Chand & Co., New Delhi, 1977.

Singh, M.K., A. Bhattacharya (eds) : *Management of Industrial Rehabilitation.* Discovery Publishing House, New Delhi, 1990.

Singh, N.N. : *Scientific Management of Small Scale Industries.* Lalvani Publishing House, Bombay, 1970.

Slatter, S : *Corporate Recovery : Successful Turnaround Strategies and Their Implementation.* Penguin, Harmondsworth, Middlesex, 1984.

Srivastava, S.S., R.A. Yadav: *Management and Monitoring of Industrial Sickness.* Concept Publishing, New Delhi, 1986.

State Bank Staff College, Hyderabad : *Rehabilitation of Small Scale Industries.* State Bank Staff College, Hyderabad, 1986.

Stepanek J.E. : *Managers for Small Industry : An International Study.* Asia Publishing House, Bombay,

1962.

–,–, *Small Industry Advisory Services : An International Study.* Asia Publishing House, Bombay, 1962.

Suri, K.B. (ed) : *Small Scale Enterprises in Industrial Development : The Indian Experience.* Sage Publications, New Delhi, 1988.

Tripathi, A.R.: *Bank Financing of Industries in India.* Tiwari Publications, Delhi, 1991.

Tulsi, S.K.: *Incentives for Small Scale Industries - An Evaluation* . Kunj Publishing House, Delhi, 1980.

Tyabji, N.: *The Small Industries Policy in India.* Oxford University Press, Calcutta, 1989.

Vepa, R.K.: *Productivity in Small Industries - Some Lessons from Japan.* Asian Productivity Organisation, Tokyo, 1969.

–,–, *Small Industry in the Seventies.* Vikas Publications, Delhi, 1971.

–,–, *Small Industry: The Challenges of the Eighties.* Vikas Publishing House, Delhi, 1983.

–,–, *Small Industry Development Programme.* Indian Institute of Public Administration, New Delhi, 1983.

–,–, *How to Succeed in Small Industry.* Vikas Publishing House, Delhi, 1984.

Viswanathan, R: *Industrial Finance.* S. Chand & Company, New Delhi, 1982.

Walters, K. (ed) : *Entrepreneurial Management : New Technology and New Market Development.* Ballinger Publishing Company, Cambridge, 1989.

World Bank : *Employment and Development of Small Enterprises.* World Bank, Washington, D.C., 1978.

Yadav, R.A. : *Financial Ratios and the Prediction of Corporate Failure.* Concept Publishing, New Delhi, 1986.

Articles

Agarwal B.K.: Sickness in Indian Industry. *Decision,* 6(1),

1979, pp. 65-73.

Agarwal P.D.: Organisational Sickness : Causes and Cures - A Case Study of the Banking Industry in India. *Prajnan*, 6(2), 1977, pp. 173-204.

Agarwal V.K.: What Do We Need to Tackle Industrial Sickness. *Yojana*, July 1-15, 1987, pp. 15-18.

Altman E.I.: Financial Ratios, Discriminant Analysis and the Prediction of Corporate Bankruptcy. *Journal of Finance*, September 1968, pp. 589-609.

Appa Rao P.B., T. Subbi Reddy: Sickness in Small Industry in Andhra Pradesh. *Decision*, 15 (3 & 4), July & Oct. 1988, pp. 235-45.

Aswathappa K., V.G. Ratnam : Turnaround Strategy in a Competitive Environment. *Indian Management*, 29(9), September 1990, pp. 34-36.

Bagchi D.: Industrial Sickness: A Growing Phenomenon. *Lok Udyog*, 18(3), June 1984, pp. 43-55.

Bamber G.J., D. Lausbury : Management Strategy and New Technology in Retail Distribution : A Comparative Case Study. *Journal of Management Studies*, 25(3), 1988, pp. 197-216.

Bhattacharya A.K.: Sickness in Medium and Large Industrial Undertakings. *State Bank of India Monthly Review*, 20(8), August 1981, pp. 315-24.

Chakravarthy P.: Executive Opinion on Industrial Sickness. *The Management Accountant*, 18(12), 1983, pp.530-33.

Cherian S.: Industrial Sickness in India : The Case of West Bengal. *Decision*, 15 (3 & 4), July-Oct 1988, pp. 191-212.

Devendra Babu M.: Sick Industries : Task Before BIFR . *Yojana*, September 1-15, 1987, pp. 18-21 & 27.

Dholakia B.H.: Industrial Sickness in India : Magnitude and Identification Criteria. *Decision*, 15(3 & 4), July & Oct. 1988, pp. 149-59.

–,–, Industrial Sickness in India : Need for Comprehensive Identification Criteria, *Vikalpa*, 14 (2), 1989, pp. 19-24.

Dwivedi R.S.: On Becoming a Sick Enterprise–Diagnosis

and Treatment. *Lok Udyog* , 17 (9), December 1983, pp. 17-25.

Frost T.F.: The Sick Organisation, Part I : Neurotic, Psychotic, Socio-pathic. *Personnel*, 62(5), May 1985, pp. 40-44.

Hambrick D.C.: R.A. D'Aveni: Large Corporate Failures and Downward Spirals. *Administrative Science Quarterly*, 33(1), 1988, pp. 1-23.

Hedge M.: Western and Indian Models of Turnaround Management. *Vikalpa*, 7(4), 1982, pp. 289-303.

Hejmadi M.: Entrepreneurship in Small Industries. *Indian Management*, 29 (11 & 12), Nov. & Dec. 1990, pp. 17-21.

Hingorani N.L.: Towards Defining a Good Account. *Commerce*, 154 (3970), June 20-26, 1987, pp. 23-26.

Hofer C.: Turnaround Strategies. *Journal of Business Strategy*, 1(1), 1980, pp. 19-31.

Joshi N.C.: Solving Industrial Sickness on War Footing. *The Journal of the Indian Institute of Bankers*, 54(4), Oct-Dec.1983, pp. 184-91.

Khandwalla P.N.: Strategy for Turning Around Complex Sick Organisations. *Vikalpa*, 6 (3 & 4), July & Oct. 1981, pp. 143-65.

Khandwalla P.N.: What can Financial Institutions Do to prevent Corporate Sickness? *Vikalpa*, 13(2), April - June 1988, pp. 11-23.

Krishnan B.: The Anatomy of a Sick Engineering Unit. *Indian Management*, 24(5), 1985, pp. 18-22.

Kumar V.: Prediction of Industrial Sickness - Need of the Hour. *The Chartered Accountant*, 30(7), January 1982, pp. 427-34.

Manimala M.J.: Turnaround Management : Lessons from Successful Cases. *ASCI Journal of Management*, 20(4), March 1991, pp. 234-54.

Marwood D.C.L.: I.C.L.: Crisis and Swift Recovery. *Long Range Planning*, 18(2), 1985, pp. 10-21.

Meena K.P.: Industrial Sickness. *Yojana*, 33(18), October

1-15,1989, pp. 4-5 & 13.

Mehta, S. S. : Guest Editorial Note. *Decision,* 15 (3 & 4) July & Oct., 1988, pp. 147-48.

–,–, Sick Industry Syndrome in India : Some Aspects, *Decision* 15 (3 & 4), July & Oct. 1988, pp. 179-90.

Mittal B. B. : Revival of Sick Unit : A Case Study. *The Chartered Accountant,* 36 (5), November 1987, pp. 432-35.

Mookerjee S. : Industrial Sickness and Revival : A Study of Selected Organisations. *Decision,* 15 (3 & 4), July & Oct. 1988, pp. 213-33.

Morris, S. : Why Do Industries Turn Sick? *Business India,* Nov. 22-Dec. 5, 1982, pp. 46-55.

Mukherjee A.R. : Sickness in Indian Engineering Industries, *The Management Accountant,* 18 (11), November 1983, pp. 467-70.

Mukherjee B. : Industrial Sickness: Propensities and Prevention. *The Journal of the Indian Institute of Bankers,* 53 (2), April-June 1982, pp. 77-82.

Muller R. : Corporate Crisis Management. *Long Range Planning* 18 (5), 1985, pp. 38-48.

Nadkarni V. N. : Sickness in Industry and its Effect on Banking. *State Bank of India Monthly Review,* 22 (6), June 1983, pp. 245-55.

Naidu L. K., A. Padmavathi : Why This Growing Sickness in Small Scale Units ? (A Case Study). *Yojana,* September 1-15, 1987, pp. 14-17.

Nair N. P. : Two Studies on Industrial Sickness (Editorial). *Indian Manager,* 13 (1), Jan-March 1983, pp. 5-12 (b).

Nakajo T, Kono T. : Success Through Culture Change in Japanese Brewery. *Long Range Planning* 22(6), 1989, pp. 29-37.

Natarajan R., G. Krishnamurthy, K.V.J. Rao: Rehabilitation of Sick Units in SSI Sector through Marketing Strategy— A Case Study. *Indian Journal of Marketing.* 15(7), 1985, pp. 13-16.

O'Neill H. M. : Turnaround and Recovery : What Strategy

Do you Need? *Long Range Planning,* 19(1), 1986, pp. 80-89.

Pal D. K. : Rehabilitation of Sick Industrial Units in the Small Scale Sector. *Chartered Secretary,* 14(5), May 1984, pp. 316-21.

Pathak K. B. : Rehabilitation of Sick SSI Units – Some Issues. *State Bank of India Monthly Review,* 29(9), September 1990, pp. 427-40.

Prahlad C. K., P. S. Thoma : Turnaround Strategy : Lessons from HPF's Experience. *Vikalpa,* 2(2), 1977, pp. 99-111.

Prasad N. S. : Curing Sickness in Industries *Indian Journal of Marketing,* 13(3), 1982, pp. 19-22.

Radford G. D. : How Sumitomo Transformed Dunlop Tyres. *Long Range Planning,* 22(3), 1989, pp. 28-33.

Rai, H. L., G. N. Brahmanandam : Sickness in Small Industry – A Diagnostic View. *Indian Journal of Marketing,* 15 (2 & 3) Oct. & Nov. 1984, pp. 25-28.

Rajagopal S. : Preventing Corporate Sickness : Improving the Working of Financial Institutions. *Vikalpa,* 14(1), 1989, pp. 65 ff.

Ramaswamy C. S. : Credit System and Industrial Sickness, *Mainstream,* 19 (46), 1981, pp. 15-17.

Ramesh T. : Problems of Small Scale Industries. *The Chartered Accountant,* 39(7), January 1991, pp. 557-59.

Rao A.V.V.S.K. : Industrial Sickness in Indian Economy. *Facts For You,* 9(12), June 1988, (Annual Number - 1988-89), pp. 22-26.

Ratnam M. V. : Sickness in Industry – How to Avoid it ? *The Management Accountant,* 19(6), June 1984, pp. 308-09.

Reddy B. B. : A.R. Reddy, B.K. Reddy : Three Pronged Attack on Sickness in Small Scale Industries, *Yojana,* Septemner 1-15, 1987, pp. 8-11 & 17.

Reddy V. R. : Problems of Small Industries in India. *Indian Management,* 29(11 & 12), Nov. & Dec. 1990, pp. 43-46.

Robertson J., R. W. Mills : Company Failure or Company

Health? Techniques for Measuring Company Health. *Long Range Planning,* 21(2), 1988, pp. 70-77.

Rose D. : Woolworth's Drive for Excellence. *Long Range Planning,* 22(1), 1989, pp. 28-31.

Ruwe D. M., W. Skinner : Reviving a Rust Belt Factory. *Harvard Business Review,* 65 (3), May-June 1987, pp. 70-76.

Sandesara J.C. : Industrial Sickness in India. *Decision,* 15 (3 & 4), July & Oct. 1988, pp. 161-65.

Schendel D. E., G.R. Patton, J. Riggs : Corporate Turnaround Strategies: A Study of Profit Decline and Recovery *Journal of General Management,* 3(3), 1976, pp. 3-11.

Seabright J.W.: Turnaround at MFI : From a Troubled Mail—Order Firm to a Leading Furniture Retailer. *Long Range Planning,* 18(4), 1985, pp. 27-32.

Sen P.K. : Trend Analysis of Financial Ratios and Forecast of Company Sickness. *Decision,* 6(1), 1979, pp. 97-118.

Shanmugham R. : Entrepreneurship in Small Scale Industry : A Case Study. *Indian Management* 29 (11 & 12), Nov. & Dec. 1990, pp. 13-15.

Sharma D. R. : Industrial Sickness : Case Study of Small Units in Kumaun Region. *Indian Journal of Marketing,* 13(8), 1983, pp. 15-18.

Sharma R. K. : Industrial Sickness in India : An Analysis. *ASCI Journal of Management,* 15(1), September 1985, pp 15-18.

Singh, A.P. : Diagnosing and Treating Industrial Sickness. *Yojana,* July 1-15, 1987, pp. 11-14.

Singh P. : Experience of Commercial Banks in Financing Sick Industrial Undertakings. *Decision,.* 6(1), 1979, pp. 23-31.

–,–, The Small Scale Sector and Issues of Management. *Indian Management,* 29(11 & 12), Nov & Dec. 1990, pp. 32-37.

Sood G.S. : Industrial Sickness : Some Issues. *Yojana,* September 1-15, 1987, pp. 4-7.

–,–, Rehabilitating the Sick Industrial Units. *Yojana,*

September 16-30, 1987, pp. 24-29.

Srivastava S.S. : Management of Industrial Sickness. *Productivity,* 24(3), Oct.-Dec. 1983, pp. 367-73.

Srivastava S.S., Kumaria R.K. : Parametric Approach in Predicting Industrial Sickness. *Management in Government,* 12(2), July-September 1980, pp. 123-32.

Turner G. : Inside Europe's Giant Companies : Olivetti Goes Bear - Hunting. *Long Range Planning,* 19(2), April 1986, pp. 13-20.

Udaya Shanker P., Rao G.U.K. : Sickness in Small Industry – Some Cases. *SEDME,* Vol. 17, June 1990, (Published by NISIET, Hyderabad, pp. 63-82.

Vittal N. : The Unusual Story of Gujarat Narmada Auto Limited : A Case Study. *Management in Government,* 20(4), Jan.-March 1989, pp. 339-48.

Weitzel W., E. Johnson : Decline in Organisations : A Literature Integration and Extension. *Administrative Science Quarterly,* 34(1), March 1989, pp. 91-109.

Whetton D.A. : Organisational Decline : A Neglected Topic in Organisational Science. *Academy of Management Review,* 5, 1980, pp. 577-88.

Yadav R. A. : Sick Industrial Companies Legislation - Remedy or Palliative. *The Chartered Accountant,* 35 (6), 1986, pp. 289-92.

–,–, Designing Management Information System for Monitoring Industrial Health. *ASCI Journal of Management,* 20(1), June 1990, pp. 1-13.

–,–, Assessment of Health of Small Scale Industries- A System Approach. *MDI Management Journal,* 3(2), July 1990, pp. 104-05.

Reports

Bhide Committee Report, 1976.

Bhucher Committee Report, 1979.

Chore Committee Report, 1979.

Economic Survey, 1987-88 to 1989-90, Ministry of Finance

Economic Division, Government of India, New Delhi.
Five Year Plan Documents (First to Seventh Plans).
Government of India, India, 1990.
Handbook of Statistics, 1989, Small Scale Industries in India, Development Commissioner (SSI), New Delhi.
High Power Committee Report, 1978.
Report on Census of Small Scale Industrial Units – Vols. I & II, Development Commissioner (SSI), New Delhi, 1977.
Report of Estimates Committee (1972-73), on Small Scale Industries (Thirty-fifth Report; Fifth Lok Sabha), Ministry of Industrial Development, Government of India, New Delhi, 1973.
Reserve Bank of India, Bombay, Report on Currency and Finance, Vol. I : Economic Review, 1978-79 to 1989-90.
Reserve Bank of India Bulletin, March 1991, (Supplement).
Reserve Bank of India, Bombay Report on Trend and Progress of Banking in India, 1978-79 to 1986-87.
Reserve Bank of India Annual Reports, 1979-80 to 1989-90.
Small Scale Industries : Twenty-five years of Progress, Development Commissioner (SSI), New Delhi, 1973.
Standing Coordination Committee Report, 1979.
State Bank of India, Financing of Small Scale Industries : Report of the Study Team, Bombay, 1975.
State Bank of India Annual Report, 1990-91.
Study Group to Frame Guidelines for Follow-up of Bank Credit, (Tandon Committee Report), 1975.
Tiwari Committee Report, 1984.

Journals

Academy of Management Review
Administrative Science Quarterly
ASCI Journal of Management
Business India
(The) Chartered Accountant
Chartered Secretary
Commerce

Decision
Facts For you
Harvard Business Review
Indian Journal of Marketing
Indian Management
Indian Manager
Journal of Business Strategy
Journal of Finance
Journal of General Management
Journal of Management Studies
(The) Journal of the Indian Institute of Bankers
Lok Udyog
Long Range Planning
Mainstream
(The) Management Accountant
Management in Government
MDI Management Journal
Personnel
Prajnan
Productivity
SEDME (Published by NISIET, Hyderabad)
State Bank of India Monthly Review
Vikalpa
Yojana

INDEX